Cormac McCarthy

McFarland Literary Companions

Cormac McCarthy

A Literary Companion

Erik Hage

McFarland Literary Companions, 9

McFarland & Company, Inc., Publishers
Jefferson, North Carolina, and London

Library of Congress Cataloguing-in-Publication Data

Hage, Erik.
Cormac McCarthy : a literary companion / Erik Hage.
p.   cm. — (McFarland literary companions ; 9)
Includes bibliographical references and index.

ISBN 978-0-7864-4310-9
softcover : 50# alkaline paper ∞

1. McCarthy, Cormac, 1933– — Handbooks, manuals, etc.   I. Title.
PS3563.C337Z68 2010   813'.54 — dc22   2010001951

British Library cataloguing data are available

Front cover: Cormac McCarthy at the premiere of *The Road*, November 16, 2009
(AP Photo/Evan Agostini); background ©2010 Shutterstock

Manufactured in the United States of America

McFarland & Company, Inc., Publishers
Box 611, Jefferson, North Carolina 28640
www.mcfarlandpub.com

Acknowledgments

Any book that addresses Cormac McCarthy's work must first and foremost acknowledge the author himself, who is providing a seemingly inexhaustible canon for critics to both muse over and admire. For nearly fifty years, McCarthy, the most resolutely individual of contemporary American writers, has plied his craft in a world far from literary circles, academies, and whatever mode of literature happens to be fashionable at the time. And like Herman Melville or William Faulkner before him, he has produced profound, timeless, and expansive novels whose depths can be plumbed again and again. Having read and reread books such as *Blood Meridian* and *The Crossing* for this project, I look forward to returning to them yet again in order to be immersed in McCarthy's narratives, imagery, and distinct thematic preoccupations. I approach this project first and foremost as a reader and appreciator of the author's work, and I am delighted to be able to share that appreciation with other readers.

I would like to extend my gratitude to my employer, the State University of New York at Cobleskill, which has afforded me a one-course release for two semesters to focus on this project. In addition, the Upper Hudson Library System of New York State's Capital Region has proved to be an invaluable resource in this endeavor (particularly the William K. Sanford Library in Colonie, New York), and I thank the libraries for maintaining such a bountiful and comprehensive collection. My appreciation also goes out to family, friends, students, and colleagues who have tolerated my immersion and, at times, savage autonomy while pursuing this project, which followed immediately on the heels of another book.

I would also like to extend my gratitude to McFarland, for bringing me into the fold and providing a platform to explore the work of my favorite living author. Thanks go out as well to all of the publishing entities (newspapers, magazines, journals, web publishers, and book companies) that have seen fit to allow me in their pages over the past decade. Those opportunities have been crucial to my development as a cultural reporter, writer, and critic, and for that I am extremely grateful.

Most importantly, I want to thank my children and soon-to-be-wife, Elizabeth Brown Mankin, whose enduring support, friendship, and love makes everything a possibility. From being a sounding board for my countless musings about whatever I'm writing about at the time, to taking me to New Mexico to experience Cormac McCarthy country firsthand, Beth has been central to this book. I wouldn't have wanted to explore the high deserts of New Mexico with anyone else.

v

Table of Contents

Preface

Cormac McCarthy: A Literary Companion is intended for readers seeking a comprehensive understanding of the author's works. The volume, organized by alphabetical entries, offers analysis of novels, stories, plays, characters, motifs, allusions, and themes, as well as commentary on corresponding events, places, and people. Many entries also include a selected bibliography for further reading.

In addition to providing commentary on the primary works, entries cover such topics as apocalyptic imagery, the American Southwest, nature, influences, loss, history, race, writing style, women, mothers, dreams, animals, the Santa Fe Institute, and the borderlands, to name some. A biographical introduction orients the reader to McCarthy's life. This volume contains two appendices. The first establishes a chronology for Cormac McCarthy's borderlands novels — that is, the Border Trilogy books (*All the Pretty Horses, The Crossing, Cities of the Plain*) as well as *Blood Meridian* and *No Country for Old Men*. The second appendix offers topical suggestions for further inquiry and study.

This volume has benefited greatly from the work of many insightful critics — both academics and journalists — who have kept alive the critical discussion regarding McCarthy's rich and powerful body of work. It is hoped that readers will take into account the suggestions for further reading and the works listed in the lengthy bibliography. Much of the scholarship and cultural criticism surrounding the author's work makes for fine reading in and of itself — though the debt is always to the primary works that inspired those insights.

Introduction

For the uninitiated reader, Cormac McCarthy constitutes an entire universe waiting to be explored. It's not surprising that he has cited Herman Melville's *Moby-Dick* as his favorite book, for much of his work has the same inexhaustible scope as that weighty tome. A rugged individualist and premiere stylist, McCarthy unflinchingly confronts human nature, particularly the dark, discomfiting regions — often without the ballast of redemption or justification. He is, as the *New York Times* put it, "a writer who renders the brutal actions of men in excruciating detail, seldom applying the anesthetic of psychology" (Woodward, "Venomous Fiction").

Early in his career, owing a great debt to William Faulkner (he even had the same editor as that Mississippi writer), he was perceived as a distinctly regionalist writer, couching his compelling, insular gothics in the hills and hollows of Appalachia. In 1985, with *Blood Meridian*, his attention shifted to the vast flatness of the West, a canvas that seemed to provide his muse and inspire larger scope and ambition. His style also crystallized into a heightened language that came off as both timeless and antiquarian, and that seemed to draw on and ultimately sublimate Melville, the Bible, and Ernest Hemingway. Now far from just being a Southern or Western regionalist, he had fashioned his own novelistic world. As Richard B. Woodward asserted, "There isn't anyone remotely like him in contemporary American literature" (*ibid.*).

By the early 1990s, as he embarked on the Border Trilogy, McCarthy had come to believe that the novel could, as he put it, "encompass all the various disciplines and interests of humanity" (*ibid.*). During the '80s and '90s, first with *Blood Meridian* and then with the famed Border Trilogy — *All the Pretty Horses*, *The Crossing*, and *Cities of the Plain* — he seemed to realize that ambition. Eminent literary critic Harold Bloom ventured that "[n]o other living novelist ... has given us a book as strong and memorable as *Blood Meridian*," regarding it "an American and a universal tragedy of blood" (pp. 254–255). Others saw in his work the knee-trembling resonance of the Old Testament, with landscapes "wide, blazing, and biblical with conflagrations" (Bradfield, "Mystery"). In his weighty parables, he summoned a different vision of the country, "a non-pop-culture America" that, while often set in the twentieth century, possessed a primordial and ageless sense of era.

McCarthy's characterizations also placed him in the lineage of great books. *Blood Meridian*'s Judge Holden, for example, an enormous, malevolent man of great intellect, eloquent oratory, and terrifyingly violent intent, is as complex, terrible, and fascinating as Melville's Ahab, Shakespeare's Iago, and Joseph Conrad's Kurtz. *The Crossing*'s Billy Parham, on the other hand, is a classic quest hero rendered anew and placed in the borderlands. And Parham's complexity lies in his actions: In book 1, when after much trial he captures a pregnant she-wolf that has been pillaging the livestock, Parham becomes possessed with the idea of setting her free across the border, in the Mexican mountains. Thus he sets out, caring for the injured wolf and towing her along on this improbable journey.

The elephant in the room, however, is McCarthy's vividly rendered violence, which often saturates his novels. (Bloom admits to first being put off by *Blood Meridian*, flinching from the "overwhelming carnage" [p. 225].) This is an ever-present element in McCarthy's work, from the grisly green skull of the decomposing, murdered father in his very first novel, *The Orchard Keeper* (1965), which becomes the book's imagistic whirlpool ("leering and coming up through the lucent rotting water with eyeless sockets"), to the American Southwest and Mexico of *Blood Meridian*, a landscape in which, as London's *Independent* put it, "human beings chop, defile, massacre, maim, and dismember one another in every conceivable fashion" (Bradfield, "Twilight Cowboy"). In *Child of God* (1973), a cave-dwelling serial killer engaging in acts of necrophilia moves gorily through the narrative, while in *Outer Dark* (1968), a shocking campfire infanticide is rendered in brutal detail. Even in the relatively recent *No Country for Old Men* (2005), a merciless and automaton-like assassin named Anton Chigurh drives the plot headlong.

In response to those who would decry such themes and imagery, McCarthy has said, "There's no such thing as life without bloodshed" (Woodward, "Venomous Fiction"). Violence and death have, in fact, become his idiom as he engages in a distinct brand of heightened (if savage) realism. Of his predecessors, he has said that he considers great only those writers who directly "deal with issues of life and death" (*ibid.*). In his Western novels he presents a different kind of history, an anti-mythology of the often-romanticized American West; his is a visceral history that renders in microscopic detail the bloodshed that "real" historical narratives politely step over. Like Joseph Conrad before him, McCarthy unfurls the great paradox of civilization — i.e., that new frontiers are tamed and "civilized" through barbaric means.

In *Blood Meridian* and other of his best novels, McCarthy's prose carries with it the discomfiting impact of a war photo — in that moment of stark reality, one forgets for a moment anything but the violent act itself.

The resonance of *Blood Meridian* and the Border Trilogy is not limited to the West. The books take up history itself as a whole "series of violent cultural transformations" (Parrish and Spiller, p. 463); this is the "universality" that Bloom has ascribed to McCarthy's work. The acts of mutilation in *Blood Meridian* are at stark odds with the high-minded, celestial ideals of Manifest Destiny or the myth of the frontier (though McCarthy does not seek to espouse causes or moralize). As a recruiting captain says in the novel, "We are to be the instruments of liberation in a dark and troubled land," with a mission to eliminate "a bunch of barbarians that ... have no least notion in Gods earth of honor or justice or the meaning of republican government" (pp. 33–35).

We can't forget, however, that McCarthy is primarily an unparalleled stylist and moving storyteller whose ambition and scope place him in the lineage of a bygone age of books. And nowhere is he more in command than in his rendering of natural landscapes and the physical world. In his very first novel, *The Orchard Keeper*, one can already sense that connection with the physical world when he describes an east Tennessee forest:

> Possum grapes and muscadine flourish with a cynical fecundity, and the floor of the forest — littered with old mossbacked logs, peopled with toadstools strange and solemn among the ferns and creepers and leaning to show their delicate livercolored gills — has about it a primordial quality, some steamy carboniferous swamp where ancient saurians lurk in feigned sleep [p. 11].

The architect of such a distinct and idiosyncratic literary style has also found a rare balance with commercial success. *All the Pretty Horses* forced the reclusive author from the shadows of literary acclaim and became a bestseller upon its release in 1992. McCarthy's novels have also been made into movies, with *No Country for Old Men* winning an Academy Award for Best Picture in 2007. He has even won favor with that arbiter of the mass market zeitgeist, Oprah Winfrey, who adopted his Pulitzer Prize–winning *The Road* (2006) into her book club and conducted a rare TV interview with McCarthy, his first ever. (To date, all of his interviews can be counted on one hand.)

His reticence to be in the public eye has made him that much more compelling to many readers. For years, only bare-bones fragments of his biography were known: He was born in Rhode Island in 1933, moved to Knoxville, Tennessee, at age four, served in the Air Force, and soon after began his long, steady ascent to a career as a successful author, the path littered with awards, grants, marriages, and accolades. And all along, he insisted on his need for privacy, avoided public appearances and remained deeply absorbed in the work of writing, not in the construction of the public persona of Cormac McCarthy.

Sitting across from Oprah in a comfortable chair in the library of the Sante Fe Institute in June 2007, finally having been dragged out into the public glare after 40-plus years of publishing, the reclusive writer slouched in his seat and politely and earnestly fielded questions. He looked and sounded like a kindly older man and gave no hint of the imagination that had produced such weighty classics and constructed a style as distinct as Hemingway's or Faulkner's.

When Winfrey questioned him about his lack of public interviews, he politely explained that talking about writing seemed kind of silly when one could actually spend that time engaged in the actual act of writing. Nevertheless, in his ten great novels, he has given the rest of us much to talk about, and much to admire; thus the reason for this particular book you are holding.

A cautionary word, however: This critical companion's intent is to facilitate and abet an interest the novels of Cormac McCarthy. The books themselves often display great complexity and a sense of darkening mystery that is difficult to broach; the novels are rarely "neat" and often depict actions that can't be resolved or explained away. In addition, critic Dana Phillips wisely asserts that the books' "moral or political worldview is bound to be disturbing to readers who ... expect novels to offer an imaginary solution to individual or social ills" (p. 452). The attempt here is to throw light on themes and stylistic tendencies, but also to honor the impressionistic gulf that must sometimes exist between McCarthy's novels and the reader (yet there is a synergy to the reader/author relationship). The aim of this work is not necessarily to wrestle down or tame the quite essential and intended narrative complexities and ambiguities.

As Phillips put it, McCarthy's work sometimes "seems designed to elude interpretation, especially interpretation that would translate it into some supposedly more essential language" (p. 434). A critical companion to these novels should celebrate the language, the gifts, and the mystery at the heart of these books in a manner that most can appreciate at some level. McCarthy, who strikes that rare balance between commercial success and literary recognition, serves many readers, and this is most of all an "appreciation" of his work.

A Brief Biography

It may be surprising to many that the writer who was to become so indelibly associated with the American Southwest — and, earlier, Tennessee — was born in the large New England city of Providence, Rhode Island, on July 20, 1933. He was third in a line of six children, and as eldest son was named Charles, after his father. (Sources vary as to whether he officially renamed himself Cormac or the family legally changed his name.) According to Richard Woodward, "Cormac, the Gaelic equivalent of Charles, was an old family nickname bestowed on his father by Irish aunts" ("Venomous Fiction").

He was preceded by sisters Jackie and Bobbie, while siblings Bill, Maryellen, and Dennis came after him. Cormac McCarthy's father was a successful attorney who graduated from Yale University; in fact, McCarthy came from roots that were not only genteel but progressive: His paternal grandfather, John Francis, after whom Cormac McCarthy would eventually name his youngest son, had gone against the grain of early twentieth-century society by sending his daughters to college, along the same path as his sons.

Cormac McCarthy did not live in Rhode Island for very long, however. At the age of four, the family moved to Knoxville, Tennessee, where his father had taken a job as legal counsel for the Tennessee Valley Authority. Charles Joseph McCarthy and Gladys Christina McGrail McCarthy and their six children eventually settled in a ten-room home located at 5501 Martin Mill Pike. McCarthy was raised as a Roman Catholic in the South, something that certainly set him apart from the majority, and he was educated in a parochial high school.

The writer's Tennessee upbringing was crucial to his development and is the root of the unflinching portraits of violence and bloodshed that would come to dominate his work. "You grow up in the South, you're going to see violence," he told an interviewer in 2007. "And violence is pretty ugly" (Kushner). As a child, he took a keen interest in the natural world that surrounded his home, another preoccupation that would come to dominate his novels, as he would become notable for distinct and uncanny descriptions of natural environments. "When I was a kid, I was very interested in the natural world," McCarthy remembered in 2007. "To this day, during casual conversations, little-known facts about the natural world will just crop up" (*ibid.*).

McCarthy entered the University of Tennessee during the 1951-1952 academic year, but then left college to join the United States Air Force in 1953, serving a four-year stint. He was stationed in Alaska for a couple of years, where he had a radio show. He also began reading ravenously, using literature as a means to fill the off-hours boredom of military life.

After the Air Force, he returned to the University of Tennessee in 1957, and while he would never achieve a degree, it was during this second attempt at college that he began to take up writing with serious intent. He became hooked after a professor tasked him with editing a textbook of eighteenth-century essays. Soon after, he appeared for the first time in print, publishing two stories in the college's literary magazine, *The Phoenix*. "Wake for Susan" appeared in the fall of 1959 and "A Drowning Incident" appeared in early 1960. During that time, McCarthy also received a grant from the Ingram Merrill Foundation. This foundation, established by celebrated poet James Ingram Merrill — son of the founder of Merrill Lynch — awarded money to writers and artists.

McCarthy permanently dropped out of college in 1961 and moved to Chicago for a short spell, working at an auto parts warehouse while writing his first novel. Around this time he married his first wife, Lee Holleman, whom he had met at the University of Tennessee. The couple had a son, Cullen, and settled in Sevier County, Tennessee. The marriage was brief, however, and McCarthy set out on a peripatetic existence, drifting to Asheville, North Carolina, and later New Orleans, living in humble abodes and scratching out a hand-to-mouth existence. (His ex-wife Lee McCarthy published a collection of poems titled *Desire's Door* in 1991; the collection included ruminations on the failed marriage.) He also continued to work on his first book.

Cormac McCarthy finally emerged as a recognized novelist with the 1965 publication of *The Orchard Keeper*, a novel that established him as an heir to the Southern tradition embodied by William Faulkner. In fact, McCarthy's editor at Random House, Albert Eskine, had been Faulkner's editor, as well as that of Robert Penn Warren and Ralph Ellison. (McCarthy had blindly submitted the manuscript to the only book publishing company of which he had known.) But some saw the debut as too fraught with, and hampered by, tones of his famous Southern predecessor Faulkner. The *New York Times* review deemed the book "impressive" but "sorely handicapped by ... humble and excessive admiration for William Faulkner" (Prescott). As if to cement the comparison, *The Orchard Keeper* garnered a William Faulkner Foundation Award for best first novel by an American writer.

But the work also displayed McCarthy's sensitivity for old and disappearing ways of life in the rural Tennessee hills — intimacy with nature, as well as hunting, trapping, and bootlegging. *The Orchard Keeper* also featured the writer's dark and grim sensibility, a lack of psychological exploration or justification, and the flair for the grotesque that would come to occupy much of his early work. In the story, which takes place before World War II, a boy named John Wesley Rattner forms a bond with Arthur Ownby, an old man with a deep connection to the land and the old ways of living, and Marion Sylder, a bootlegger who is the unknown murderer of John Wesley's father. At this stage of his career, critics firmly placed McCarthy in the Southern Gothic tradition embodied not only by Faulkner but Flannery O'Connor as well.

But *The Orchard Keeper*, like all of his first five novels — up through *Blood Meridian* (1985) — sold poorly upon initial release (only moving a few thousand copies).

McCarthy continued to pull down grants, however, allowing him to eke out an existence and to continue writing. One such award, a travel fellowship from the American Academy of Arts and Letters, allowed him to head by ocean liner to Ireland, reportedly to research his family history for a possible book. While on board he met an English woman named Anne DeLisle, who was working as a singer and dancer on the ship. The two married in England in 1966, and on the back of a Rockefeller Foundation grant they traveled around Europe and settled for a time on the island of Ibiza, about 80 kilometers off the coast of Spain, in the Mediterranean Sea. (The island was a relatively bohemian artistic settlement at the time.)

Here McCarthy finished *Outer Dark* (1968), his second novel. The book firmly established the unremitting darkness of McCarthy's vision and clearly showed that he was willing to tap into uncomfortable regions that others avoided. He centered the novel around an incestuous union between a brother and sister, a union that results in a baby. There is a dreamlike and archaic atmosphere to the haunting narrative of *Outer Dark*, as well as an arduous journey motif and a cast of malevolent characters. These qualities presaged *Blood Meridian* and the Border Trilogy decades down the road, though *Outer Dark* stands apart as McCarthy's most turgid and "problematical" work, and it doesn't possess the powerful immediacy of many of his narratives.

In 1967, Cormac McCarthy and his second wife moved back to the writer's native Tennessee, taking up residence near Knoxville, where they lived first at a pig farm and later in a dairy barn that McCarthy had refurbished. DeLisle claimed years later that they lived in virtual poverty. He did, however, receive a Guggenheim Fellowship to subsist on while writing his next book, *Child of God* (1973), a grotesque and uncanny tale about a serial killer/necrophiliac named Lester Ballard who lived in a cave with the bodies of his dead victims.

Child of God was based on actual news reports out of Sevier County, Tennessee, and in a lengthy and admiring essay on the book in August 1974, *The New Yorker* tagged McCarthy as a novelist "whose fate is to be relatively unknown and often misinterpreted" (Coles, p. 90), a prediction that the immediate, if not long-term, future certainly bore out. What was most interesting about McCarthy's rendering of Lester Ballard was that the writer was able to somewhat humanize such a character without casting a wholly sympathetic eye on him or his atrocities. It is a vivid, grotesque, and even darkly humorous book.

In 1974, director Richard Pearce sought out McCarthy to write the screenplay for *The Gardener's Son*, a television drama about a South Carolina mill owner who is murdered in the 1870s by a disturbed young man with a wooden leg. (The boy is hanged for the crime.) The film premiered on PBS in 1977, starring Brad Dourif, Ned Beatty, and Kevin Conway as members of two feuding families, the affluent Greggs and blue-collar McEvoys.

In 1976, McCarthy left Tennessee, separated from his second wife, and moved to El Paso, Texas. The writer "showed up in El Paso around January 1976 ... unannounced and his arrival completely unnoticed. He was a 43-year-old writer of three out-of-print novels, a man twice divorced, living exclusively off of literary fellowships," piped a 1992 *Texas Monthly* profile. "He began to be seen in pool halls and bowling alleys on the south side of town, as well as in various Mexican restaurants, always with some esoteric book under his arm" (Draper).

The geographical shift would also resonate in his writing, which would soon turn to the Southwestern borderlands and Western literary and historical motifs — opening up a whole new world for McCarthy's novels. But, first, 1979 saw the release of a Knoxville-centered novel, *Suttree*, which McCarthy was said to have been toiling at on and off for two decades. It was also considered to be a tangentially autobiographical work, making it a rarity in the McCarthy canon. In the novel, the title character balks at his privileged upbringing, abandons his wife and son, and seeks out an existence among degenerates, outcasts, and other such characters while carving out an existence as a fisherman on a houseboat on the Tennessee River. The ambitious and trenchant *Suttree* would weather comparisons to James Joyce's *Ulysses* and would later be hailed by some as McCarthy's greatest novel, running up against frequent and competing claims for *Blood Meridian*. While still married to McCarthy, DeLisle had typed up the lengthy manuscript of *Suttree*, and in the wake of their official divorce in 1978, the two remained friends.

While residing in the U.S.-Mexican borderlands, McCarthy reportedly undertook rigorous research of the region and its history, including scouting trips into Mexico. He also mastered Spanish, which would often crop up in the dialogue of his future books. Despite having several commercially unsuccessful novels under his belt, his financial circumstances were vastly improved by a 1981 MacArthur Fellowship, the award more commonly known as the "genius grant." The fellowships are bestowed upon individuals from a wide range of disciplines — the sciences, the arts, the humanities — who, based on their accomplishments and potential, are awarded a substantial sum of money (in McCarthy's case, over $200,000).

The fellowship was a clear indication that, despite his meager sales and reclusiveness, McCarthy was gaining great respect in high literary circles. Among the writers recommending him for the award were Nobel Prize winner Saul Bellow and acclaimed Southern novelist and historian Shelby Foote. Nevertheless, despite such honors and accolades, McCarthy remained a defiantly private person. He gave no interviews, avoided public appearances, and steered wide of traditional milieus such as literary circles and university lecturing gigs. "Cormac has staked out a life completely outside the literary system," claimed his agent Amanda Urban in 1992 (Draper).

During the 1980s McCarthy wrote a screenplay called *Whales and Men* that has yet to see publication or production, though it can be located in the Cormac McCarthy Papers in the Southwestern Writers Collection of Texas State University–San Marcos library. (The work was most likely written in the early 1980s, as it references the year 1984.) The screenplay is a deep, dialogue-driven meditation on the nature of whales, particularly how they communicate, with a locale that shifts from Florida, to Ireland, to Sri Lanka. In *Whales and Men,* according to Edwin T. Arnold, "Whales come to represent the unknowable in nature, perhaps even the sacred mystery that man senses but cannot comprehend" (*Whales and Men* synopsis).

But *Blood Meridian, or The Evening Redness in the West,* released in 1985, would become the author's grand achievement of the 1980s and the product of all of his borderlands immersion. It was also the book that truly galvanized his literary reputation (though celebrated writers such as Foote and Bellow had been singing McCarthy's praises before that book ever came to fruition). *Blood Meridian* was a vast, epic, bloody, and phantasmagoric narrative about a motley band of scalp hunters running amok in the American Southwest and Mexico during 1849 and 1850. The heightened and archaic prose, epic scope, and lofty ruminations drew comparisons to McCarthy's favorite novel, Herman Melville's *Moby-Dick: or; The Whale* (1851). The novel also contained one of his greatest, vilest characters, Judge Holden, a monstrous, hairless, compellingly astute killer who comes to seem immortal by book's end. But *Blood Meridian* only gathered critical steam in the following decades; at the time of its release, it received little recognition and only sold a few thousand copies. McCarthy was still very much a cult figure and "writer's writer." Nevertheless, *Blood Meridian* would be discovered by many readers in subsequent years, and eminent literary critic Harold Bloom would even come to rank it among the greatest American novels of all time, deeming it the continuation of an American literary heritage that coursed straight out of Melville and Faulkner.

With *Blood Meridian*, McCarthy had firmly hammered out a novelistic worldview that would come to dominate subsequent novels as well, a gaze characterized by stark pessimism, apocalyptic imagery, and deliberations on the inevitable violence of the human condition. The latter aspect meant that McCarthy's narratives were sometimes (and necessarily) charged with frank, brutal, and startling descriptions of the most unimaginable bloodshed and killing. Bloom recalled that he initially "flinched at the overwhelming carnage" in *Blood Meridian* (p. 255) and wasn't able to clearly ascertain the greatness of the work until he could see beyond that element. All of McCarthy's Western novels also came to be characterized by deep philosophical musings on history, God, and the very nature of being.

These qualities were certainly evident in McCarthy's next novel, *All the Pretty Horses* (1992), which took up the same borderlands locale 100 years after the time of *Blood Meridian*. But they were combined with a more accessible narrative upheld by recognizable romance and adventure tropes. Only McCarthy himself knows whether this was a calculated attempt to launch his reputation out of relative obscurity — and that's exactly what happened. *All the Pretty Horses,* the first volume in the proposed Border Trilogy, not only showed commercial vitality by becoming a bestseller but also was critically lauded, pulling down both a National Book Award and a National Book Critics Circle Award.

McCarthy, then nearly 60 years old, was still living in El Paso at the time, in a modest stone house near a shopping center. Just prior to the release of *All the Pretty Horses* he granted his first major interview, to Richard Woodward from the *New York Times*. He only relented after his publisher had implored him to submit to the publicity in order to help promote the new book and the pending Vintage reissues of his older novels.

For devotees of McCarthy, it was an opportunity to glimpse the personality of the enigmatic and mysterious writer for the first time. The portrait that Woodward painted of McCarthy certainly seemed a stark contrast to his complex and dark novels:

> A compact unit, shy of six feet even in cowboy boots, McCarthy walks with a bounce, like someone who is also a good dancer. Clean-cut and handsome as he grays, he has a Celtic's

blue-green eyes set deep into a high-domed forehead. "He gives an impression of strength and vitality and poetry," says [writer Saul] Bellow, who describes him as "crammed into his own person." ... For such an obstinate loner, McCarthy is an engaging figure, a world-class talker, funny, opinionated, quick to laugh ["Venomous Fiction"].

The profile also revealed that McCarthy had reestablished a relationship with his son, Cullen, in recent years, and that he didn't have many "literary" friends, preferring to keep company with such scientists as Nobel Prize–winning physicist Murray Gell-Mann and whale biologist Roger Payne, both of whom he had met through the MacArthur Fellowship association. (McCarthy did, though, admit to becoming acquainted with novelist Edward Abbey before his death in 1989.) The *New York Times* interview didn't augur an era of openness and accessibility for McCarthy, however, and it would remain his sole interview — and one that critics continually ransacked for information — for the next 13 years. (In his seventh decade and well into the next millennium McCarthy finally opened up a bit.)

At the time of the *New York Times* piece, McCarthy was immersed in composing *The Crossing* (1994), the second border book and a novel that would stand out as the most weighty, complex, and multifaceted volume of the trilogy. In July 1993, the world would get a first glimpse of that endeavor in *Esquire* magazine, which featured the first section of that larger work, there entitled "The Wolf Trapper." The novel introduced a new protagonist, Billy Parham, and went back in time about ten years before the action of *All the Pretty Horses*, to a period just before and during World War II. The narrative consisted of three "crossings" over the border, deep into Mexico and back again, giving it the quality of an epic literary voyage such as Homer's *Odyssey*.

In the first, Billy traps an elusive and pregnant she-wolf that has been feeding on ranch livestock and then somehow sets his mind upon freeing the wolf in the mountains of Mexico, prompting an unceremonious break with his family and an arduous and unlikely journey. After that, Billy returns to find that his parents have been murdered and the family's horses stolen, so he and his younger brother, Boyd, set off into Mexico to recover the horses. During the final crossing, Billy returns for his brother, who had remained in Mexico to be with a young Mexican woman that he and Billy had rescued, only to find that Boyd had become a legendary vigilante and had been killed. Billy then sets out to return Boyd's corpse across the border. But the mere summary of these journeys barely hints at the thematic scope and the countless people Billy meets along the way, as well as the vivid imagery and deep musings that are interwoven in the narrative.

In the early 1990s, Cormac McCarthy had begun making regular trips to Santa Fe to visit the Santa Fe Institute, a place that would eventually become a sort of home base for him. McCarthy's physicist friend, Murray Gell-Mann, and a group of other scientists had founded the institute in 1984. Housed in an old convent in the hills outside of Santa Fe, it became a haven for thinkers from varying disciplines to come together and ponder the complexities of existence. McCarthy has made no bones about preferring the company of scientists to that of other writers or artistic types. "Science is very rigorous," he once said. "When you hang out with scientists and see how they think, you can't do so without developing a respect for it.... When you say something, it needs to be right. You can't just speculate idly about things" (Kushner).

McCarthy became a de facto writer-in-residence of the institute, and he even eventually relocated from El Paso to Santa Fe to be closer. At times he was viewed as a curiosity among so many notable scientific minds. "People who know my work walk in and they're kind of confused as to why I'm there," he said, "but that's OK. They soon get over that" (*ibid.*). Gell-Mann has said of McCarthy's daily presence at the institute, "He has a long-standing interest in a great many things and he knows an immense amount about them ... if he weren't so shy, he could probably ask penetrating questions" (Woodward, "Cormac Country").

Richard B. Woodward, interviewing McCarthy for the second time — this time for *Vanity Fair* in 2005 — for what would become McCarthy's second major interview, opened the article by painting this colorful picture:

> The parking lot at the Santa Fe Institute, in New Mexico, features rows of vehicles typical of American academia — S.U.V.'s and minivans, a few older model BMWs and Mercedeses, a Toyota Prius, and an inordinate amount of Subarus and Hondas.... Standing out from the crowd is a red Ford F-350 diesel pickup with Texas plates. Equipped with a Banks Power-Pack that boosts the 7.3 liter engine to more than 300 hp, it has a stripped down profile in back, like a wrecker's, with no winch.... The owner of the truck, the novelist Cormac McCarthy, would also seem not to belong here. He is the lone fiction writer at the institute, and his books, although they constitute one of the towering achievements in recent American literature, are often horrifically violent ["Cormac Country"].

In 1997, McCarthy received the Texas Institute of Letters Lon Tinkle Lifetime Achievement Award. The following year, four years after the publication of *The Crossing*, the final Border Trilogy book, *Cities of the Plain*, finally appeared. This time the narrative did not offer journeys that strayed deeply into Mexico, but hewed close to the border, in the vicinity of the title cities of El Paso and Juárez, Mexico. The novel brought together the protagonists from the first two books, Billy Parham and John Grady Cole, who appeared here working together at a New Mexico ranch not far from the titular cities.

Billy, now in his late 20s, assumes a brotherly/mentor role toward the younger John Grady, who falls in love with a young, epileptic prostitute in Juárez and tries to free her from her pimp so that he can marry her. But again, as so often happens in the work of McCarthy, things end terribly and Grady perishes from wounds sustained in a knife fight with the pimp. The novel has a more subtle, wistful, and elegiac cast than the previous two books, and because it does not possess the immediacy of *All the Pretty Horses'* romance and adventure or *The Crossing's* epic and harrowing overtones, it was not as well received.

Cities of the Plain had actually first seen life as a screenplay, over ten years before the first Border Trilogy volume, 1992's *All the Pretty Horses*, was released. In fact, according to the *New York Times*, McCarthy and director friend Richard Pearce (from *The Gardener's Son* association) had tried to get the film made.

The late 1990s ushered in the era when McCarthy's novels began to be much more coveted as potential Hollywood properties. Around this time, production began on the 2000 film version of *All the Pretty Horses*, directed by Billy Bob Thornton and starring Matt Damon and Penélope Cruz. For the most part, the movie was poorly received, and

Thornton made no bones about his anger over having had to cut out a full hour of story from the final version.

Well into his sixties, McCarthy also became a father again. John Francis McCarthy was born to the writer and the significantly younger Jennifer Winkley, who would become his third wife. "He dotes on his son, whose bedroom is stuffed with books, maps, and models," wrote Richard B. Woodward in 2005. "One has the sense that he wants to atone for his shortcomings as a parent earlier in life. He seldom saw his first son, Cullen, after his first marriage dissolved" ("Cormac Country").

In 2001, McCarthy's *The Stonemason: A Play in Five Acts* was staged in Houston. He had conceived the piece years earlier, and it was published by Ecco Press in 1994. (In 1992, an intention to mount a production of the play in Washington, D.C., at the Arena Stage, had fallen through.) McCarthy was not directly involved in the 2001 production but did make a rare appearance to witness the staging of the play, which, according to critic and close McCarthy follower Edwin T. Arnold, appeared in a much abbreviated form. "Drama is the hardest to write," Cormac McCarthy said regarding this turn to a different medium. "Novels and other forms of literature are difficult, but drama is the hardest. It's unusual to get two outstanding playwrights in a century" (Arnold, "Stonemason Evening"). The play went up for one night only on October 12 at the Arts Alliance Center in Clear Lake, Texas.

Arnold describes McCarthy's presence at the performance:

> He comes in quickly and unobtrusively with his brother Dennis. They are both wearing sports coats and jeans, and the resemblance between the two is obvious. When the lights dim, McCarthy, his wife Jennifer, and Dennis sit near the back of the room, inconspicuous members blending into the anonymous audience, waiting for the play to begin ... the audience stands at the end of the performance, applauding and nodding their heads in approval. McCarthy, of course, chooses not to come forward when he is introduced at the end, but he does smile and wave his hand so that the audience can see him ["Stonemason Evening"].

While this condensed version of McCarthy's stage drama omitted and altered many elements, *The Stonemason: A Play in Five Acts*, as written by McCarthy, tells of the close bond between a young black construction worker, Ben Telfair, and his stonemason grandfather, Papaw. The play intercuts two dramatic sections; in one Ben delivers stirring monologues that pay tribute to Papaw. The other more traditional staging presents the Telfair family living together in a house in Louisville, Kentucky, in the early 1970s, delving into topics such as racism, infidelity, drug abuse, and suicide.

According to the *New York Times*, the "breakdown of the family in the play mirrors the recent disappearance of stoneworking as a craft" (Woodward, "Venomous Fiction"). "Stacking up stone is the oldest trade there is," said McCarthy in 1992, showing his typically keen interest in archaic practices. "Not even prostitution can come close to its antiquity. It's older than anything, older than fire. And in the last 50 years, with hydraulic cement, it's vanishing. I find that rather interesting" (*ibid.*).

McCarthy's next book, *No Country for Old Men* (2005), was a surprising departure. (According to the Southwestern Writers Collection, which houses McCarthy's papers, the book's genesis was as a screenplay in the 1980s [Witliff].) The novel dealt with a familiar geographical locale, the borderlands, but acknowledged a new dark force that had consumed the region: drug trafficking. Set in 1980, it was typically violent but also turned out to be McCarthy's briskest and most readable work to date, assuming the dimensions of a white-knuckle crime thriller. Lauded filmmakers Joel and Ethan Coen (*Fargo*; *O, Brother Where Art Thou?*; *The Big Lebowski*) snapped up the rights to the novel and adapted it into a screenplay. The Coen brothers would also direct the film. The movie, released in 2007 and starring Tommy Lee Jones and Josh Brolin, stayed remarkably true to McCarthy's book, and the reception to this film was far different from that to the movie version of *All the Pretty Horses*; in fact, the movie won scores of awards and pulled down eight Academy Award nominations, bagging four statues, including best picture, director, and screenplay adaptation.

McCarthy, becoming cautiously more accessible, could be seen in attendance at the Oscars, standing and applauding when the film won for best picture. The camera even focused directly on him in his seat (son John at his side) when producer Scott Rudin thanked him from the stage. During the press run-up to the movie, McCarthy again showed willingness for publicity: In October of 2007 *Time* magazine ran a short article that was basically an informal conversation between the Coen brothers and Cormac McCarthy. They discussed the film as well as American cinema in general.

McCarthy also made another foray into theater in 2006 with *The Sunset Limited: A Novel in Dramatic Form*, which premiered onstage in May at the Steppenwolf Theater in Chicago and then opened for a short run in October in New York City, where it was well-received. The *New York Times* review described it as "a poem in celebration of death" and compared it to the work of Samuel Beckett (Zinoman). The play consists of two characters, named "BLACK" and "WHITE," monikers that represent both the characters' race and their opposing outlook on existence. (Here, as he so often does, McCarthy works with contradiction: BLACK possesses the more idealistic outlook of the two.) At the outset, we learn that BLACK, a reformed convict, has recently saved WHITE, a professor, from throwing himself in front of a train. BLACK is a man of faith who espouses the teachings of the Bible, while WHITE, an atheist and nihilist, shows that he is the antithesis of his moniker: "I yearn for the darkness. I pray for death," he says. "Real Death. If I thought that in death I would meet the people I've known in life I don't know what I'd do. That would be the ultimate horror" (p. 57).

During this period, McCarthy claimed to be working on a few novels at once, and he promptly followed up *No Country for Old Men* with *The Road* (2006), one of his grimmest, most horrifying works (and as one critic pointed out, "that's saying something" [Barra]). The post-apocalyptic tale describes a man and his son undertaking a relentless journey across a charred landscape that has been obliterated by some unnamed and cataclysmic catastrophe. McCarthy finally delivered what he had been suggesting for so long: the end of the world. The two central figures endure starvation, exposure to the elements, and hordes of tribal cannibals in their quest to reach the sea.

The narrative itself is stripped-down and stark (especially when compared to the Border Trilogy), but won McCarthy his biggest accolade yet, the Pulitzer Prize (2007); it was also a national bestseller. In the UK, it scored the prestigious James Tait Black Memorial Prize, Britain's oldest literary award. TV mogul Oprah Winfrey even picked *The Road* as a choice for her book club, and in perhaps the strangest twist in the story of the publicity-shy writer, McCarthy agreed to be interviewed by the talk-show host on her program in June 2007. Oprah traveled to McCarthy's favorite haunt, the Santa Fe Institute, to tape an interview with him in the institute's library.

Flak Magazine described the televised image of the two sitting across from each other in chairs, discussing the writer's work: "For McCarthy's longtime fans, the prospect of finally seeing the man on TV, but with You-Go-Girl icon Oprah Winfrey in the opposite chair, is the very essence of cognitive dissonance" (Danzen). For fans, it was the first time to see and hear McCarthy, who, at 73 years of age, came off as kindly, down-to-earth, and humble. When Winfrey asked him if he was "passionate" about writing, McCarthy, slouching in an easy chair in a pressed denim shirt, responded, "I don't know. Passionate sounds like a pretty fancy word. I like what I do.... You always have this image of the perfect thing which you can never achieve" (Winfrey). When Winfrey inquired about the inspiration behind *The Road*, McCarthy explained that he and his young son John, to whom he dedicated the book, were staying in a hotel in El Paso when the idea came to him. "I went and stood at a window, and I could hear the trains coming through, a very lonesome sound" (*ibid.*). He said he had an image in his head of what the landscape would look like in the wake of apocalypse, with fires burning on a hill.

After the Hollywood success of *No Country for Old Men*, *The Road* was quickly picked up as a film property. Australian John Hillcoat (*The Proposition*) directed the movie, and Viggo Mortensen of *Lord of Rings* fame portrayed the father. The film was shot in locales that suited the barren, post-apocalyptic setting of the novel. Production began in February 2008 in and around Pittsburgh, and scenes were also filmed in New Orleans and on Mount St. Helens. In a May 2008 *New York Times* profile on the production, one member of the crew explained that Pennsylvania was chosen "because it offered such a pleasing array of post-apocalyptic scenery: deserted coalfields, run-down parts of Pittsburgh, windswept dunes." The article added that "Chris Kennedy, the production designer, even discovered a burned-down amusement park ... and an eight-mile stretch of abandoned freeway, complete with tunnel." This latter location was "ideal for filming the scene where the father and son who are the story's main characters are stalked by a cannibalistic gang traveling by truck" (McGrath). The completed film was initially planned for release in November 2008, but was withheld until November 2009.

Cormac McCarthy's name broke across the national news wires for an altogether different reason in January 2009, when his childhood home, long abandoned, was destroyed by fire — just as Knoxville preservationists were turning an eye toward restoring it as a literary landmark. One local news story noted that there had been reports of "homeless people squatting" in the vacant building, and the attending fire chief said that the "interior was disgustingly dilapidated." In addition, the house "was hidden from the street by a thick wall of bamboo and honeysuckle" (Stambaugh). For close readers of McCarthy, all of this sounded like life imitating art, as the descriptions conjured the author's "Knoxville novel" *Suttree*. In fact, there is even a scene in the novel where the central figure explores a similarly once-noble home that has fallen to ruin and become a haven for squatters (*Suttree*, pp. 134–136).

In early May of 2009, McCarthy received another in a long line of honors. *USA Today* reported, "The author of *The Road*, *All the Pretty Horses* and several other novels was named the winner ... of the PEN/Saul Bellow Award for lifetime achievement in American fiction" ("Author Cormac McCarthy Receives PEN Award"). As the awarding organization itself noted, the honor "goes to a distinguished living American author of fiction whose body of work in English possesses qualities of excellence, ambition, and scale of achievement over a sustained career which place him or her in the highest rank of American literature" (PEN American Center). The judges who chose McCarthy were Claudia Roth Pierpont, Philip Roth, and Benjamin Taylor.

Predictably, McCarthy did not show up in person to accept the honor; Ajai Singh "Sonny" Mehta, a publisher and editor-in-chief at his book company, Knopf, accepted for the author, briefly thanking the PEN organization for recognizing McCarthy's work. In the citation, the judges lauded McCarthy as a "self-transformer," an artist whose career was "driven at the inmost by a will to change." The statement also admired how the "phenomenal career of Cormac McCarthy embodies just such a self-transformation. Between *Suttree*, his Knoxville novel of 1979, and *Blood Meridian*, his 1985 novel of mid-nineteenth-century Texas and Mexico, the Southern writer has become a Western writer" (PEN American Center).

As of this writing, in the summer of 2009, Cormac McCarthy is said to be at work on a new novel—set in New Orleans and with the working title *The Passenger*—and allegedly has two other books underway as well. News of this broke in May 2009, when an archive of Cormac McCarthy's papers went public at the Texas State–San Marcos library, as part of the Southwestern Writers Collection. The Southwestern Writers Collection purchased the archives for two million dollars, according to the Associated Press ("Texas State Acquires Cormac McCarthy Archives"). The London *Guardian* reported on May 18, 2009, that the "author's notes, handwritten drafts and correspondence for each of his 10 novels are included in the archive" (Flood).

Among these items are such treasures for enthusiasts as "[h]and-drawn and photo-copied maps of Saltillo and Zacatecas ... as part of McCarthy's research for *All the Pretty Horses*" as well as "correspondence between McCarthy and a doctor" regarding an initial draft of a scene in which a rural Mexican physician treats Boyd's gunshot wounds in *The Crossing*: "From a literary standpoint, there is no doubt that the scene well depicts the adversity Boyd faces in the character of the Mexican physician who intervenes," writes the doctor to McCarthy. "However, from a purely medical view, it doesn't tie together." The doctor also "provided information about the period appropriateness for some of the medical instruments used in the novel" (*ibid.*).

While these materials are a testament to the diligence and thoroughness with which McCarthy pursues real-life accuracy, the unfinished manuscript of *The Passenger*, which is included in the collection as well (with restricted access until publication), presents a different kind of testament: to that of the restless, enduring artistry of Cormac McCarthy, who—40-plus years after the publication of his first novel and 50-plus years since he first set out to be a writer—continues to seek out new literary terrain.

Cormac McCarthy: A Literary Companion

Ab

Ab Jones, a featured character in the novel *Suttree* (1979), drives McCarthy's most sobering storyline regarding race relations in the South. Throughout the novel, Ab remains locked in an obsessive, pitched, and violent struggle with the Knoxville police force, a war of attrition that eventually leads to his death in a police beating.

Fittingly, Ab is named after the biblical character Abednego, a Jew from the Book of Daniel who, in an act of ethnic intolerance, is thrown into a fiery furnace along with two other resisters. In this biblical story, the three Jews were condemned to death for refusing to worship a golden idol of King Nebuchadnezzar, but they emerged unscathed from the furnace because of the intervention of God.

Drawing the parallel to Southern race relations even tighter, Martin Luther King, Jr., in his "Letter from a Birmingham Jail" (1963), cites this biblical episode as an exemplar for civil disobedience — "evidenced sublimely in the refusal of Shadrach, Meshach and Abednego to obey the laws of Nebuchadnezzar, on the ground that a higher moral law was at stake." But King also delineates the manner in which Ab Jones diverges from both the biblical Abednego and King's own enterprise when he exhorts, "So the question is not whether we will be extremists, but what kind of extremists we will be. Will we be extremists for hate or will we be extremists for love? Will we be extremists for the preservation of justice or will we be extremists for the cause of justice?"

Ab's is ultimately a self-destructive brand of resistance, driven by obsessive hatred. "He want to kill his enemies is what he want," Miss Mother tells Suttree. "Which enemies?" Suttree asks her. In her wordless response the old sorceress reveals the futility and scope of Ab's enterprise against institutionalized racism: "She gestured with one hand, extending her arm and suggesting the world that stood beyond the thin board walls ... a gesture both grave and gracious that acknowledged endless armies of the unbending pale" (*Suttree*, p. 229). But Ab himself is not deluded about the futility and mindlessness of his battle, and his obsessive compulsion: "You aint got nothin for it but a busted head. You caint do nothin with them motherfuckers," he says. "I wouldnt fight em at all if I could keep from it" (p. 204).

Ab ultimately can't keep from it because the sense of injustice is so firmly branded into the fiber of his past. He describes to Suttree how he was shot by a white man as a teenager "cause I whipped him. I didnt know no better" (*ibid.*). That same white man was murdered and Ab was wrongly imprisoned for the crime and forced to endure severe beatings in jail.

Ab's shortened appellation also calls to mind "Ahab," from one of McCarthy's favorite works, Herman Melville's *Moby-Dick*. Ab's obsession with the massive "unbending pale" calls to mind Ahab's obsessive quest for the white leviathan. Here, an analogy can be drawn between the white whale and the Knoxville judicial body politic that Ab confronts — this particular usage of "body politic" having its roots in Thomas Hobbes' fittingly titled treatise (for this purpose) *Leviathan* (1651). In fact, Melville actually quotes from *Leviathan* in his novel about the white whale, borrowing Hobbes' first lines for the opening "Extracts" section of *Moby-Dick*: "For by Art is created that great LEVIATHAN called a COMMON-WEALTH, or STATE, (in latine CIVITAS) which is but an Artificiall Man" (Hobbes, p. xviii). And, indeed, Ab's actual fate is much more in line with Ahab's, though his civil disobedience reflects his biblical appellation, Abednego.

See also Race; *Suttree*; Suttree, Cornelius

Abbey, Edward

When Cormac McCarthy finally submitted to his first major interview, with the *New York Times* in 1992, he confirmed what many had often suspected: a general disdain for the literary world as well as the professional and social circles that writers of his caliber often inhabit. In particular, McCarthy noted how he preferred the company of scientists to that of other writers. Nevertheless, wrote Richard Woodward in 1992, "One of the few [writers] he acknowledges having known at all was the novelist and ecological crusader Edward Abbey," noting how, "[s]hortly before Abbey's death in 1989, they discussed a covert operation to reintroduce the wolf to southern Arizona" ("Venomous Fiction").

The plans for the wolf may have never materialized, but the association makes sense, as both writers are indelibly associated with the landscape of the Southwest and have been recognized as rugged individualists driven by their own respective visions and not afraid to work outside of the structures and orders of mainstream society. In fact, Abbey may have been the more extreme — or at the least the more vocal — of the two.

Abbey was not only a novelist but a staunch wilderness defender who often espoused extreme measures. "I feel rage and outrage quite often," he told the *Washington Post* not long before his death. "I'd gleefully take part in a violent revolution — I'd love to go down to city hall in Tucson and tear it down. I'm getting more radical as I get older" (Sipchen). In writing, he also displayed a powerful affinity and sensitivity for the Southwestern landscape that rivaled McCarthy's. "Alone in the silence, I understand for a moment the dread which many feel in the presence of primeval desert," he wrote in *Desert Solitaire: A Season in the Wilderness* (1968), "the unconscious fear which compels them to tame, alter or destroy what they cannot understand, to reduce the wild and prehuman to human dimensions" (p. 240).

Also like McCarthy (and like many Americans who once "settled" the West) Abbey came to the region from Appalachia, having grown up the son of a miner in Home, Pennsylvania. After serving in the Army, Abbey headed west in 1946, where he studied English and philosophy at the University of New Mexico. Soon after, he set out to become a writer, supporting himself through whatever jobs he could pick up. For nearly 20 years on and off, he worked for the U.S. Forest Service and the National Park Service. He also worked on highways, on an assembly line, as a roughneck in the oil fields, and as a ditch digger. "For most of those years," he has said, "I was living right around the official poverty line" (Sipchen).

Abbey would go on to pen 19 books, including his most well-known, the 1975 novel *The Monkey Wrench Gang*, about radical environmentalists planning the destruction of Glen Canyon Dam in Arizona. Two of his other, earlier books were made into movies, *The Brave Cowboy* (1956), which became the 1962 Western film *Lonely Are the Brave* (with Kirk Douglas), and *Fire on the Mountain* (1962), released as a movie of the same title in 1981.

But Abbey's legacy remains that of a controversial figure and a writer and spokesperson not afraid to go after sacred and romanticized institutions in the Southwest, including cattle ranching. "I have a deep, instinctive sympathy for the rancher and the small miner and the small logger," he said in 1988. "But our society is so huge, and so totally overpopulated, in my opinion, that there's no longer enough room on public lands for a privileged minority — cattle ranchers and to a lesser extent, miners and loggers" (Sipchen).

He had even harsher words for larger industries. "With bulldozer, earth mover, chain saw and dynamite, the international timber, mining and beef industries are invading our public lands ... bashing their way into our forests, mountains and rangelands and looting them," he wrote. "This for the sake of short-term profits in the corporate sector and multimillion-dollar annual salaries for the three-piece-suited gangsters" (*One Life at a Time*, pp. 29–30).

In the preliminary remarks to his essay collection *One Life at a Time, Please*, he fittingly wrote, "If there's anyone still present whom I've failed to insult, I apologize" (*ibid.*, p. 5). Edward Abbey died on March 14, 1989, from a circulatory ailment at his home in Oracle, Arizona.

All the Pretty Horses

All the Pretty Horses (1992) was the novel that pulled Cormac McCarthy out from the shadows of critical acclaim (and his reputation as a "writer's writer") and straight into the crucible of mass appeal. It was also the first book of the projected Border Trilogy that would come to include *The Crossing* (1994) and *Cities of the Plain* (1998). Despite its mass popularity, however, the novel was still critically lauded and scored both a National Book Award and a National Book Critics Circle Award.

In fact, McCarthy's greatest achievement with the book was hedging his own powerful and idiosyncratic style with a more accessible narrative — without compromising either. His previous book, *Blood Meridian* (1985), the first to take up the U.S.-Mexico borderlands as a geographical locale, showcased his complex mastery and will deservedly go down as one of the (if not *the*) most powerful works he has produced. *All the Pretty Horses*, however, as critic Stephen Tatum points out, offers, among other things, "a more linear and sparer departure-return adventure plot, a more pivotal romance subplot, and fewer extended inset stories" (p. 21). This differentiates it not only from *Blood Meridian* but also from the next book in the trilogy, *The Crossing*.

One of the ways in which McCarthy finds success is through the paradoxical capability of the novel. There are elements of the story that fall in line with boilerplate Westerns and classic romance, but through the prism of McCarthy's style those very elements are also questioned and even undermined as they are presented. Or, as Vince Brewton would have it, "in the Border Trilogy, McCarthy has undertaken to tell authentic westerns using the basic formulas of the genre while avoiding the false sentimentality, uncritical nostalgia, and unearned happy endings that often characterize the genre" (p. 133).

The very title of the book is pulled from a lullaby; it has a toothless, childlike ring to it that paradoxically cuts against the grain of the violent realities that the central figure, the teenager John Grady Cole, confronts across the border in Mexico. And even as the novel presents images of the romanticized Western, it sets up a pattern of questioning that very romance. We get a clue to this early on as John Grady Cole stares at a painting in the dining room of the family ranch, which is destined to be sold off to big oil interests. The oil painting is a vividly dramatic rendering of horses busting through a corral, with flowing manes and "wild" eyes. With his keen horseman and rancher's eye, Cole notices how the individual horses seem a mix and match, a Frankenstein-like patchwork of actual breeds. There are traces of Andalusian, Barb, and Steeldust in the horses, "but nothing else matched and no such horse ever was that he had seen" (p. 16). Cole had "once asked his grandfather what kind of horses they were" and his grandfather tersely responded, "picturebook horses," and "went on eating" (*ibid.*).

Here we see the narrative emerges as the "romantic" epic journey of Cole and his stalwart pal Lacey Rawlins into the deeper regions of Mexico. McCarthy presents a journey story in the tried-and-true tradition of innocence to experience (think Mark Twain's *Adventures of Huckleberry Finn* or countless Westerns), yet there is a constant, active layer to the narrative that also questions and even sometimes undermines the artifice of familiar tropes, or, as literary critic Neil Campbell suggests, McCarthy's text enters into "a dialogue with the myths of the West ... [following] their strange logic to dark conclusions, to the point where the myths turn in on themselves, implode and begin to deconstruct" (p. 218).

In another scene that functions much like that of the horses painting, Cole's mother — who is bound and determined to sell off the family ranch upon her father's death, thereby dashing Cole's dreams — is starring in a play at a theater in San Antonio. When Cole secretly slips in to the performance, he watches it "with great intensity. He'd the notion that there would be something in the story itself to tell him about the way the world was or was becoming but there was not." He finds "there was nothing in it at all" (p. 21). McCarthy hedges the more familiar elements of his own story — adventure, cowboys, romance — with a sense of the artifice of such dramatic devices. *All the Pretty Horses* grips us and wraps us up in Cole's journey from innocence to experience, while all the time telegraphing to us that there is no moral, lesson, or even redemption — here too there is nothing to tell the reader "the way the world was or was becoming."

John Grady Cole seems to take that critical mindset from the play into Mexico, and while Rawlins revels in the idea of the two of them as desperados on the run, Cole is more pragmatic and skeptical. In a humble mud-hut store in Reforma, the first Mexican town the boys encounter, they elbow up to the counter as if they are in a nineteenth-century Western saloon. Rawlins, drinking, plays every bit the cowboy: "I don't know what that shit is, he said. But it tastes pretty good to a cowboy. Let us have three more here" (p. 50). Later, in the same scene, we see Cole's more flat, realistic attitude: "Rawlins shook his head. Drinking cactus juice in old Mexico, he said. What do you reckon they're sayin at home about now? / I reckon they're sayin we're gone, said John Grady" (p. 51).

However, neither Cole's attitude nor the narrative's mode of questioning should be mistaken for intellectual aloofness from the more romantic, familiar elements of the story. In fact, in the Edenic horsemen's paradise of the Hacienda de Nuestra Señora de la Purísima Concepción, Cole becomes the vaunted breaker of wild horses that he has always dreamed of being and falls into a passionate romance with Alejandra, the rich, educated daughter of hacendado Don Hector. Likewise, McCarthy's prose often exults in the familiar devices of both the action-adventure and romantic motifs, skirting dangerously close to purple prose at times: "When she reached him he held out his hand and she took it. She was so pale in the lake she seemed to be burning. Like foxfire in a darkened wood," writes McCarthy. "Her black hair floating on the water about her, falling and floating on the water ... and then she turned her face up to him. Sweeter for the larceny of time and flesh, sweeter for the betrayal" (p. 141).

But this is one side of the paradoxical capability that is the book's strength. The reader becomes caught up in familiar motifs rendered masterfully — gripping adventure and engrossing, idyllic romance — yet the book seamlessly merges those motifs with McCarthy's powerfully singular style and his unique thematic and philosophical preoccupations (particularly with violence and a worldview that frequently teeters toward nihilism). Those critics who would question the clichéd über-masculinity of the adventure and the exotic, paradise-like glow of McCarthy's Mexico miss the fact that his prose has already presented that question for them.

Consider this scene he paints of Cole having returned from Mexico, in which he seems to vanquish the notion of antique cowboy mythology: "he drifted north again, trailing the horses in the bar ditches along the edge of the black top roads, the big semi's blowing them up against the fences" (p. 298). There's a stirring anachronistic effect to Cole awkwardly leading his horses along the narrow shoulder of a bustling modern highway while large tractor trailers blow by, a portrait that runs counter to the numerous previous passages of him heroically thundering across the plains on his horse, often bloodied and with bullets whipping through the air, in what seems a much more old-fashioned, mythical universe,

Like much of the Border Trilogy, *All the Pretty Horses* is cast in a blurred temporal border between the old and the new — and this is also true of the borderlands themselves during the time marked out in the book (1949–1950). The Mexican Revolution, an armed struggle on horseback, had ceased only two decades before, and its reverberations are still all over the Mexico that Cole encounters. In Texas, Cole's father is physically and psychologically debilitated from his injuries from the more recent World War II, the great modern, mechanized conflict. (*The Crossing* will actually take us backward, into a time just before and during that war.)

The old is giving way to the new, but the past still resonates. We witness this in the opening passage, with Cole attending the funeral of his grandfather, the last ancestral vestige of the family ranching tradition. His mother is destined to inherit the ranch and, like many others in west Texas, sell it off to big oil interests, signaling the death of an old way of life. Leaving his grandfather's coffin-side, Cole encounters a train, "boring out of the east like some ribald satellite of the coming sun howling and bellowing in the distance" (p. 3).

Its passage through this dying existence heralds the historical universality of this theme, what the *New York Times* has termed "that brief moment between a culture's existence and extinction — this is the border that McCarthy's characters keep crossing and recrossing" (Mosle, p. 16). Much like the land once used for ranching is giving way to oil companies and military interests, so too did the Comanche who once inhabited this land find themselves cast into obsolescence by the modernizing push of Manifest Destiny and the strikingly loud modern trains sweeping across the ancient plains. We see the narration sifting through all of those historical layers in the opening sequence: The funeral of his grandfather, a narrated history of the family ranching generations since 1872, the appearance of Cole's war-injured father, the pounding train, and a horseback ride along an old Comanche trail, where Cole can palpably feel the "riders of that lost nation" in the night, "all of them pledged in blood and redeemable in blood only" (p. 5).

Cole is also part of a generational cycle "redeemable in blood only," and here McCarthy picks up one of his great borderlands themes: the historical successions of bloodletting and violence. He picked this up in his preceding novel, *Blood Meridian*, an "American ... tragedy of blood" that unflinchingly describes "overwhelming carnage" (Bloom, p. 255) in the Tex-Mex borderlands 100 years before the time of *All the Pretty Horses*. Even 100 years down the road, however — and into the modern era — we find that Cole's personal path from innocence to experience must run a gauntlet of blood, much like his tragically wounded war veteran father before him and much like preceding generations. Cole's grandfather had seven brothers, none of whom had lived past 25: "They were drowned, shot, kicked by horses. They perished in fires.... The last two were killed in Puerto Rico in eighteen ninety-eight" in the Spanish-American War (p. 7).

In Mexico, which provides the canvas for his trajectory into adulthood, he experiences the consummation of true romantic love, but just as importantly, he also experiences the blood consummation, where he must kill or perish in a knife fight. The narrative intertwines violence and romantic love, like twisting gyres. Long after Cole and Alejandra's love has been condemned by the girl's grand-aunt and guardian, Dueña Alfonsa, the two choose to privately meet in the city of Zacatecas for what will be their last encounter. The girl leads him to a small, open plaza. "My grandfather died here," says Alejandra. "Where?" asks Cole. "Here. In this place," she answers. "In the revolution," finishes Cole, knowingly (p. 253). The image of the two young lovers standing on the spot of her young grandfather's killing during the revolution shows the intertwining of violence and romance.

McCarthy is hesitant to mythologize, though; violence is a matter of fact, and standing at the site of her grandfather's death the girl delivers just that, the facts, in a Joe Friday succession of clauses, boiled down to the quick: "There was no mother to cry. As in the *corridos*. Nor bird that flew. Just the blood on the stones. I wanted to show you. We can go" (*ibid.*). It is also fitting that Alejandra reveals a prophetic dream vision of Cole's own violent death to him in the plaza, a death that will happen just as she describes in the trilogy's final book, *Cities of the Plain*, when he is knifed to death over his love for a Mexican prostitute.

The death of Jimmy Blevins, the mysterious man-child companion of Cole and Rawlins who gets them into so much trouble, is represented in a similarly unvarnished, unromantic fashion. He is led off and unceremoniously shot behind a stand of trees, like a sick animal. As he is taken away, Cole "watched the small ragged figure vanish limping among the trees with his keepers," writes McCarthy. "There seemed insufficient substance to him to be the object of men's wrath. There seemed nothing about him sufficient to fuel any enterprise at all" (p. 177). He perishes out of sight, to the sound of just "a flat sort of pop. Then another" (p. 178). Without proselytizing, McCarthy seems to be stripping away any gloss to reveal only the act, both the inevitability and the mindlessness of it.

A tale that Alejandra's grand-aunt, the Dueña Alfonsa, relates to Cole further highlights the co-mingling of violence and love in the novel, and here McCarthy's story intersects with "real" historical events. Alfonsa tells how, as a teenager, she had deeply fallen in love with Gustavo, the younger brother of Francisco Madero, the genteel, educated Mexican president whose assassination in 1913 led to the bloodiest epoch in the Mexican Revolution. Gustavo, like his brother a politician and revolutionary, was captured by Federalist forces and released to an angry mob, where, as many historical sources report, he was tortured and killed. But McCarthy uses his descriptive powers to imagine the gory details that histories politely step over. Historical narrative has the potential to "legitimize" mindless violence or render it almost rational by giving it neatness and order and fitting it into a cause-and-effect sequence of events.

By contrast, Alfonsa's narration of the event highlights the senselessness of it by relating the specific details, and this historical footnote becomes part of a larger "mindless cycle of violence" (Eaton, p. 159) that constitutes McCarthy's borderlands history. It is important to note that McCarthy's narrative avoids preaching, instead relying on a maddening objectivity in his descriptions of bloodshed. As Timothy Parrish and Elizabeth Spiller point out, the historical violence in McCarthy's border books is not aimed at the "compensatory pleasures of self-accusation." Rather, McCarthy's renderings "remind us of how particularizing versions of history ... deny how we have become to be who we are" (p. 461). We see that veil pulled back in Alfonsa's unflinching descriptions of Gustavo's death:

25

When he begged them again to cease one of them came forward with a pick and pried out his good eye and he staggered away moaning in his darkness and spoke no more. Someone came forward with a revolver and put it to his head and fired but the crowd jostled his arm and the shot tore away his jaw. He collapsed at the feet of the statue of Morelos. Finally a volley of rifle shots was fired into him. He was pronounced dead. A drunk in the crowd pushed forward and shot him again anyway. They kicked his dead body and spat upon it. One of them pried out his artificial eye and it was passed among the crowd as a curiosity [p. 237].

In Alfonsa's rendering, all the ideals and politics that underpin the revolution dissipate into thin air and we are left with nothing but these monstrous acts, which she narrates in a seemingly empirical manner. And she shares with Cole her view of history as an endless, inevitable cycle of violence: "What is constant in history is greed and foolishness and a love of blood and this is a thing that even God — who knows all that can be known — seems powerless to change" (p. 239). Her narration of Gustavo's death calls to mind postcolonial critic Homi Bhabha's meditations on the violence of colonial contact, how he describes the remembering of it as "never a quiet act of introspection or retrospection [but] a painful re-membering, a putting together of the dismembered past to make sense of the trauma of the present" (p. 90). However, in McCarthy's world, there is no "sense" to be made; violence is both a fact of life and a driving historical force, and his characters often stare into that abyss without redemption or moralizing.

Violence is also a generational rite of passage for John Grady Cole, much like it was for his great-uncles and his own father. His consummation comes when he is forced to defend himself against assassination in a Mexican prison. In an act that cruelly mirrors romantic consummation, he thrusts the knife into his combatant's heart and "snapped the handle sideways and broke the blade off in him" (p. 201). He ends up in a blood-drenched embrace as the other young man "dropped to his knees and then pitched forward into the arms of his enemy" (*ibid.*).

Killing and passionate romance: This is quite an evolution from the narrative's beginnings. For Cole and Rawlins, Mexico had started out as a blank space on the map (p. 34), a space onto which they projected their romantic notions of an existence that adhered to old-fashioned cowboy principles — and they got a lot more than they bargained for. As Katherine Sugg suggests, "For McCarthy's Anglo characters, this Mexican landscape figures opportunities that had been shut down in the United States by the 1950s, specifically World War II: open pastures and freewheeling cowboys working outside the constraints of corporate and urban culture" (p. 118). In the U.S., Cole had simply been a disenfranchised young man with divorced parents whose girlfriend had just broken up with him — a west Texas teen in a town being taken over by oil corporations. In Mexico, he realized his adult ambition to be a vaunted trainer of wild horses, he found (and lost) the kind of passionate love that few experience, and he and Rawlins also engaged the bloody "realities" of existence.

Nevertheless, one motivating force that drives John Grady Cole throughout *All the Pretty Horses* is his overwhelming and peculiarly obstinate sense of justice — and this ultimately prevents the novel from pitching into outright pessimism. He shares this quality with the Border Trilogy's other protagonist, Billy Parham of *The Crossing* (though

Billy is a more complex case, and seems a bit more debauched and cynical by the time of *Cities of the Plain*). When the two unite in the third trilogy book, Cole's unwavering, stubborn commitment to his own justice compass ultimately leads to his death.

In this book, Cole's compass drives the action and therefore the conflict: his need to run away after his mother dissolves the ranch; his refusal to abandon the boy Blevins, who is a lightning rod for trouble (as well as a literal lightning rod); his refusal to let go of the relationship with Alejandra; and his stubborn need to recover his, Rawlins' and Blevins' horses and seek retribution upon a corrupt Mexican official. In a traditional Western or in a more conventional "hero" narrative, this essentially heroic quality might lead to some sort of satisfying resolution or redemption, but again the paradoxical quality of McCarthy's narrative rears its head, for, as one critic put it, "in the context of McCarthy's trademark pessimism (call it realism), the individual cannot truly win against the world" (Brewton, p. 136).

McCarthy's borderlands novels are not a binary world of good and evil and conflict and resolution. Therefore, in a landscape where mindless violence is a fact of life and where boundaries — both cultural and temporal — are often blurred, the "heroic" figure is cast adrift; there is no saving the day, no resolution and gallant ride over the final horizon.

Thus, we see Cole, in some sort of baptismal image, crossing the Rio Grande nude and on horseback, having fully emerged from his ordeal in Mexico. When he reaches United States soil, McCarthy paints a pathetic, discomfiting, vulnerable image that cuts against the grain of any heroic cowboy ideal: "he thought about his father who was dead in that country and he sat the horse naked in the falling rain and wept" (286). Here again we also get a sense that Cole's violent ordeal is a part of a larger historical cycle, as he finds out that this day is Thanksgiving, a holiday that harkens back to the country's Puritan roots and the roots of Manifest Destiny.

But while the traditional history of the American colonial enterprise has a rhetorical power to justify bloodshed in the name of nation and even religion, *All the Pretty Horses* traces the more arbitrary reasons for violence. When Cole says to the captain that shot Blevins, "You didn't have to kill him," the captain offers an anecdote by way of explanation in which he implies that, as a boy, he exacted violence upon a prostitute who refused him sex simply so his friends wouldn't laugh at him when he returned. The captain uses this analogy to explain why Blevins' fate was inevitable: "That has always been my way in this world. I am the one when I go someplace then there is no laughing" (p. 181). In more blunt terms, it was simply a matter of ego.

We essentially find Cole, and later Billy Parham in *The Crossing*, adrift in a state of unrelenting dislocation and emptiness at the end of the first two borderlands novels. Our last image of Billy in *The Crossing* is of him sitting in the middle of a highway weeping. Cole is cast in a similarly pessimistic light. Toward the end of *All the Pretty Horses* Cole and his old buddy Rawlins have a final exchange in which Rawlins proclaims, "This is still good country." Cole responds, "Yeah. I know it is. But it ain't my country." Rawlins then asks, "Where is your country?" to which Cole curiously responds, "I dont know where it is. I dont know what happens to country" (p. 299).

Here, the idea of "country" seems to telescope from the immediate surrounding environs of Tom Green County to a larger sense of "nation" during the course of the exchange. McCarthy also makes implicit the historical cycles of nation-building violence as Cole rides off in the final pages. First, he passes a group of "indians camped on the western plain," who simply stare at him: "They stood and watched him pass and watched him vanish upon that landscape solely because he was passing. Solely because he would vanish" (p. 301). This scene recalls the ride along the old Comanche trail at the beginning of the book, where the ghosts of the old warriors are palpable. The word "vanish" is loaded, though, as the Native Americans have all but vanished from the plains. The text suggests that Cole and his ilk (cowboy/rancher) are vanishing as well. The final passage, which repeats some imagery from the Comanche trail ride early in the novel, is both apocalyptic and soaked in the colors of the bloody past, recalling the title image in *Blood Meridian*, the weighty prequel to the Border Trilogy: "The desert he rode was red and red the dust he raised.... A wind came up and reddened all the sky before him," writes McCarthy. "He came at evening upon a solitary bull rolling in the dust against the bloodred sunset like an animal in sacrificial torment. The bloodred dust blew down out of the sun (p. 302).

This final image is followed by the shadows of Cole and horse melding into one another and seeping into the "darkening land, the world to come" (*ibid.*). This unsettling conclusion reminds us just how distinctive, powerful, and unusual a reading experience the Border Trilogy truly is and is illustrative of the relentless dark weight of the books. Dana Phillips explained how McCarthy's "worldview is bound to be disturbing to readers who ... expect novels to offer an imaginary solution to individual or social ills" (p. 452), which we can feel in the dark, unresolved final passage.

Beyond thematic concerns, however, we cannot forget the remarkable language of Cormac McCarthy. True, he hedged his singular style with a book that for the first time in his career provided many accessible and familiar elements, yet all of those master flourishes are still present as well. We see this in the apocalyptic and loaded image of the twisting bull in the previously cited passage, which seemed to herald an end to the ranching way of life, but we can even see a kind of serene economy in his description of a prison knife slashing: "he held [a switchblade] at waist level and passed it three times across Rawlins' shirt while Rawlins leaped three time backwards with his shoulders hunched and his arms outflung like a man refereeing his own bloodletting" (p. 189). At many points in the book, the reader also experiences the hallmark omniscient voice that occasionally breaks into a McCarthy narrative in a stentorian *basso profondo*:

> [T]he captain inhabited another space and it was a space of his own election and outside the common world of men. A space privileged to men of the irreclaimable act which while it contained all the lesser worlds within it contained no access to them. For the terms of election were of a piece with its office and once chosen that world could not be quit [p. 179].

This is the booming, antiquarian voice that we will hear even more prominently in *The Crossing*. McCarthy also renders the relationship between John Grady Cole and horse in one long stream of prose that is itself all muscle and sinew and that delves into the very interior of the animal:

> [I]nside the vaulting of the ribs between his knees the darkly meated heart pumped of who's will and the blood pulsed and the bowels shifted in their massive blue convolutions of who's

28

will and the stout thighbones and knee and cannon and the tendons like flaxen hawsers that drew and flexed and drew and flexed at their articulations and of who's will all sheathed and muffled in the flesh and the hooves that stove wells in the morning groundmist and the head turning side to side and the great slavering keyboard of his teeth and the hot globes of his eyes where the world burned [p. 128].

This is the uncanny language that has roots in William Faulkner but that McCarthy has fashioned in his own image over the decades. Many critics were enchanted by McCarthy's style upon the release of the book in May of 1992. Major American newspapers such as "the *New York Times, Los Angeles Times, Chicago Sun-Times,* and the national magazines *Time* and *Newsweek*" praised it, and "in dramatic contrast to the fate of McCarthy's previous novels, *All the Pretty Horses* appeared on the *New York Times* hardback national bestseller list" (Tatum, p. 69). The *New York Times* noted how, "[p]owered by long, tumbling many-stranded sentences, his descriptive style is elaborate and elevated.... McCarthy seems to be pulling the language apart at its roots." The critic also pointed to what he termed McCarthy's "archaisms": "His diction and phrasing come from all over the evolutionary history of English and combine into a prose that seems to invent itself as it unfolds, resembling Elizabethan language in its flux of remarkable possibilities" (Bell, "The Man Who," p. 9).

Newsweek saw in John Grady Cole one of McCarthy's noblest characters, suggesting that he "partakes of violence with the greatest reluctance and wears its memory with genuine remorse. This young man — gentle, stubborn and honorable — ranks with his creator's greatest achievements" (Jones, p. 68). Meanwhile, the *Washington Post* heralded the thematic scope and universality of the book: "Like classic literary journeys before it — from Jason and the Argonauts chasing the golden fleece to Huck and Jim floating down the Mississippi — this is a trip that covers much more than just geography" (Tidmore, p. X1).

Also, in the back of everyone's mind, of course, was the idea that *All the Pretty Horses* wasn't simply the culmination of something — of simply bringing to the masses the unusual gifts of Cormac McCarthy after nearly 30 years of publishing. This was the first stage of the towering Border Trilogy. Readers hadn't seen the last of John Grady Cole, who would tragically reemerge in the final volume, *Cities of the Plain,* and an introduction to another compelling and enigmatic young man from the American Southwest was just around the corner.

See also The Dueña Alfonsa; Blevins, Jimmy; Cole, John Grady; Rocha, Alejandra

• *Further Reading*

Arnold, Edwin T. "'Go to Sleep': Dreams and Visions in the Border Trilogy." *A Cormac McCarthy Companion: The Border Trilogy,* eds. Edwin T. Arnold and Dianne C. Luce. Jackson: University Press of Mississippi, 2001.

Bell, Madison Smartt. "The Man Who Understood Horses." *The New York Times Book Review,* May 17, 1992, p. 9.

Brewton, Vince. "The Changing Landscape of Violence in Cormac McCarthy's Early Novels and the Border Trilogy." *Southern Literary Journal* 37, no. 1 (Fall 2004), pp. 121–143.

Busby, Mark. "Into the Darkening Land, the World to Come: Cormac McCarthy's Border

Crossings." *Myth, Legend, Dust: Critical Responses to Cormac McCarthy*, ed. Rick Wallach. Manchester, UK: Manchester University Press, 2000.

Sugg, Katherine. "Multicultural Masculinities and the Border Romance in John Sayles's *Lone Star* and Cormac McCarthy's Border Trilogy." *The New Centennial Review* 1, no. 3 (Winter 2001), pp. 117–154.

Tatum, Stephen. *Cormac McCarthy's* All the Pretty Horses: *A Reader's Guide*. New York: Continuum Books, 2002.

Tidmore, Kurt. "Lighting Out for the Territory." *Washington Post Book World*, May 3, 1992, p. Xl.

Wegner, John. "Wars and Rumors of Wars in Cormac McCarthy's Border Trilogy." *A Cormac McCarthy Companion: The Border Trilogy*, eds. Edwin T. Arnold and Dianne C. Luce. Jackson: University Press of Mississippi, 2001.

The American Southwest

Patricia Nelson Limerick, a leading historian of the American West, has written of the "habit of mind that has long burdened western American history: the desire to squeeze very complicated events into simple categories" (foreword, p. xvi). She points out that "Americans have worked diligently, kneading the stories until the complexities of the events ... have been smoothed, flattened, compressed, and generally made manageable" (*ibid.*). In neatly codifying the events that led to the American claim on the region, Limerick points out how the turgid, complicated "swirl of encounters, transactions, and conflicts" is tamed into false dichotomies: "the familiar pairings of 'whites versus Indians,' 'good guys versus bad guys,' 'winners versus losers'" (*ibid.*, p. xix). Furthermore, she notes an American tendency to not face "up to the bitter reality of violence embedded in landscapes that Americans would later come to see as places of natural innocence, separated from the tragedy of history" (*ibid.*).

With his historically fraught, diligently researched books about the U.S.-Mexican borderlands — particularly *Blood Meridian* (1985) — Cormac McCarthy has done much to move against this tendency and to engage the messy complexities and pervasive violence that are the history of the American Southwest. Indeed, with its potent descriptions of savagery and exacting body counts *Blood Meridian* taps into areas that few other novels about the West have dared broach. The narrative broadly ranges about the contested lands that would eventually form the American Southwest and northern Mexico, a cultural stew of indigenous tribes, Anglos of various European descents, the occasional African American, and Spanish-speaking peoples. But the "sides" and allegiances here are muddy at best, as testified to by McCarthy's central representation of the band of scalpers, the Glanton Gang, a motley, multi-racial crew that includes a black man and some "Delaware" (Lenape) Indians (along with a host of Anglo degenerates from many walks of life). Further complicating this civilizational portrait is the nature of their vocation, which contractually binds them to furnish Apache scalps to the governors of the Mexican states of Chihuahua and Sonora.

During this time (1840s and '50s), these northern Mexican regions were in pitched

conflict with the Apache and Comanche and employed bands of mercenaries to eliminate the natives. These mercenaries, typically from the United States, used scalps as
receipt for what was at the time significant payment. The rationale for using U.S. bounty
hunters was simple: At the time, Anglo relations with the Apache in particular were
more cordial than Mexican relations with the natives; therefore, a common pattern for
the "bounty killers was to meet with a band of Apaches and then ... suddenly attack
their unsuspecting trade partners" (Jacoby, p. 102). Notorious bounty scalp hunters of
the period included the Northern Ireland–born James Kirker and infamous James Johnson, who is credited with sparking the scalp industry boom.

The Mexican War directly preceded the period that McCarthy addresses in *Blood
Meridian*, and most readings of that conflict focus on the finely demarcated lines between
the primary combatants, Mexico and the United States, but the indigenous people of
the region were a major factor too. Historian Donald Emmet Worcester points out that
by the onset of the conflict, "conditions in northern Mexico were appalling; the Apaches
and Comanches had gravely weakened Mexico's capacity to defend the region" (p. 43).
In fact, Worcester points out that during the war "Apaches destroyed a number of towns
in Sonora and forced Mexican troops to abandon the presidio of Tubac" (*ibid.*).

Raids of Mexican ranches and livestock were a cornerstone of subsistence for
the Apache and Comanche, and early on in *Blood Meridian* we encounter a large
band of Comanche riding a Mexican plunder trail with "several thousand head" of
stolen cattle, horses, and mules (p. 51). McCarthy describes this "legion of horribles,
hundreds in number" as decked out in haphazard accoutrements, heterogeneous cos-
tumes of plunder that allegorize the confusing multiculturalism and fraught violence of
the borderlands: "skins of animals," "silk finery," "braided cavalry jackets," a "stovepipe
hat," "an umbrella," "a bloodstained weddingveil," a conquistador's armor "deeply dented
with old blows of mace of sabre [sic] done in another country by men whose very
bones were dust" (p. 52). Here, too, the author unabashedly details a "bitter reality of
violence" that Limerick claims Americans are hesitant to face up to — the Comanche
raiders descend upon Captain White's outfit, scalping and mutilating the would-be
agents of Manifest Destiny, "hacking and chopping at the naked bodies, ripping off
limbs, heads, gutting the strange white torsos and holding up great handfuls of viscera"
(p. 54).

But early Apache and Comanche relations with white settlers (1820s, '30s, '40s),
who were still interlopers to the region, were often more "marked by mutual accommo-
dation than irreconcilable differences," likely because they had a common enemy in Mexico (Jacoby, p. 101). Many Americans, for example, had no problem trading for loot that
was plundered in raids of Mexico. This of course changed as Americans evolved into
permanent and populous settlers in the 1850s after the war-ending Treaty of Guadalupe
Hidalgo and the Gadsden Purchase vastly extended the young American republic into
regions that Mexico once claimed. This led to a rampant displacement of all Native
American communities by a massive influx of settlers, displacement that, as Larry
McMurtry indicates, "accelerated sharply in the 1840s and 1850s" (p. 2).

Blood Meridian, opening in the late 1840s (around 1847), thrusts the reader into
this turbulent historical borderlands, with the Glanton Gang modeled on a real-life

band of scalpers described in gang member Samuel Chamberlain's account, *My Confession: Recollections of a Rogue*. And McCarthy's contribution to the historical conversation is important, despite its literary tack, for as Karl Jacoby, author of *Shadows at Dawn* (2008) — a penetrating study of the 1871 Camp Grant Massacre — points out, "the borderlands between history and storytelling ... much like the U.S.-Mexico border itself, has not always been as clearly demarcated as some might expect" (p. 6).

Jacoby's own engagement of the Camp Grant Massacre, like McCarthy's work, confronts the complexities of cultural relations in the borderlands, showing how a "combined force of Anglo Americans, Mexican Americans, and Tohono O'odham Indians" ransacked an Apache reservation located in Arizona, "sixty miles northeast of Tucson, killing a large number of women and children" (Jacoby, p. 2). This is the same strange egalitarianism we find in McCarthy, a world in which savagery cuts across cultures and leads to unexpected allegiances and battle lines.

In fact, the first glimpse of the Glanton Gang yields up a sight akin to the "legion of horribles" that overwhelmed Captain White's outfit earlier in the novel. The gang is described as "visciouslooking humans ... bearded, barbarous, clad in the skins of animals," and the "trappings of their horses [are] fashioned out of human skin and their bridles woven up from human hair and decorated with human teeth." The riders' own adornments consist of "scapulars or necklaces of dried and blackened human ears," looking altogether like a "visitation from some heathen land" (*Blood Meridian*, p. 78). The Apache and Comanche clearly have nothing on this crew when it comes to savagery, and the notion that a governor's contract could contain such violence is foolish — of course, the scalpers eventually turn against and slaughter all that crosses their path: peaceful Indians, women, children, Mexican soldiers and citizens. (Many historical accounts point out that in their zeal to collect bounties scalp hunters descended upon any and all with black hair: Mexicans, other indigenous people, etc.)

As mentioned, *Blood Meridian* thrusts us into the period just after the Mexican War, a time when the United States had absorbed almost half of what was once Mexico's territory. This is the hot crucible of Manifest Destiny, a time of remarkable expansion allegedly divined "by Providence," as editor and columnist John L. O'Sullivan wrote in 1845. (The latter passages of *Blood Meridian* leap ahead to the winter of 1878.) For many who come to McCarthy's novel, however, the historical poignancy will not be as prominent a feature as the vividly rendered bloodletting that courses through the pages. Harold Bloom defends this aspect, proclaiming that "[none] of [*Blood Meridian*'s] carnage is gratuitous or redundant; it belonged to the Mexico-Texas borderlands of 1849–1850" (p. 255).

It is also captivating that McCarthy's rendering of the historical Southwest not only confronts the unreal violence and intercultural convolutions that Patricia Nelson Limerick has accused others of glossing over, but it comes two years before Limerick's own groundbreaking re-rendering of Western history, 1987's *The Legacy of Conquest: The Unbroken Past of the American West*. McCarthy seems to have been step-for-step — if not in front of — many of the early "new Western" historians.

Another commonality that McCarthy shares with the most trenchant Western historical scholarship is the idea of the U.S.-Mexico borderlands as space of liminality and not as a clearly demarcated separation between cultures. Karl Jacoby, who is at the forefront of a newer generation of Southwestern historians, noted in 2008 how the border "never completely separated the communities on either side," and furthermore how the eras of Mexican and American claim on the region "do not divide neatly at some point moment in time, but rather bleed into one another, mutually constructing the borderlands of the nineteenth century — and beyond" (p. 95). That the newly established border in the 1850s — which took years to map out — passed through the heart of active native communities presents yet another conundrum to the idea of demarcation.

For Cormac McCarthy, liminality becomes the very milieu of the Border Trilogy that came upon the heels of *Blood Meridian*, and an important force in his reimagining of the Western. For the American cowboy protagonists John Grady Cole and Billy Parham, living in the middle of the twentieth century, the multicultural history of the borderlands has bold resonance; they move easily between Spanish and English dialogues, and in Mexico they consistently rub up against the after effects of the Mexican Revolution (1910–1920), absorbing the tales and violent lessons of that epoch. In that country, they experience intimate encounters with people of all stripes: rural poor, aristocrats, artisans, gypsies, workers, bureaucrats, felons, Mennonites, Mormons, *serranos* (mountain people). Billy even embodies the racially mixed nature of the borderlands; riding his horse, he sings "old songs his father once had sung ... and a soft *corrido* in spanish from his [Mexican maternal] grandmother" (*The Crossing*, p. 125).

Though the trilogy leaves behind the 1800s for a more modern milieu (the 1940s and 1950s), the past is always a stalwart presence. Only a few pages into the first book of the trilogy, John Grady Cole rides an old Comanche trail (in 1949) and that prior race is still palpable: a "ghost of nation passing in a soft chorale ... bearing lost to all history and all remembrance like a grail the sum of their secular and transitory and violent lives" (*All the Pretty Horses*, p. 5). Cole's own violent family history in the region rises to the surface in the early pages as well. His family ranch was built in 1872, and his grandfather was the only of eight male siblings to escape an early death. The rest surrendered to the afflictions of frontier life, having been "drowned, shot, kicked by horses. They perished in fires. They seemed to fear only dying in bed" (*ibid.*, p. 7). In McCarthy's borderlands, lives and ways of existence are transitory, but violence is constant.

National identity is not so constant in these liminal border spaces, however. Political scientist Benedict Anderson, in the book *Imagined Communities* (1991), mapped out national identity as a mere invention, and this is an attitude that resounds in the Border Trilogy as well. John Grady Cole, having just emerged from his ordeal in Mexico, is asked, "Where is your country?" He responds, "I dont know ... I dont know where it is. I dont know what happens to country" (*All the Pretty Horses*, p. 299). The slippery nature of national identity in the borderlands is hinted at before John Grady and Rawlins even enter Mexico. They encounter a Tejano (a Texan of Mexican descent), whom McCarthy paradoxically chooses to describe as a "Mexican," and they ask him about Mexico: "The Mexican shook his head and spat. I never been to Mexico in my life" (*ibid.*, p. 34).

It is not only "country" but ways of life and means of existence that surrender to the transitory nature of the borderlands. From *Blood Meridian* to *All the Pretty Horses*, the reader is swept through momentous changes that impact the societies of the region. Vast fenceless deserts and plains are filled with railroads and cordoned off into ranches; the ranches in turn are leased or sold to become oil fields. (*The Crossing* also references atomic testing in the open spaces of New Mexico). By the third decade of the twentieth century, some small "cattle towns" became cities and centers of oil industry and the "vast cattle country of the panhandle and Permian Basin was opened to the petroleum industry" (Hinton and Olien, p. 166). By the time that John Grady Cole rides across the early pages of *All the Pretty Horses*, the oil industry had a firm foothold and the *vaquero* (cowboy) way of life was rapidly diminishing.

Amidst the influx of industry the border itself has been more a place of constant cultural and commercial exchange and less of a line of separation. Free trade between the U.S. and Mexico occurred in "certain communities after 1858," and, beginning in 1885, the *Zona Libre* policy extended that agreement along the entirety of the border (Martínez, p. xvi). The Mexican government discontinued the *Zona Libre* in 1905, but Prohibition saw Americans flocking into Mexico in the 1920s. The World War II and Korean War years heralded a boom in tourism into Mexico, while the United States' demand for cheap Mexican labor as well as "the pattern of large-scale Mexican immigration into the Southwest that began in the 1940s" continues to this day, despite U.S. governmental efforts to curb it (*ibid.*).

In addition, border cities such as Juárez and El Paso, the titular *Cities of the Plain* (1998) of the final trilogy book, have developed interdependent economies, relying upon shoppers from across the border for subsistence. Since World War II, the United States government has also stimulated the American Southwest by deep military investments in installations and industry throughout the region. Northern Mexico, as "an extension of the U.S. Southwest" benefitted from this external funding as well as from "national industrialization policies promoted from Mexico City." These factors culminated in El Norte becoming "one of the most modern and prosperous regions within the Mexican republic" (Martínez, p. xviii).

But as we see in standard histories and in McCarthy's novels, the borderlands relationship between the United States and Mexico has been one of conflict and interdependence. *No Country for Old Men* (2005), which is set in the Texas border country in 1980, offers new, terrible testimony to this. Sheriff Bell, in one of his italicized inner-monologue chapters, laments, "*I think if you were Satan and you were settin around tryin to think up somethin that would just bring the human race to its knees what you would probably come up with is narcotics. Maybe he did*" (p. 218). In what the *Wall Street Journal* has called a "neo–Western" novel, drug trafficking has replaced the Glanton Gang as the new marauding evil of the Southwest.

An alarmingly large percentage of the illegal drugs that enter the United States are still smuggled across the border, but here we see U.S.-Mexico borderlands' interdependence rear its head again, as a June 2009 article reported that "90 per cent of the weapons seized in Mexico originate in the United States" (Diebel). And has the region truly come so far since the days of the Glanton Gang and other bands of bounty scalpers? McCarthy has consistently used the borderlands to point out the continuity of violence in human civilizations. Therefore, the author surely would not express the same shock as U.S. Senator John F. Kerry, Senate Foreign Relations Committee chairman, who noted in a March 2009 El Paso panel meeting that drug-related killings and beheadings were occurring "just a stone's throw across the Rio Grande from where we're sitting this morning" (Quinones).

While introducing the Obama administration's National Southwest Border Counternarcotics Strategy in June 2009, United States attorney general Eric Holder claimed, "Drug trafficking cartels spread violence and lawlessness throughout our border region and reach into all of our communities, large and small." He also called for "increased cooperation between the U.S. and Mexican governments as well as enhanced communication within U.S. law enforcement agencies" ("Obama Administration Announces National Strategy"). The same article outlining this initiative describes how "[a]cross the border, thousands of Mexican soldiers patrol Ciudad Juárez, which has had about 2,000 [drug cartel-related] slayings in 14 months" (*ibid.*). This, of course, is the very same Juárez that McCarthy analogized to the "cities of the plain" in the novel of the same name — the biblical cities of Sodom and Gomorrah that God saw fit to destroy because of irreversible corruption and evil.

Sheriff Bell of *No Country for Old Men*, a traditional, old-school Texas law enforcer, finds himself ill-equipped to deal with this new menace of the American West. He notes to a newspaperman how, of 19 felony charges in his remote region the previous year, only two were non–drug-related: "In the meantime, I've got a county the size of Delaware that is full of people who need my help" (p. 95). Bell suggests, however, that this malevolence is of a whole new breed, one unforeseen by history. He says that he once thought that he was dealing with the same kind of criminal that his grandfather had to deal with back when "they was rustlin cattle." But he came to a different view: "I ain't sure we've seen these people before. Their kind. I dont know what to do about them even. If you killed em all they'd have to build an annex to hell" (p. 79).

Bell's view seems to veer from McCarthy's, however, for his borderlands novels place humanity on a historical continuum. There's a reason why McCarthy describes the ancient, rock-carved pictographs that Llewelyn Moss passes by in the opening passages. The etchings are described as "perhaps a thousand years old. The men who drew them hunters like himself. Of them there was no trace" (p. 11). How much different, one should ask, is this novel's bounty hunter Anton Chigurh from the bounty scalpers in *Blood Meridian*? Human existence is transitory, the five books that constitute McCarthy's borderlands work tell us, but the evil — from scalpers to war, to genocide, to drug-cartel beheadings — remains the same.

See also All the Pretty Horses; Blood Meridian; Borderlands; *Cities of the Plain; The Crossing; No Country for Old Men;* Violence.

• *Further Reading*

Jacoby, Karl. *Shadows at Dawn: A Borderlands Massacre and the Violence of History.* New York: Penguin Press, 2008.

Limerick, Patricia Nelson. *The Legacy of Conquest: The Unbroken Past of the American West.* New York: W.W. Norton & Company, 1988.

Martínez, Oscar Jáquez. *U.S.-Mexico Borderlands: Historical and Contemporary Perspectives*. Lanham, MD: Rowman & Littlefield, 2003.

Animals

Animals often figure prominently in Cormac McCarthy's fiction, taking on mystical significance or even mirroring human nature. At other times, McCarthy portrays a striking intimacy between animals and men. The animals in McCarthy's novels also represent a link to an older, natural order and a vanishing (or vanished) way of life.

Two of the more prominent examples of McCarthy's rendering of animals show up in *All the Pretty Horses* (1992) and *The Crossing* (1994), but animals are an important motif throughout most of his fiction. The representations are clearly myriad and diverse, but the one thing that can be asserted for certain is that the overarching tendency is to elevate animals to positions of great significance; they inhabit a space that, while often overlapping with the human realm, is distinctive and important.

In fact, since McCarthy takes the slant that human existence is corrupted and fleeting in the overall order of things, one could argue that animals occupy a higher hierarchical status in McCarthy's fictional worldview. In *Cities of the Plain* (1998), they certainly occupy a high moral and ethical ground. As John Grady puts it, a horse "won't do one thing while you're watching him and another when you ain't.... A good horse has justice in his heart. I've seen it" (p. 53). It's also quite significant that in *The Road* (2006)— a dying world that is utterly devoid of natural life — the last image is of a "muscular and torsional" brook trout who lived in "deep glens where ... all things were older than man and they hummed of mystery" (p. 287). He suggests a natural world with infinite roots, before humankind.

In *All the Pretty Horses* John Grady Cole is virtually defined by his relationship to horses, and there are moments of striking intimacy between him and horses in the novel. In one passage, McCarthy depicts John Grady breaking a green colt and sitting astride it as it lay on the ground, its muzzle pressed to his chest and its "hot sweet breath ... flooding up from the dark wells of its nostrils over his face and neck like news from another world" (p. 103). Here we witness not only the intimacy between man and horse, but the mystical — even esoteric — light ("another world") in which McCarthy casts horses. They also show up in that hue in John Grady's dreams, where the young man himself is running with the horses "and they moved all of them in a resonance that was like a music among them ... that resonance which is the world itself and which cannot be spoken but only praised" (p. 162).

McCarthy also explores a metaphysical kinship between horses and men. An old man named Luis, a veteran of the Mexican Revolution, tells John Grady and Rawlins, "the souls of horses mirror the souls of men more closely than men suppose ... horses also love war" (p. 111). But in a world in which mechanized, modern warfare is encroaching, and in a geographical region where the cowboy lifestyle is headed toward obsolescence, the horses in the Border Trilogy also come to embody an old and vanishing way of life.

Wolves assume a similar place of significance in *The Crossing*. The ranchers discuss how the cattle, in their domestication and defenselessness, "puzzle" the wolves, who kill the cattle in a much more savage manner than they do wild quarry, "as if they were offended by some violation of an old order. Old protocols" (p. 25). Like the horses or the brook trout, they provide a link to an ancient order in McCarthy's books. They also show up as mystical creatures, such as when Billy consults an old trapper, who warns him that the wolf is a being "of great order and that it knows what men do not: that there is no order in the world save that which death has put there" (p. 45).

In *Cities of the Plain*, the reader again experiences John Grady Cole's intimate relationship with horses. In fact, in one exchange, both John Grady and Billy Parham come to agree that "a horse knows what's in your heart" (p. 84). Of course, the interest in animals in McCarthy's work is an outcrop of his characterizations — McCarthy often creates people who are particularly attuned to the natural world and all it contains (much like the author himself). Let us not forget that opening image of the boy Billy Parham in *The Crossing*: "He carried Boyd before him in the bow of the saddle and named to him the features of the landscape and birds and animals in both spanish and english" (p. 3). Even as the novels take us down deep avenues of philosophical and theological exploration, animals often provide a ballast for the characters — a sense of certainty in an uncertain world.

Billy also experiences moments of intimacy with the pregnant she-wolf that echo John Grady Cole's relationship to horses, and this happens at the same two levels: in both the dream world and the tangible world. In a dream, Billy can feel wolves' muzzles and their breath against his face (p. 295). But his literal encounters with the pregnant she-wolf are also depicted in arrestingly intimate terms: "When he touched her her skin ran and quivered under his hand.... He talked to her about his life" (p. 89).

Ultimately, though, the wolf attains a different brand of significance than horses; the wolf, unlike the wild horses, is not something that can be broken or otherwise mastered, and Billy's attempt to essentially domestic one and bend it to his will ends terribly. When Billy cradles the dead wolf's head in his lap, McCarthy notes that he is reaching out to hold "what cannot be held" (p. 127). In this way, as Wallis R. Sanborn points out, the vanishing wolves in *The Crossing* become "a negative metaphor for man's ceaseless appetite for control over the natural world" (p. 131). Since McCarthy is also frequently preoccupied with existences that are headed toward extinction, it must be noted that the vanishing wolf — as a threat to cattle — has been pushed toward extinction by the ranching enterprise, just as the ranching way of life is also giving way.

All the Pretty Horses and *The Crossing* are not alone in their deliberation on animals; this is a motif that McCarthy began working with quite early on. In fact, in his first novel, *The Orchard Keeper*, a panther appears as a phantasm-like presence, more myth than thing — here again it represents an old order, a dying way of existence in which humans were closer with, and more attuned to, nature. Yet the panther of *The Orchard Keeper* also seems weakened by its proximity to and dependence upon humans: It sleeps in an outhouse (and smells of it), feeds on prey lodged in man-made traps, and is attacked unawares by an owl. (A panther, a.k.a. mountain lion, also makes a brief appearance as a phantasm-like being that is talked about but never seen in *Cities of the Plain*.) The feline is a potent symbol in the novel, though, and the wild and vital being of the panther is contrasted with a blighted and sickly litter of kittens, which represent domestication. The domestic cat also shows up as a mystical being in the novel, an animal that the souls of the dead sometimes inhabit, according to local lore.

• *Further Reading*

Sanborn, Wallis R. *Animals in the Fiction of Cormac McCarthy.* Jefferson, NC: McFarland, 2006.

Apocalyptic Themes

McCarthy's apocalyptic worldview can perhaps best be expressed by the character Judge Holden, who, gesturing to the ruins left by the ancient Anasazi, says, "They quit these parts, routed by drought or disease or wandering bands of marauders, quit these parts ages since and of them there is no memory" (*Blood Meridian*, p. 146). Then comes the kicker: "This you see here, these ruins wondered at ... do you not think this will be again?" (*ibid.*, p. 147).

McCarthy's poetic vision always weighs the historical ebb and flow of civilizations (particularly the ebb), which is why the reader constantly glimpses mnemonic traces of the past in his novels: Anasazi ruins in *Blood Meridian* (1985); rock pictographs etched by ancient hunters in both *Cities of the Plain* (1998) and *No Country for Old Men* (2005); John Grady Cole's palpable sense of old indigenous warrior races on an ancient horse trail in *All the Pretty Horses* (1992). The beginning of *Blood Meridian* is even preceded by a news clipping from the *Yuma Daily Sun*, describing a three-million-year-old fossil skull that "shows evidence of having been scalped" (*Blood Meridian* preface page). The clipping is presented to introduce this story of hired borderlands scalpers in the 1850s, and seems to implicitly say to the reader, "Look how far we have *not* come."

In McCarthy's borderlands novels there is always the looming awareness that civilizations will rise and civilizations will fall, but what is constant is war, brutality, and death. This is why his books, particularly his works concerning the Southwest and Mexico, are littered with apocalyptic themes and images—until, of course, he delivers the death of *all* civilizations in the post-apocalyptic rendering *The Road* (2006). Considering all of this, it is difficult not to think of Cormac McCarthy when considering this passage, written by Native American writer Louise Erdrich in 1984:

> In our worst nightmares, all of us have conceived what the world might be like *afterward* and have feared that even our most extreme versions of a devastated planet are not extreme enough. Consider, then, that to American Indians it is as if the unthinkable has already happened, and relatively recently. Many Native American cultures were annihilated more thoroughly than even a nuclear disaster might destroy ours [Wong, p. 48].

This is what Judge Holden is speaking of; but what makes it compelling in the space of the narrative—and such a powerful literary device—is that the Judge is immersed in the very "unthinkable" described above by Erdrich. As a hired expunger of Indians, he is engaged in annihilation with the other members of the Glanton Gang. But Judge

Holden is the only character in the novel that carries a full awareness of the dimensions, scope, and continuity of the enterprise — of the link between the three-million-year-old scalping, the Glanton Gang, and the devastation of which Erdrich speaks. The Judge is aware of the historical continuum, is aware that he is an agent of the "unthinkable." And perhaps his awareness holds the key to Judge Holden's immortality — perhaps he is, in fact, the *embodiment* of these civilizational qualities. In this way, he lives up to the claims at the end of the novel: "He never sleeps. He says that he will never die" (*Blood Meridian*, p. 335).

Prior to the Western novels, we had already seen apocalyptic stirrings in McCarthy's work — in *Suttree*'s (1979) purgatorial wasteland, for example, and in the compelling image of the hopeless Culla Holme at the end of *Outer Dark* (1968), wandering a supernatural road and landscape whose description anticipates *The Road*, nearly 40 years later: "The road went on ... and for miles there were only the charred shapes of trees in a dead land ... a spectral waste out of which reared only the naked trees in attitudes of agony and dimly hominoid like figures in a landscape of the damned" (*Outer Dark*, p. 242). But McCarthy's apocalyptic intonations found a true home when he turned to the American West, a locale where, as Erdrich has pointed out, the unthinkable has happened "only recently." And it's no mistake that McCarthy begins *Blood Meridian* with the 1850s, in the crucible of massacre. For, as Larry McMurtry reminds us, this "process" of Native American displacement that began in the 1830s "accelerated sharply in the 1840s and 1850s, [and] was mostly completed, insofar as the native tribes were concerned, by 1890" (McMurtry, p. 2).

This is not to say that McCarthy's apocalyptic vision is entirely focused on the Indians of the United States and Mexico. Most readers of McCarthy understand that he takes an egalitarian view of violence and posits it as a condition of humanity, not race or culture. (In fact, in *Blood Meridian*, our first glimpse of the indigenous warriors shows them unleashing unspeakably brutal slaughter on a band of white men.) In an interview, McCarthy dismissed the global threat of climate change, claiming "[w]e're going to do ourselves in first" (Kushner). Such is his view of the overall human condition.

The Border Trilogy stays in the same locale as *Blood Meridian* but takes us away from the genocide of the 1850s and into the twentieth century. The author nonetheless continues to mark out genocidal moments on the human continuum. *The Crossing*, in fact, ends with the blinding flash of an atomic bomb testing in the New Mexico desert. McCarthy does not visit the Japan where those bombs are eventually dropped, but we are peripherally aware, at the end of this "cowboy" story, of yet another unthinkable slaughter pending. Also, the bloody specter of massacres during the Mexican Revolution, which took place decades before, casts a weighty pall over the three books.

Beyond direct allusions to events, McCarthy consistently delivers up foreboding and suggestive apocalyptic imagery. A blighted and crippled dog that howls a sound "not of this earth" immediately before the atomic test in *The Crossing* (p. 424) calls to mind the sickly litter of kittens in his first novel, who appear "as if they might have been struck ... by some biblical blight" (*The Orchard Keeper*, p. 180) or the "enormous lank" hellhound at the end of *Suttree*, who initiates an unusual shift to a first-person voice that may simultaneously be omniscient: "I have seen them in a dream, slaverous and wild and their eyes crazed with ravening for souls in this world" (p. 471).

This quote raises the point that these apocalyptic images so often come to the characters in cryptic dreams. In *The Crossing* (1994), for example, Billy has a sleeping vision of "God's pilgrims laboring upon a darkened verge ... returning from some dark enterprise" (p. 420), while the same character, now an old man, has a similarly apocalyptic vision in *Cities of the Plain* "of figures struggling and clamoring silently in the wind. They appeared to be dressed in robes.... He thought they might be laboring toward him across the darkened desert" (p. 289). Yet the vision, this time a dreamlike but waking one, turns out to be "only rags of plastic wrapping hanging from a fence where the wind had blown them" (*ibid.*).

Alan Bilton has argued that "there is a remarkable continuity of symbolism, theme, and authorial voice, with a kind of apocalyptic grandeur present in McCarthy's fiction from the onset" (p. 133). Indeed, readers can trace an apocalyptic imagistic strain from McCarthy from the 1960s into the new millennium, despite certain authorial shifts in style, intent, and geographical locale. To support this assertion it is worth mentioning again the fact that Culla Holmes' final moments in *Outer Dark* have distinct strains of *The Road*, nearly 40 years later. While it is this tendency to dwell in apocalyptic themes that often gets Cormac McCarthy labeled a nihilist, it is undoubtedly also part and parcel of the soaring aesthetic vision for which the writer has come to be lauded.

And if one can trace a streak of nihilism in McCarthy, he comes off as a pragmatic sort of nihilist. "There's no such thing as life without bloodshed," he said in a 1992 interview. "I think the notion that the species can be improved in some way, that everyone could live in harmony, is a really dangerous idea," he added. "Those who are afflicted with this notion are the first ones to give up their souls, their freedom. Your desire that it be that way will enslave you and make your life vacuous" (Woodward, "Venomous Fiction").

See also Dreams; Style; The Mexican Revolution; The American Southwest

Ballard, Lester

Child of God's Lester Ballard could easily be termed Cormac McCarthy's most surprising protagonist. First, the obvious: As a serial killer who performs sex acts on corpses that he keeps stashed away in his cave, he plumbs depths of depravity that are even alarming for McCarthy. But in this unique and idiosyncratic novel, the author also casts Ballard as a child of God, just like everyone else. "Ballard may be an extreme case," observes one critic, but McCarthy presents him as "inescapably one of us, bone of our bone" (Bryant, p. 221).

In fact, it isn't until fairly deep into the narrative that Lester begins to undertake the unthinkable. The early pages are invested in detailing his star-crossed relationship with the human world in which he lives — and how his pathetic attempts to reach out for human contact only deepen his misery and isolation. His overtures to court a girl by bringing an idiot child in her care a live bird ("a playpretty") end with the child chewing off the bird's legs, while his initial attempts to assist a passed-out prostitute culminate in his being falsely accused of rape and imprisoned for nine days. And upon his release from jail, the community powers-that-be seem to preordain his descent. "I guess murder is next on the list ain't it," says the sheriff. "Or what things is it you've done that we ain't found out yet" (*Child of God*, p. 56).

But the most surprising aspect of Lester Ballard emerges during his descent into malevolence; as the plot thickens we witness a deep soulfulness arising out of his character that was not present in the grotesque hick of the early pages. In one passage late in the narrative, the reader encounters a more developed, multi-dimensional Lester overlooking a valley, observing — as an omniscient narrator describes — the "diminutive progress of all things ... fields coming up black and corded under the plow, the slow green occlusion that the trees were spreading" (p. 170). Lester then begins to cry, consumed by the heightened realization that his life is moving against the grain of all thriving, living things.

This hollow epiphany is reinforced in a dream: "Each leaf that brushed his face deepened his sadness and dread. Each leaf he passed he'd never pass again. They rode over his face like veils" (*ibid.*). Later, he hides from a "churchbus" in a ditch and spies "at the last seat in the rear a small boy ... looking out the window," his face pressed against the glass. Lester's twinge of familiarity grows to a shattering realization: "[I]t came to him that the boy looked like himself. This gave him the fidgets and though he tried to shake the image of the face in the glass it would not go" (p. 191). In an unexpected turn, Lester too can see through his own debasement to the "child of god" that he is — and, more significantly for this moment, that he *was*.

Edwin T. Arnold describes it well: In these moments, McCarthy "opens Ballard's heart to us in all its twisted yearning" ("'Go to Sleep,'" p. 42). Or, as another critic asserts, "Without delving into sentimentality, McCarthy nonetheless demands our consideration for such an essentially unsympathetic character" (Pacientino, p. 199).

See also Child of God

Bellow, Saul

Saul Bellow (1915–2005), one of the most revered writers of the twentieth century, was a great advocate for McCarthy's work, long before the younger writer came to wider public notice. Bellow has been awarded both the Pulitzer and Nobel prizes for his writing, as well as the National Medal of Arts. In addition, he is the sole writer to have won the National Book Award three times (and the only writer to have been nominated six times). He was also the first American to receive the International Literary Prize. Bellow is most known for his books *Herzog* (1964), *Henderson the Rain King* (1959), *Humboldt's Gift* (1975), *The Adventures of Augie March* (1953), *Seize the Day* (1956), and *Ravelstein* (2000).

Bellow championed McCarthy while sitting on the 1981 MacArthur Fellowship panel (the "genius grant") that honored the writer. He lauded McCarthy's "absolutely overpowering use of language, his life-giving and death-dealing sentences" (Pilkington, p. 125).

Bellow's own work, like McCarthy's, was committed to a specific and recurring geographical locale, in this case, his native Chicago. (As a child Bellow had moved there from Quebec, where he was born.) Of Bellow, English novelist Malcolm Bradbury has said, "His fame, literary, intellectual, moral, lay with his big books," works "filled with their big, clever, flowing prose, and their big, more-than-lifesize heroes ... who fought the battle for courage, intelligence, selfhood and a sense of human grandeur in the postwar age of expansive, materialist, high-towered Chicago-style American capitalism" (Gussow and McGrath). Novelist Philip Roth claimed, "The backbone of 20th-century American literature has been provided by two novelists — William Faulkner and Saul Bellow.... Together they are the Melville, Hawthorne, and Twain of the twentieth century" (Cornwell).

After Bellow's death, the writer's estate (aided by a grant from author/philanthropist Evelyn Stefansson Nef of Washington, D.C.) established the PEN/Saul Bellow award at the PEN American Center, which was to be given biennially to "a distinguished living American author of fiction whose body of work in English possesses qualities of excellence, ambition, and scale of achievement over a sustained career which place him or her in the highest rank of American literature" (PEN American Center). Philip Roth was the first recipient, in 2007; Cormac McCarthy was the second, in 2009.

Blevins, Jimmy

The character sketch of Jimmy Blevins in *All the Pretty Horses* (1992) can be seen as an inheritance of McCarthy's earlier, Southern writing and of what have been termed his "Southern gothic" tendencies. One critic, discussing the work of Southern gothic master Flannery O'Connor — for which McCarthy's early novels have great affinity — noted "the strong, unresolved tension and dualities [that were] characteristic of the grotesque" (Flora, MacKethan, and Taylor, p. 323). McCarthy's first Southern novels employed the grotesque to great effect; in fact, the character Gene Harrogate in *Suttree* (1979) anticipates Blevins. In both, one witnesses the tensions and dualities of the grotesque precisely embodied in one single character.

Even though McCarthy moved his vision away from the South to the American Southwest and Mexico in *All the Pretty Horses*, the boy-man Jimmy Blevins possesses that same "unresolved tension" — but to an even more unsettling degree. As readers, it is difficult to reconcile the more comic and childlike episodes involving Blevins with the more dead-serious elements, particularly his role as murderer and con-man and his heart-wrenching execution at the hands of Mexican authorities. This, of course, fits the larger "paradoxical capability" of the novel itself, which develops obvious tropes on the one hand (Western tropes, romantic tropes, comical tropes), while also purposefully undermining and troubling those motifs. Blevins' effect in the novel is to vividly appear and reappear and then ultimately leave behind a discomfiting void. What did we ultimately know about Blevins? Not much, really; he remains a cipher who meets a terrible end, his true name and origin a mystery.

At the outset Blevins, simply termed "the kid" (reminding one of the *Blood Meridian* protagonist), is an adolescent tagalong who latches onto the older teens, John Grady Cole and Lacey Rawlins. Soon enough, though, we realize that this "kid about thirteen years old" (*All the Pretty Horses*, p. 39) actually embodies the cowboy fantasy that for Cole and Rawlins is only a mere posture early in the novel. He is a dead shot, putting a hole in the center of Rawlins' tossed billfold, and actually emerges as the real American desperado of the novel: a genuine murderer and horse thief. (The irony is that the older boys jokingly attempt to scare Blevins when they first meet him by flipping a coin "to see who gets to shoot him" [p. 40].)

Before things go horribly wrong for Blevins, though, McCarthy represents him in a grotesquely comic light; for example, Blevins — fraught with lightning phobia and resolved that it's a family curse to be struck — tries to out-gallop a thunderstorm and is found trembling in "stained undershorts" in a small hollow beneath a tree (pp. 69–70). Similarly, Blevins — having drunk too much — repeatedly falls off his horse like some kind of rodeo clown: "Whoo, he said when he saw them. I'm drunkern shit" (p. 66).

Even before Blevins' imprisonment, however, disturbing undercurrents move against his passage through the narrative. With Blevins still reduced to only his undershorts, the boys share a meal with Mexican laborers, and one worker (whispering in prurient tones and eyeing Blevins) offers John Grady money for the boy, asking how much he will take for "the blonde" (*el rubio*) (p. 76).

By the time that John Grady and Rawlins re-encounter Blevins in a Mexican prison, he has evolved into a truly unsettling combination of identities and become a character embodying "strong, unresolved tension and dualities characteristic of the grotesque" (Flora, MacKethan, and Taylor, p. 323). He is a 13-year-old boy, a horse thief, a comic foil, a gunslinger, an object of pedophilic interest, a con-man of mysterious origins, and, to the Mexican authorities, "the assassin Blevins" (p. 167). Unsettling the portrait even more, the Mexican captain who proclaims him "the assassin" also notes to John Grady, "He dont have no feathers." John Grady is at first confused: "What?" But when the captain repeats it John Grady understands that he is talking about pubic hair: "I wouldnt know about that. It dont interest me," John Grady replies (p. 167).

Ultimately, though, all of these identities of Blevins are consumed in a portrait of pathos, as the two older boys find him completely hobbled in prison, having had his feet "busted ... all to hell" in some kind of primitive torture session (p. 161). And his fate in *All the Pretty Horses* is to be consumed like so many others in the mindless savagery that McCarthy meditates upon without moralizing. Blevins dies offstage; "just a flat sort of pop" marking his end, not a blaze of glory (p. 178). The last words that need to be said about him come as John Grady meditates upon his figure being dragged off to slaughter: He "watched the small ragged figure vanish limping among the trees with his keepers. There seemed insufficient substance to him to be the object of men's wrath ... nothing about him sufficient to fuel any enterprise at all" (p. 177).

See also All the Pretty Horses; Harrogate, Gene; Southern Gothic

Blood Meridian, or The Evening Redness in the West

Blood Meridian, or The Evening Redness in the West (1985) has often been deemed Cormac McCarthy's masterpiece (though the Pulitzer Prize–winning *The Road*, ambitious *Suttree*, and remarkable Border Trilogy certainly present arguments against that claim). It was also his first work set in the Southwestern borderlands, a region that would become the central locale for his novels in later years, and with which he would become inextricably linked. (It would also become his longtime home; he initially settled in El Paso, Texas, and later Santa Fe, New Mexico.)

Esteemed literary critic Harold Bloom declares in a definitive essay on the novel, "I venture that no other living American novelist, not even [Thomas] Pynchon, has given us a book as strong and memorable as *Blood Meridian*" (pp. 254–255). The critic also goes so far as to place McCarthy in a lineage of the greatest American novelists ever: "The fulfilled renown of *Moby-Dick* and of *As I Lay Dying* is augmented by *Blood Meridian*, since McCarthy is the worthy disciple of both [Herman] Melville and [William] Faulkner," writes Bloom in his 2000 book, *How to Read and Why* (p. 254).

Blood Meridian is also McCarthy's most directly historical novel, taking up the tale of the Glanton Gang, a notorious band of mercenary scalp hunters who operated in the Southwestern United States and Northern Mexico in the period following the Mexican-American War (a.k.a. the Mexican War, 1846–1848). And while McCarthy does obviously take license with history, his book is based on an actual account, *My Confession: Recollections of a Rogue*, by Samuel Chamberlain, onetime member of the real-life Glanton Gang.

That gang, led by John Glanton, a veteran of the Mexican-American War, was initially hired by the Mexican state of Chihuahua to eliminate Apache in the region, the scalps serving as gruesome receipts for what was then substantial payment. The brutal, motley group of outcasts consisted of "Sonorans, Cherokee and Delaware Indians, French Canadians, Texans, Irishmen, a Negro and a full-blooded Comanche," according to Chamberlain's book (p. 268). The parallel here to McCarthy's favorite novel, Herman Melville's *Moby-Dick*, must have struck him, for, as one academic put it, "In both of these novels, a ragtag group of men made up of many races and creeds becomes involved in a hunt led by a madman" (Rebein, p. 118).

Certainly *Blood Meridian* is fraught with tones of Melville, particularly in the uncanny character of Judge Holden, whose high oratory and inscrutability calls to mind Ahab. In fact, Melville's description of Captain Ahab in chapter 16 of *Moby-Dick* as "a grand, ungodly, god-like man" who had "been in colleges, as well as 'mong the cannibals" (p. 79) contains the same contradictory blend of savagery and refinement that characterizes Judge Holden. (Also, note how the McCarthy novel's full title echoes the syntax of many titles during that time: *Moby-Dick: or, The Whale*.)

Chamberlain's account must also have appealed to McCarthy's consistent fascination with gory acts of brutality, which he had been known to render in wondrously imaginative detail in his previous Southern-based works. The sheer bloodletting of *Blood Meridian* takes it into regions that *Moby-Dick* never explored, and the novel is a landscape in which, as London's *Independent* put it, "human beings chop, defile, massacre, maim, and dismember one another in every conceivable fashion" (Bradfield, "Twilight Cowboy"). But while many of the atrocities in the novel can be ascribed to the American Southwest of the 1800s, the book must be seen as greatly an imaginative work; Judge Holden is a minor figure in Chamberlain's account, for example, and contains only some of the traits that McCarthy ascribed to the character.

Blood Meridian is also an opportunity for McCarthy to not only take up the theme of what he sees as the innate violence of humanity, but to invest that preoccupation in a new geographical locale, one that offers a rich storehouse of material for his meditations. In turning away from the American South of his early novels and toward the Southwest, *Blood Meridian* can be seen as a prequel to the Border Trilogy. (In fact, some critics refer to the "Tetralogy," including it in the sequence.) Thus *Blood Meridian* also marks the beginning of a slow turn for McCarthy from critically celebrated, cult figure to a well-known author of highly lauded, award-winning bestsellers, though that full culmination would come with the second book about the Southwest, 1992's *All the Pretty Horses*.

McCarthy has said that he initially moved to El Paso and undertook the writing of this novel with the idea that "no one had taken [the Western novel] seriously and as a subject for literary effort" (Kushner). Therefore, McCarthy has often been accused of writing revisionist Westerns, an assertion that rings only partially true. For, as literary critic Neil Campbell pointed out, *Blood Meridian* is simultaneously "a Western and an anti–Western" (p. 218). Campbell rightly hailed it as an "excessive, revisionist, and contradictory narrative" that "both rewrites the histories of the West ... and maintains and utilizes many of the Western archetypes familiar in this genre of writing" (p. 217).

As he would later do in the Border Trilogy, McCarthy also uses the borderlands geography to explore liminality, paradox, and contradiction, using the "opportunity" innate in that part of the country: For example, the contradiction of westward expansion — i.e., "civilizing" through barbarism — or the contradiction at the heart of the Mexican-U.S. border, a place that both allows and discourages contact between neighboring cultures. Of course, there is also the very liminality of the borderlands civilization itself, caught between two very different cultures but somewhat of a hybridization of both. (In the nascent period taken up in *Blood Meridian* there is actually a hybridization of many cultures — European, African American, Native American, Mexican — an idea expressed in the multicultural makeup of the Glanton Gang itself.)

But again, while many academic critics seek to outline a strain of revisionist history in McCarthy, it is important to note that there is nothing as transparent as proselytizing or some form of postcolonial activism in his work. Beyond the soaring rhetoric of Judge Holden, McCarthy achieves his own ends through a relentless brand of objectivity, rendering the brutal details of violence in a frank, uniquely vivid, and seemingly dispassionate manner.

In addition, the narrative takes a distinctly unsentimental view of the indigenous people of the region, separating it even more from many postcolonial renderings. McCarthy presents a violent humanity as a whole — across races, creeds, and cultures. Consider the reader's first glimpse of the Indians, when a band of cattle- and horse-raiding Comanche wipe out an army company that the kid, the unnamed protagonist of the novel, has joined:

> A legion of horribles, hundreds in number, half naked or clad in costumes attic or biblical or wardrobed out of a fevered dream with the skins of animals and silk finery and pieces of uniform still tracked with the blood of prior owners, coats of slain dragoons, frogged and braided cavalry jackets, one in a stovepipe hat and one with an umbrella and one in

white stockings and a bloodstained weddingveil ... and all the horsemen's faces gaudy and grotesque with daubings like a company of mounted clowns, death hilarious, all howling in a barbarous tongue and riding down upon them like a horde from a hell more horrible yet than the brimstone land of christian reckoning [*Blood Meridian*, p. 52].

And then there is the over-the-top savagery they unleash against the small army company, atrocities that seem both prelude and parallel to the kind of acts later committed by the Glanton Gang:

passing their blades about the skulls of the living and the dead alike and snatching aloft the bloody wigs and hacking and chopping at the naked bodies, ripping off limbs, heads, gutting the strange white torsos and holding up great handfuls of viscera, genitals, some of the savages so slathered up with the gore they might have rolled in it like dogs and some who fell upon the dying and sodomized them with loud cries to their fellows [p. 54].

The *New York Times* book review, reacting to the violence in the narrative, noted how these depictions distance us "not only from the historical past, not only from our cowboy-and-Indian images of it, but also from revisionist theories that make white men the villains and Indians the victims. All men are unremittingly bloodthirsty here, poised at a peak of violence" (James, p. 31). (The review rightly saw that violent peak as the "meridian"—i.e., zenith—cited in the title.) In a 2008 edition of *Modern Fiction Studies*, David H. Evans also pointed out that "McCarthy's novel is such that it tends to shred any critical container one attempts to put it in" (Evans, p. 864), further cautioning against a straight revisionist reading of the book. Dana A. Phillips added these cautionary words regarding the vivid bloodletting in the novel: "In McCarthy's work," she wrote, "violence tends to be just that; it is not a sign or symbol of something else" (p. 435).

It is important, however, not to let the technicolor brutality of *Blood Meridian* drown out its significant literary merits. Even champion of the book Harold Bloom admitted that his initial attempts to appreciate the work "failed, because I flinched at the overwhelming carnage that McCarthy portrays" (p. 255). Yet in his final estimation he allowed that "none of its carnage is gratuitous or redundant; it belonged to the Mexico-Texas borderlands in 1849–1850" (*ibid.*). As to what makes *Blood Meridian* such a great work of literature, Bloom pointed out how the prose of the novel "soars, yet with its own economy, and its dialogue is always persuasive, especially when the uncanny Judge Holden speaks" (p. 256). He also regarded the giant, hairless, brilliant, and terrible judge—whose numerous atrocities include molesting and murdering children—as immortal. (Holden is the only remaining member of the Glanton Gang alive at book's end.)

Bloom also took up the parallel with *Moby-Dick*, posing the idea that the judge, because of his immortality, wasn't equivalent to Captain Ahab (a popular comparison) but to the white whale itself: "As another white enigma, the albino judge, like the albino whale, cannot be slain," he wrote (p. 259). (A side note: There is no indication in *Blood Meridian* that the judge is actually albino.) But perhaps a more apt interpretation would posit Judge Holden as a conflation of the whale *and* Ahab; this would certainly suit the McCarthy tendency to blur boundaries and seek out compelling and intentional ambiguities.

The seven-foot leviathan of a judge has unmistakably Ahab-like qualities, and beyond his apparent immortality there is also compelling enough imagery to support the judge's kinship to the whale itself. Regarding the latter, Bloom cites a passage in which the judge visits the kid in a dream: "A great shambling mutant, silent and serene. Whatever his antecedents he was something wholly other than their sum.... Whoever would seek out his history ... must stand at last darkened and dumb at the shore of a void" (*Blood Meridian*, pp. 309–310).

The judge's oft-mentioned paleness also calls to mind Melville's meditations on whiteness in *Moby-Dick*. McCarthy describes the "blinding white" pallor of the judge (p. 79), and this whiteness adds to his terrifying aspect. In the chapter "The Whiteness of the Whale," Ishmael relates that when "divorced from more kindly associations, and coupled with any object terrible in itself" whiteness heightens "that terror to the furthest bounds" (Melville, *Moby-Dick*, p. 182). And it is the whale's whiteness that "above all things appalled" Ishmael (*ibid.*, p. 181).

Judge Holden also inhabits *Blood Meridian* as a partially supernatural entity. His entry into the Glanton Gang comes after he miraculously appears on the plain, calmly sitting on a lone rock in the middle of nowhere (tellingly during the "meridian" of the day). "And there he set," relates the defrocked priest Tobin to the central figure, the kid, "No horse. Just him and his legs crossed, smiling as we rode up. Like he'd been expectin us" (p. 125). On Holden's rifle is inscribed the Latin saying: "et in Arcadia ego," a saying that translates to "even in Arcadia I am present," which sounds like a platitude issued from the lips of a personified death. Adding to the mysterious and supernatural qualities of Holden, the kid mentions that he had once seen the judge in Nacogdoches, before he joined the Glanton Gang, and Tobin responds, "Every man in the company claims to have encountered that sootysouled rascal in some other place" (p. 124).

The judge also seems ageless; when he murders the kid at the end of the novel, the kid is in his 40s, but the judge seems to have not changed or diminished in strength one iota and claims he is immortal. (If human, he would be an old man at this point.) In Judge Holden the reader beholds an embodiment of what critic Alan Bilton has termed the "metaphysical grounding" of McCarthy's Western novels: "We are dealing with what is beyond us, with what is implacably inhuman; an awful (in every sense of the word) notion of the sublime" (p. 97).

Judge Holden is such a bewitching character that it's easy for critics to leave aside significant discussion of the protagonist of the novel, the kid, who remains a true enigma throughout despite the fact that the narrative traces the arc of his maturity, beginning with *Blood Meridian*'s very opening lines: "See the child. He is pale and thin, he wears a thin and ragged linen shirt" (p. 3). McCarthy's rendering of his protagonist echoes Melville's use of Ishmael in *Moby-Dick*, in that the kid will be the focus at times, but then will fade into the background as the novel takes up a wider view of the Glanton Gang. Pages will fly by with nary a mention of the kid, even in the midst of a bloody skirmish, and then the attention will again return to him. (Ishmael, though, is allowed the perspective of first-person narration; the kid is not.)

This gives McCarthy's narrative a telescoping effect, as the focus zooms in and out, drawing away from the trials of this individual to the larger trials of the Glanton Gang for long stretches and then returning to the kid. In *Moby-Dick*, however, the reader does ultimately get more of a sense of Ishmael, as Melville draws the narrative tightly enough around the character's first-person observations and delves into his psychology enough to bridge the gulf between character and reader. McCarthy, keeping with his maddeningly objective tendency to keep out of his characters' heads (unless describing their dreams), never lets us that close to the kid. Bloom wrote that "though the kid's moral maturation [later in the novel] is heartening, his personality remains largely a cipher, as anonymous as his lack of a name" (Bloom, p. 257). And in a subtle, metafictional capacity, the kid's tendency to lay low in the narrative is reflected in his very character. "Was it always your idea that if you did not speak you would not be recognized?" asks the judge of him (*Blood Meridian*, p. 328).

Because the kid fades into the background and becomes anonymous at times, the reader is not sure to what extent the protagonist participates in the more atrocious violent episodes; it seems that the kid's moral turmoil and development is happening offstage. When he does come to the forefront in the final stages of *Blood Meridian*, it is in opposition to Judge Holden — as a force against the evil that the judge represents — and, of course (keeping with McCarthy's pessimistic outlook) Judge Holden prevails and kills him. In McCarthy's dark worldview, the kind of timeless evil that Judge Holden represents must ultimately triumph.

In his weighty rhetoric, Holden also offers a way to read *Blood Meridian*. He espouses to the Glanton Gang the "degeneracy of mankind," proclaiming that man's "spirit is exhausted at the peak of its achievement. His meridian is at once his darkening and the evening of his day" (pp. 146–147). The book's title, *Blood Meridian, or The Evening Redness of the West*, contains this contradiction; that is, the idea that a culture's high point — for example, the opening of the American West, or British imperialism, or the "victorious" bombing of Hiroshima and Nagasaki — can also be its nadir because of the brutality exacted to achieve that peak.

The very character of Judge Holden also embodies this contradiction: He is truly the most degenerate and villainous character in the novel, yet he is also the most "refined" as well. In fact, he represents the best that "civilization" has to offer in his intellectual capacity; his musical, dancing, and artistic ability; his multilingualism; his legal and diplomatic acumen; and his capacity to philosophize, converse, and reason. Yet he is a murderer and child molester, and a man who will commit arbitrary and unspeakable acts of brutality simply to preoccupy himself. But McCarthy suggests that in these savage qualities is a validation and embodiment of civilizational history, going back longer than recorded time, as the newspaper snippet from 1982 that precedes chapter 1 indicates. In that paragraph we read that anthropologists have discovered "a 300,000-year-old fossil skull" that "shows evidence of having been scalped" (p. 1).

These meditations on historical violence and the succession and extinctions of civilizations are something that would preoccupy McCarthy in the decades to come, in the three books of the upcoming Border Trilogy, for example — in which memories of the bloody Mexican Revolution are cast like a pall across the pages — or in his Pulitzer Prize–winning *The Road* (2006), in which he presents a post-apocalyptic world devoid of the markings of humanity. This thematic preoccupation took root in *Blood Merid-*

ian, which — despite its accolades and growing reputation in ensuing decades — did not find more than a cult audience upon its initial release. McCarthy wouldn't taste any mainstream success until his next book, 1992's *All the Pretty Horses*, which commenced the Border Trilogy and offered a more accessible narrative.

At the time of its release, in 1985, *Blood Meridian* was reviewed and lauded by few. The *Washington Post* outright panned it, focusing mostly on the blood and gore and offering this dismissive appraisal: "A bunch of men ride around for a while, they camp for a while, they philosophize for a while, they kill for a while. It's all in a day's work, but it sure makes for a slow day" (Yardley, p. B2). The *New York Times* write-up was more positive, but ultimately ambivalent, with the critic acknowledging, "If *Blood Meridian* is ultimately a failure, it is an ambitious, sophisticated one" (James, p. 31). Nevertheless, the novel would gather critical momentum as the years passed and as more readers discovered — and fully embraced — the work of Cormac McCarthy.

But the passage that readers and critics alike have continually struggled with is the novel's brief and mysterious epilogue, in which a lone figure progresses "over the plain by means of holes which he is making in the ground. He uses an implement with two handles and he chucks it into the hole and he enkindles the stone in the hole with his steel hole by hole striking the fire out of the rock which God has put there" (p. 337). Many interpretations take the approach that the man is using a post-hole digger to erect fences, the steel of the tool striking rocks and creating sparks. With him on the plain, though, are wanderers, some "in search of bones" and "others who do not search" (*ibid.*), a cryptic image that is not explained. Harold Bloom suggests that the passage depicts a Promethean figure that may rise up one day against the malevolence that the judge represents, but a more practical interpretation suggests that ranches are rising up across the very plains that were soaked in blood for so many years, ushering in a new epoch and pushing out an old one. The gatherers in the work crew are clearing away the bones and therefore all evidence of the past or what has transpired.

As a reviewer once wrote of *Cities of the Plain* (1998), McCarthy is preoccupied with "that brief moment between a culture's existence and extinction" (Mosle); thus the passage seems to freeze that moment in time between the peak historical violence of the West marked out in *Blood Meridian* and the encroaching dominance of the ranch cowboy. The latter is an existence that the Border Trilogy will explore and ride to extinction as well, as modernization, military interests, and the oil industry impinge upon the ranches and plains. The epilogue is in fact the perfect setup for the next novel, *All the Pretty Horses*, where McCarthy takes us 100 years into the future, to 1949. We land on a long-standing family ranch, originally built in 1872, that is about to be sold off to big oil interests, leaving the teenage John Grady Cole riding those fenced-in plains as his heritage fades into oblivion. And in the evening, when the sun reaches that evening redness in the West mentioned in *Blood Meridian*'s title, that sinking point just above the horizon, John Grady rides an old Comanche war trail that is now pasture, and he can feel the past described in *Blood Meridian*: he can sense the ghost nation of warriors "pledged in blood and redeemable in blood only ... passing in a soft chorale across that mineral waste to darkness bearing lost to all history and all remembrance like a grail the sum of their secular and transitory and violent lives" (*All the Pretty Horses*, p. 5).

That is the true heart of *Blood Meridian*'s epilogue; the description of the movement across the plain, the clearing away of the bones and digging of holes for fence posts, is at once ceremony and industry. It is a ritual played out in the brief moment between existences, the extinction of one, the ascension of another. Mostly, though, it is a ceremony for those "transitory and violent lives" of the past — and those to come.

• *Further Reading*

Bloom, Harold. *Blood Meridian* section in *How to Read and Why*. New York: Scribner, 2000, pp. 254–263.

Chamberlain, Samuel. *My Confession: Recollections of a Rogue*. Lincoln: University of Nebraska Press, 1987.

Donoghue, Denis. "Teaching Blood Meridian." *The Practice of Reading*. New Haven, CT: Yale University Press, 2000, pp. 258–278.

Josyph, Peter. "Tragic Ecstasy: A Conversation with Harold Bloom about Cormac McCarthy's *Blood Meridian*." *Southwestern American Literature*, volume 26, number 1, Fall 2000, pp. 7–20.

Luce, Dianne. "Ambiguities, Dilemmas, and Double-Binds in Cormac McCarthy's *Blood Meridian*." *Southwestern American Literature* 26, no. 1 (Fall 2000), pp. 21–46.

The Borderlands

Throughout his career McCarthy has used the "borderlands" as both a literal and metaphorical region. Even before he took up the border between Mexico and the United States as a geographical muse, his prose dwelled in figurative borderlands. The Knoxville, Tennessee, landscape of *Suttree* (1979) comes off like a blurred boundary between life and death, or a "terrestrial hell" (p. 14), and Cornelius Suttree seems to always be standing on the death border, staring at the land on the other side. Critic Edwin T. Arnold describes the novel's figurative terrain as "a state of purgatory" ("Go to Sleep," p. 43), and the novel's opening invocation deems the environs "interstitial" — an in-between region.

Immediately after *Suttree* Cormac McCarthy turned his gaze away from Tennessee and toward the literal Southwestern borderlands. This was a geographic milieu that proved to be his muse, and it is both the literal and the symbolic qualities of the border region that McCarthy explores in his work, particularly in the Border Trilogy.

One borderland that McCarthy explores in his Southwestern works is the boundary between storytelling and history. This is an amorphous region, which even for historians, "much like the U.S.-Mexico border itself, has not always been as clearly demarcated as some would expect," writes historian Karl Jacoby (p. 6). Jacoby also indicates how the "seeming inevitability of the western story ... has long desensitized us to both the region's violence and its other ways of being" (p. 6). McCarthy's novels, particularly *Blood Meridian* (1985), therefore have much historical value in that they face up to the pervasive slaughter and discomfiting cultural complexities that form the historical bedrock of the American Southwest.

As a literal place, it provides McCarthy with two rich and different cultures in proximity to each other. When John Grady Cole in *All the Pretty Horses* or Billy Parham in *The Crossing* enters Mexico, each is moving into a whole different realm, one fraught with different concerns (still reeling in the wake of the Mexican Revolution, for example) and not as modernized as the United States they have left behind.

Indeed, they often seem to be going back in time when they cross over the border. Nevertheless, the separation between the two cultures is not always clear, as the borderlands themselves are a place of hybridization, a place where the two cultures seem, at times, to have melded. We see, for example, John Grady and Billy's ability to shift back and forth between two different languages, and thus the reader must negotiate nontranslated dialogues in Spanish.

There is also a deeper resonance to this idea of a "borderlands." At the most obvious level, the characters often seem poised between two cultures or in that nether region in which a border is caught between existence and obliteration. In the Border Trilogy, as well as in *Blood Meridian*, we see the ebbing and flowing of cultures and ways of life. Early in *All the Pretty Horses*, John Grady rides a trail upon which he can sense the spirits of the Native American cultures that once made this same passage, even as his own traditional way of life — as a cattle rancher — is poised to slip into the void. It is these successive layers of dead and dying civilizations with which McCarthy is concerned, and he often catches those civilizations on the border — very much present but also receding into extinction. This is true of *No Country for Old Men* (2005) as well; the reader experiences Sheriff Bell's meditations on how his traditional lawman's ethos and cowboy roots are out of step and time with the 1980s borderlands atmosphere of drug trafficking.

There are other borders that the books seem to be blurring: The line between life and death, past and present, waking and dream worlds. Furthermore, academic Mark Busby adds that McCarthy employs the border as "a metaphor for a complex and oxymoronic melding of nihilism and optimism, good and evil, illusion and reality" as well as the "complex intertwining of positive and negative forces" (p. 227). Busby also notes how McCarthy's metaphoric border serves as an "ongoing dialectic between the forces of death and life, end and beginning, and other apparent dualities ... the border living in a world of between" (*ibid.*).

See also The American Southwest; *The Crossing*

• *Further reading*

Busby, Mark. "Into the Darkening Land, the World to Come: Cormac McCarthy's Border Crossings." *Myth, Legend, Dust: Critical Responses to Cormac McCarthy*, ed. Rick Wallach. Manchester, UK: Manchester University Press, 2000.

"The Boy" (*The Road*)

The nameless boy in Cormac McCarthy's Pulitzer Prize–winning novel *The Road* (2006) is what author William Kennedy, reviewing the book for the *New York Times*, has described as a "designated but unsubstantiated messiah." The father of the boy deems that the child is not only his "warrant" (and all that stands between him and death), but "the word of God" itself: "If he is not the word of God God never spoke" (p. 5). At another point, the father sits "beside him and stroke[s] his pale and tangled hair. Golden chalice, good to house a god" (p. 75).

McCarthy teases out this idea of the boy's messianic possibility throughout the two characters' arduous, suffering-laden trudge across a post-apocalyptic universe. But it is not only the father who champions this perspective. We see a shift in the boy late in the novel, a strengthening of resolve, and finally the proclamation from his own mouth. "You're not the one who has to worry about everything," the father says. "He looked up... Yes I am, he said. I am the one" (p. 259).

Nevertheless, if the boy is a messianic figure, he is one that is disconnected and adrift from all ecclesiastical forms; for all religions, all cultural structures, and all evidence of the world that housed such beliefs has been obliterated: "On this road there are no god-spoke men," the father meditates. "They are gone and I am left and they have taken with them the world" (p. 32). And the father dredges up a fundamental and crucial difference between him and his son when he internally poses the question, "How does the never to be differ from what never was?" (p. 32). With all cultural and societal forms pitched off into the void, every person is a blank slate. "Are you a doctor?" one of the bad guys asks the man. "I'm not anything," he responds (p. 64). In a later passage, the old man, Ely, asks the man and boy, "What are you?" but "[t]hey'd no way to answer the question" (p. 162). Encountering traces of other people, the boy asks who they could be. "I don't know. Who is anybody?" answers the father (p. 49).

But the boy is a different kind of—and ultimately more genuine—*tabula rasa* than the man. The boy represents the "what never was" in the father's ontological question. By contrast, the man hangs on to his memories of the world that once was but is "never to be" again. When a morning forest fire stirs reminiscences of old sunrises in a happier world, it moves "something in him long forgotten." He chides himself, "Make a list. Recite a litany. Remember" (p. 31). And a childhood memory of a day at the lake hunting for firewood with his uncle becomes for the man a source of strength to draw from: "the perfect day of his childhood ... the day to shape the days upon" (p. 13).

The man's trudge down the titular road, pushing the burdened shopping cart filled with scant worldly goods, is likewise plagued by daydreams of a past life. Of the boy's mother, he "could remember everything of her save her scent" (p. 18). He is able to pull up tangible traces, her stockings and "thin summer dress": "Freeze this frame," he commands. "Now call down your dark and your cold and be damned" (p. 19).

The boy, however, was born after the devastation of humanity. His only glimpse of another child is for a brief second in a destroyed neighborhood, and he has a difficult time wrapping his head around ideas that were once basic to the human condition—sayings like "as the crow flies," the notion of geographical "states," the sensation of drinking a soda.

In this boy's blankness McCarthy suggests a certain purity; he is an untainted boy, unpolluted by the once-dominant humanity that brought about its own end. He is driven by a deep and abiding compassion for all he encounters—a skeletal dog, an old man reduced to a "pile of rags" (p. 62), the child he briefly glimpsed: "What about the little boy? He sobbed. What about the little boy?" (p. 86). Unfettered by the spiritually corrupt detritus of the former world, "the 10-year-old messiah ... is compassion incarnate," writes William Kennedy. Nevertheless, McCarthy, in his typically inchoate manner, never fully resolves the issue of the boy's messiah-hood, an issue that a more conclusive ending would have put to rest.

And it is primarily the novel's conclusion that Kennedy is bemoaning when he condemns "the scarcity of thought in the novel's mystical infrastructure," for it is the novel's pensive, evocative, and esoteric ending that leaves the boy an "unsubstantiated messiah" (Kennedy). "Of the boy's becoming, or his mission — redeeming a dead world, outliving death?— nothing is said," complains Kennedy.

The inconclusive handling of the boy fits the Cormac McCarthy vision in many ways, however. The author's canon is filled with agonizingly open-ended conclusions, many of them flatly bleak. (It must be mentioned that next to *The Orchard Keeper* [1965] and *Suttree* [1979], *The Road* actually possesses one of McCarthy's most relatively uplifting conclusions.) In addition, in order to substantiate the boy's messianic nature, McCarthy would have to pose some kind of ecclesiastical order, something that *The Road* resists, despite the father's constant inner cries to God. (As McCarthy once said in a rare interview, "I don't think you have to have a clear idea who or what God is in order to pray" [Winfrey].) To clearly and distinctly substantiate the boy as a messiah and define his mission would also fly in the face of something that McCarthy has been suggesting in his novels for decades: That human beings have the capacity to ponder the deepest metaphysical questions but not to fully penetrate them.

See also "The Man"; *The Road*

Chigurh, Anton

If one is to look for comparison within McCarthy's catalogue to cold-blooded assassin Anton Chigurh, only the fearsome and multifarious Judge Holden from *Blood Meridian* (1985) will do. Chigurh, the bounty hunter from *No Country for Old Men* (2005), may not crest the same operatic heights as Holden, but like the judge, he "embodies the violence and evil that Mr. McCarthy sees at the heart of the human enterprise" (Kakutani). A critic from Spain has described him as an "implacable mercenary who takes his job far beyond the limits of his profession, a morbid philosopher of murder for whom there are no exceptions to his errand of extermination" (Brancano, p. 77). McCarthy himself has simply said that the *No Country for Old Men* assassin is "pretty much pure evil" (Woodward, "Cormac Country").

Because of his penchant for forcing victims to choose their destiny by coin toss, Chigurh has also been called a "symbol of the terrifying randomness that in the author's view governs the universe" (Woodward, "Bernard Madoff and Anton Chigurh"). Yet Chigurh doesn't see the outcome as random, but destiny; as he tells Llewelyn Moss' widow after the coin toss and before he kills her, "A person's path through the world seldom changes and even more seldom will it change abruptly. And the shape of your path was visible from the beginning" (p. 259). The coin, it seems, only confirms what destiny has already prescribed. "When I came into your life your life was over. It had a beginning, a middle, and an end. This is the end," proclaims Chigurh (p. 26).

Chigurh's rhetoric casts him as a leaner and more athletic version of Judge Holden. "Suppose two men at cards with nothing to wager save their lives. Who has not heard such a tale? A turn of the card," espouses the judge in *Blood Meridian*. "The whole universe for such a player has labored clanking to this moment which will tell if he is to die at that man's hand or that man at his" (p. 249). In Judge Holden's rhetoric, we see McCarthy working with the same themes he will continue to explore through the character of Anton Chigurh.

But while both are similarly minded bounty hunters in the American Southwest, separated by a century and a half in historical context (and by two decades in the book-publishing world), in many ways the *No Country for Old Men* assassin is a more stoic and Spartan version of the judge. Holden is a renaissance man who embodies the American enterprise (including the unthinkable violence of the nineteenth-century borderlands), but Chigurh is somewhat more human, and an ascetic: "You think I'm like you. That it's just greed. But I'm not like you. I live a simple life," he tells Wells (p. 177). Chigurh also acts according to his own strict underlying code. "You can't make a deal with him," says Wells, who is the character best acquainted with Chigurh. "You could even say that he has principles. Principles that transcend money or drugs or anything like that" (p. 153).

Chigurh is more than just a highly principled killer, however — his psychosis is such that he sees himself as an agent of destiny, as one carrying out the will of the universe. He tips his hand to the dimensions of his underlying complex when he instructs Carla Jean that one "might find it useful to model himself after God. Very useful, in fact" (p. 256). And note the manner in which Chigurh enacts a murder, only a few pages into the novel, cueing us into his worldview: "He placed his hand on the man's head like a faith healer ... the man slid soundlessly to the ground, a round hole in his forehead" (p. 7). There is a zeal, purity, and unwavering consistency in the way that he conducts himself and carries out his murderous tenets. As Carla Jean begs for her life and attempts to reason with him, Chigurh responds, "You're asking that I make myself vulnerable and that I can never do. I have only one way to live. It doesnt allow for special cases" (p. 259). Part of that terrible purity of vision is eradicating any who would oppose it: "There's no one alive on this planet that's ever had even a cross word with him," notes Wells. "They're all dead. These are not good odds" (p. 153). In these ways, Chigurh could be seen as an analogy for religious extremism (though the "religion" is of his own devising).

Much like Judge Holden, Chigurh has unique and compelling aspects that push him beyond the quotidian novelistic killer. The judge's uncanny dancing, fiddling, intellectual, and lingual capacities set him apart from the other brutal killers in the Glanton Gang. And even though Chigurh's brutish weapon of choice, a pneumatic air gun typically used on cattle, shows what little regard he has for human life, a London *Observer* review also described how "[m]uch of the horror of the Chigurh character comes from the sense that he is not only a sort of intellectual but an aesthete. He studies the faces of his victims as they die" (Mars-Jones, p. 15).

Indeed, Chigurh sometimes becomes a student, appreciator, and intimate of his quarry. On the trail of Carla Jean, he roams through her house, studying various items; he empties her bureau drawer, paws through her personal effects, "[w]eighing these things in his hand like a medium who might thereby divine some fact concerning the owner" (p. 204). Chigurh also pores over photograph albums and even sleeps in her bed. None of these aspects quite elevate him to the grandiose terribleness that is Judge Holden, but the judge's representation suits the bloody baroque of the novel he inhabits, just as Chigurh's potent portrayal suits the lean, pared-down drive of *No Country for Old Men*.

See also Moss, Llewellyn; *No Country for Old Men*; Sheriff Bell

Child of God

Taken at a purely thematic level, *Child of God* (1973) is surely Cormac McCarthy's most shocking novel. In the book, Lester Ballard, an Appalachian Mountain–dwelling killer in Sevier County, Tennessee, preys on young women, living with the corpses of his victims in a cave and engaging in acts of necrophilia with them. The idea is beyond morbid, and McCarthy — in his typically bracing manner — doesn't flinch from the most gory of details. As a corpse is recovered from the cave at book's end, "Gray soapy clots of matter fell from the cadaver's chin. She ascended dangling.... A gray rheum dripped" (p. 196). Surely this is the stuff of which a million B-grade horror movies are made or the literary terrain of Stephen King or Thomas Harris (*The Silence of the Lambs*).

But when Cormac McCarthy applies his unique sensibilities and literary predilections to a subject, understandings of genre often collapse. Much later, in 2006's *The Road*, he took up a post-apocalyptic tale, but what emerged stood far apart from such post-apocalyptic renderings as Stephen King's *The Stand* (1978) or Richard Matheson's *I Am Legend* (1954). There is something less fantastical in McCarthy's detailing of events. He grounds the novel in a father and son relationship that cuts to the core of the fears and anxieties of any parent. He labored over such scenes as the father simply trying to fix the wheel of the dilapidated shopping card that hauls their few possessions. What makes everything stand out is the utter plausibility of it. Similarly, in his Border Trilogy, he presents us with undeniable "Westerns" that are as much "anti–Westerns" steeped in pessimistic realities and deep ontological waters.

Although written much earlier than those novels — and though it is much less dense and probing than later McCarthy works — we see that same impulse in *Child of God*. What pulls it away from being pure horror is McCarthy's use of perspective. His use of a grotesque, caricatured style early on adds a peculiar sense of levity. This is a stirring contrast to the light in which McCarthy presents Lester later in the novel; here the elegiac, melancholy tone compellingly humanizes the killer and, as Edwin T. Arnold puts it, "opens Ballard's heart to us in all its twisted yearning" ("Go to Sleep," p. 42). McCarthy also pitches the reader straight into Lester's existence, his more mundane comings and goings as well as his hardscrabble life of hunger, pain, and exposure to the elements, aligning us in tenuous empathy with him.

In addition, the book operates at a level of social examination, as Lester's marginalization and then utter estrangement from societal and familial structures precede his malevolent, cave-dwelling existence. And though it would be overly simplistic — and patently ridiculous — to suggest a cause and effect of larger implications in Ballard's estrangement, Edward J. Pacientino rightly asserts that "[w]ithout delving into sentimentality, McCarthy nonetheless demands our consideration for such an essentially unsympathetic character" (p. 199).

But to elaborate on the first point, the issue of the novel's "grotesqueness"— particularly in the novel's early stages — when we first encounter Lester Ballard he is standing "straddlelegged" and urinating on the ground. This is the reader's introduction to the protagonist, relieving himself and making "in the dark humus a darker pool wherein swirls a pale foam with bits of straw" (p. 4). As if we had not encountered enough of Lester's toilet activities, a mere few pages later we find that he has "trod a clearing in the clumps of jimpson and nightshade and squatted and shat." Never one to leave a scene undone, McCarthy is careful to note that as Lester "pulled his trousers up from the ground ... green flies clambered over his dark and lumpy stool" (p. 13). We also encounter Lester's acquaintance, the dumpkeeper, whose chosen names for his nine daughters include Urethra and Hernia Sue. They are described as "gangling progeny with black hair hanging from their armpits" (p. 26).

This is the gross levity with which McCarthy imbues *Child of God*, for as Pacientino points out, there is both a "comic and tragic" element to the novel (p. 199). We see this when Lester, trying to court one of the dumpkeepers' daughters, brings an "idiot child" the gift of a captured bird as a "playpretty," and the child bites the bird's legs off. "He wanted it to where it couldn't run off," Lester says (tipping a hand toward his own intrinsic understanding of the act). Nevertheless, the grossly comic slant is often pushed into unsettling regions, for example, when the dumpkeeper catches his daughter fornicating with a boy. He beats her with a stick, but then he experienced the "[h]ot fishy reek of her freshened loins.... Next thing he knew his overalls were about his knees and he was mounting her. Daddy quit, she said. Daddy. Oooh" (pp. 27–28). A conventional horror novel might spend early moments building tension or foreshadowing; *Child of God* comes out of the blocks with toilet descriptions, incest, and grotesque hillbilly caricatures.

It is this slant of McCarthy's Southern writings that many critics and readers alike find off-putting. But, as Mark Royden Winchell indicates, McCarthy's "reputation as a serious artist is such that critics are inclined to give him the benefit of the doubt and assume that some higher seriousness redeems his gross sensationalism" (*Reinventing*, p. 79). There might not be an elevated seriousness at work here, but the effect within the narrative is to establish Lester as a fairly innocuous figure early on and to establish a lighter comic milieu. There is no build-up of narrative tension or sense of what is to come. Who is Lester Ballard, after all, when the reader first meets him? He is not only a "child of God much like yourself perhaps" (p. 4), but his transgressions are of a slimy garden variety: He's a peeping tom who spies on couples at the local lover's lane, seeking voyeuristic gratification.

In fact, his entry into necrophilia is represented as a chance happening. He doesn't even kill his first victim, but comes upon a young couple, dead and entangled in flagrante, in an idling car (presumably asphyxiated). Something breaks free in the social reject who has never felt a sensual touch, and he becomes a "crazed gymnast laboring over a cold corpse. He poured into that waxen ear everything he'd ever thought of saying to a woman" (p. 88). The idea to bring the girl's corpse back to his dwelling is an afterthought. He leaves, runs back to rob the corpses, leaves again, and then, *finally*, gets the idea to recover the girl's body.

Lester is seeking the sensual world from which he is locked out, and readers may find it troubling that he is not represented as a psychotic at this stage, but simply as a hopeless outcast and weirdo. Lester, as the *Companion to Southern Literature* points out, is "odd" and "eccentric" but ultimately as "bleakly human" as previous Southern gothic characters like William Faulkner's Snopeses or Popeye. In fact, when Ballard ends up in the state mental hospital, he is placed in a cell next to "a demented gentleman who used to open folks' skulls and eat the brains" with a spoon, but Ballard, presuming himself made of different stuff, "had nothing to say to a crazy man" (p. 193).

As so often occurs in McCarthy's work, there is a paradox or "twist," and the twist in *Child of God* is that Lester Ballard becomes more human and multidimensional as he moves deeper and deeper into monstrous depravity. Late in the novel, before his capture, Lester overlooks a valley, watching the "diminutive progress of all things ... fields coming up black and corded under the plow, the slow green occlusion that the trees were spreading." He then "let his head drop between his knees and he began to cry" (p. 170). That night he also has a beautiful but ominous pastoral vision in a dream: "Each leaf that brushed his face deepened his sadness and dread. Each leaf he passed he'd never pass again. They rode over his face like veils" (*ibid.*).

Toward the end of the novel the reader witnesses levels of emotional depth and self-awareness in Lester that were unimaginable at the outset. For example, when he sees a "churchbus" wheeling by in the night as he lays hiding in a ditch: "a small boy was looking out the [rear] window ... [Lester] was trying to fix in his mind where he'd seen the boy when it came to him that the boy looked like himself. This gave him the fidgets and though he tried to shake the image of the face in the glass it would not go" (p. 191). This leads us to the strangest realization about *Child of God* and McCarthy's most engaging "twist": It is as much bildungsroman as work of grotesque horror; it just happens to be about a serial killer. In fact, we witness his self-realization when, having escaped, he presents himself back at the hospital desk and makes a statement that has greater implications than the obvious: "I'm supposed to be here, he said" (p. 192).

But there is a disturbing corollary to this "progress," for as Lester is cast out of social forms and progresses deeper into nature — from living in a house, to an overgrown shack, to a cave — he becomes more "human," but he also is driven deeper into the dark recesses of "human nature" — that is, the sexual and violent drives that are, in McCarthy's worldview, inherent in the human condition (if often buried). We see this paralleling of nature and the human condition as Lester walks through the winter forest: "Disorder in the woods, trees down, new paths needed. Given charge Ballard would have made things more orderly in the woods and in men's souls" (p. 136).

And Lester, just another child of God, is not a deviation from the larger human order. As old Mr. Wade puts it when asked if "people was meaner" back in an older era:

"I think people are the same from the day God first made one" (p. 168). Critic Arthur Saltzman claims, "The greater threat [in *Child of God*] is not that such lapses from humanity survive and function ungoverned; it is that they are not lapses but manifestations that must be accommodated within any honest definition of the human" (p. 897). Here, though, they remain buried deep in the psyche (the allegory of Lester's cave) but rise to the surface as the social forms and constraints collapse around Lester — home, community, etc.

In *Child of God* there is what Georg Guillemin terms "societally sanctioned" barbarism as well, which explains the meticulous details of students studying Lester's corpse at the state medical school: He was "flayed, dissected, eviscerated. His head was sawed open and his brains removed. His muscles were stripped from his bones.... His entrails were hauled forth and delineated." And at the end of the examination, "Ballard was scraped from the table into a plastic bag" (p. 194). Here we experience what Mark Royden Winchell describes as "the exploiter of corpses becoming an exploited corpse" (*Reinventing*, p. 237).

Nevertheless, Lester, despite his corporal self having been disposed of, is actually incorporated into the social order and community of Sevier County, completing the journey of the bildungsroman. Ballard may not be alive at book's end, but the short chapters of oral testimony interspersed throughout the early part of the book — testimony from a later point in time than the narrative action — show that, after his death, Lester becomes a part of the fabric and folklore of the community through the tales they tell about him. The irony is that his atrocities have made him more a part of the social order than he ever was back when he was a harmless peeping tom. He is now simply catalogued among other town eccentrics in these front-porch tales.

In fact, for the speakers, Lester's story calls to mind wild local tales of others, and the teller often segues into stories of other people, like "old Gresham" (p. 22) and "that Trantham boy" (p. 36). (It is also interesting that Ballard is "never indicted for any crime" [p. 192].) As a legend, Ballard finds a more meaningful, posthumous existence in society, and the community shows much more interest in him in the wake of his atrocities than they ever did in his lifetime. Vince Brewton claims that "although Ballard's existence may be confined to the margins of the social order, storytelling reinserts him ... into the heart of the community" (p. 125). This is quite an evolution from the shadowy, inchoate community member, the "misplaced and loveless simian shape," who once surreptitiously crept around peering into car windows (p. 20).

Upon release of the book, the *New York Times* reviewer, like many, was taken aback by the thematic material of *Child of God* and put off by its handling. The critic saw a novel that was "lacking in human momentum or point" and declared that the "sour diction of this book ... does not often let us see beyond its nasty 'writing' into moments we can see for themselves, rendered. And such moments, authentic though they feel, do not much help" (Brickner). The reviewer summed up *Child of God* as an "essentially sentimental novel that no matter how sternly it strives to be tragic is never more than morose" (*ibid.*). Not all reviewers were immune to the novel's charms, however, and based on the book the *New Yorker* offered a lengthy, thoughtful piece on McCarthy at a time when he was still an obscurity. The *New Republic* and the *Washington Post Book World* also saw something powerful in Cormac McCarthy's unusual vision and idiosyncratic style, and the book, very much in popular release, has continued to find new readers.

• *Further reading*

Guillemin, Georg. *The Pastoral Vision of Cormac McCarthy.* College Station: Texas A&M University Press, 2004.

Sullivan, Nell. "The Evolution of the Dead Girlfriend Motif in *Child of God* and *Outer Dark.*" *Myth, Legend, Dust: Critical Responses to Cormac McCarthy,* ed. Rick Wallach. Manchester, UK: Manchester University Press, 2000.

Winchell, Mark Royden. *Reinventing the South.* Columbia: University of Missouri Press, 2006.

Cities of the Plain

Readers that have attentively followed the previous two books of the Border Trilogy — *All the Pretty Horses* (1992) and *The Crossing* (1994) — will find themselves disoriented in the opening pages of the trilogy's finale, *Cities of the Plain* (1998). The novel finally brings together the individual heroes of the previous two books, John Grady Cole (*All the Pretty Horses*) and Billy Parham (*The Crossing*). Each of those characters' border crossings and ordeals in the previous novels left them at the end of the previous books consumed by a vast, cosmic sadness — and in the midst of a grim and inevitable shift that was bound to consume all that they loved, including their very way of life. *Cities of the Plain* has a narrower scope than the preceding books. John Grady Cole and Billy Parham had ranged far and wide in their adventures, particularly into the depths of Mexico; here, however, they both work at a ranch in New Mexico in 1952 — a ranch headed toward extinction like so many before it — and in proximity to the titular "cities of the plain," El Paso, Texas, and Juárez, Mexico.

In fact, while ranging about at night during their ranch labor or while sitting around a campfire, the two cowboys often take in a sweeping, panoptic view of the neighboring cities in the distance, lashed together in uneasy symbiosis and butted up against opposite sides of the border: "Far out on the plain below the lights of the cities lay shimmering in their grids with the dark serpentine of the river dividing them" (p. 156). The environs of these cities of the plain constitute the literary geography of Cormac McCarthy's novel. The title itself is an unsettling biblical reference to Sodom and Gomorrah. In the Scriptures, God destroyed those cities because of the corrupted nature of the humanity within them; therefore, the novel's title summons not only heavenly wrath but the corruption of human nature. The evocation of these cities is undoubtedly "deeply and indelibly imbued with a mysterious and dreadful meaning" (Abbott, p. 577). (Thus the "serpentine" image of their boundary line in the previous quote.)

Moreover, this allusion suits McCarthy's larger enterprise in the trilogy — i.e., deliberating on the inevitable ebb and flow of civilizations caught up in the bloody epochs that constitute history. Just as the Native Americans headed toward obsolescence, and just as the Mexicans were pushed out of the land that constitutes the American Southwest, so too is the *vaquero* — the cowboy — fading as a once prominent presence of these plains. But, as the *New York Times* review of the novel suggested, McCarthy's Border Trilogy opens the aperture enough to suggest a universal resonance (and a universal fate) that extends beyond the Southwest, often through references to the Mexican Revolution and World War II and the looming, modern U.S. government presence on these plains. (The ranch land is soon to be bought by the government.) McCarthy is concerned not just with the history of the American Southwest but with all the "'cities of the plain' ... that once flourished and were destroyed," writes Sara Mosle. "That brief moment between a culture's existence and extinction — this is the border that McCarthy's characters keep crossing and recrossing, and the one story, as he's forever writing, that contains all others (p. 16).

But beyond its thematic link with the other two volumes in the trilogy, *Cities of the Plain* also works on two other levels. On one hand, it is a wistful, softer-focus story of kindness between people and of tragic personal relationships. Several cowboys in the novel live with one foot in the past, missing loved ones who have died, including Billy, who lost his brother Boyd in *The Crossing*. This makes *Cities of the Plain* a much different book from the action/adventure romance of *All the Pretty Horses* or the darkly complicated saga of *The Crossing*. *Cities of the Plain* also works at a deeper level, though, problematizing notions of narrative conventions and myth-making and returning to *The Crossing*'s deliberations on the nature of being. At this level, the *Cities of the Plain* seeks to finish the work of the Border Trilogy, though one should not expect anything as finite as conclusion or resolution from a McCarthy narrative.

But first we must return to what makes this particular narrative a disorienting departure from the previous two novels of the trilogy; for the emotional and philosophical distance that John Grady and Billy have traveled seems absent from the opening pages of *Cities of the Plain*, which thrust us into a Juárez whorehouse in 1952. The reader does not witness the moment when Billy and John Grady finally meet and is not privy to the circumstances of that meeting; rather, when we encounter the two they have already been working together at the Alamogordo, New Mexico, ranch for a time and are simply out for a night on the town at a favored bordello.

From Billy, we get no sense of the travails, monstrous grief, or accumulated, esoteric wisdom that was poured in his ear in the multitudinous quests of *The Crossing*. Instead, now older at 28, he swaggers into the house of ill-repute in the opening lines and launches into wisecracking, teasing the younger John Grady, and making bawdy comments regarding the qualities of the assembled prostitutes.

Nevertheless, as the novel progresses, we come to realize that Billy is the trilogy's true enigma and most inscrutable figure. We know what John Grady is — he is that Western cowboy archetype who embodies a sort of fierce individualism. As John Updike describes it, "an antisocial extreme of individualism" (p. 349). John Grady still has that sense of exaggerated justice we found in *All the Pretty Horses*; he stands fiercely by his principles and pursues an unyielding line of destiny based on those principles (leading to his tragic demise). But he is a hero of an old and familiar trope cast into a new and increasingly unfamiliar world. McCarthy, as always, presents us with conflict and paradox, and the character of John Grady, this lone figure and relative outlaw, is bound to run up against failure in a Border Trilogy "where the very possibility of individual or collective secession from the structures of the world ... is relentlessly problematized" (Holloway, p. 19). Thus, the succession of "doomed enterprises" (a term from *The Crossing*) in the three volumes: John Grady's love affair with Alejandra, Billy's failed attempt to free a trapped she-wolf in the mountains of Mexico, Billy's failed attempt to save his brother Boyd, John Grady's failed attempt to rescue and marry the young prostitute, and Billy's failed enterprise to steer John Grady from death.

Billy doesn't drive the action in *Cities of the Plain*, and he often seems more like an observer than a participant in the story; in fact, he seems to have settled into a life on the margins, never — for example — having any sort of romantic relationship beyond his whorehouse forays. When he does step in, it is to protect John Grady, who in his obstinacy and unyielding sense of purpose reminds him of his brother Boyd.

But it is the lone enigma Billy that we are left with in the trilogy's final pages, an epilogue which zips forward in time to him at 78 years old, living an indigent life and sleeping beneath a highway overpass. His last job had been as an extra in a movie, a role for which he was surely chosen because of his "authentic" weathered and aged cowboy appearance. He has become a player in the myth of the West, despite being the keeper of a rich personal history of the borderlands.

Writer/literary critic Leslie Fiedler once declared, "We have always been, insofar as we are Americans at all, inhabitants of myth rather than history" (Winchell, *Too Good to Be True*) and the most potent landscape for that myth has been the American West. But McCarthy's work in the trilogy actually does a great deal to demythologize the borderlands, even as he presents new, problematizing myths of his own. One comes away from the reading experience with the notion that history is as much a myth-making endeavor as the "*corridos*," the Mexican narrative folk songs often alluded to in the trilogy that took up historical events, tragedies, and heroism, becoming a "distinctive and artistically powerful master cultural poetics of the northern Border," particularly during the Mexican Revolution (Limón, p. 9). But there is also a suggestion in *Cities of the Plain* that the stories that we tell ourselves, our written histories, are simply structured myths, like the ballads sung around campfires by guitar-strumming Mexican rebels.

Cities of the Plain explores these individual and personal myths as well. Billy, as an old man in the epilogue, has a different vantage point on the life he has lived, a distant perspective, much like the many nights on the range when the characters observe those glittering cities of the plain from an objective distance. On one such night, Billy observed, "There's a lot of things that look better at a distance," to which John Grady agreed, adding, "The life you've lived, for one." Billy's life might not look "better" to him at 78, but he can see it better and the view is not comforting.

Toward the end of the novel, Billy awakes on his concrete bed beneath the overpass and thinks of his dead sister and of the death of his brother Boyd in Mexico. "In everything that he'd ever thought about the world and about his life in it he'd been wrong" (p. 266), writes McCarthy. Billy, it seems, had been an inhabitant — a prisoner perhaps — of his own personal mythology. Decades before, when Billy had attempted to negotiate with Eduardo on John Grady's behalf, the pimp who would become John Grady's killer had imparted that very wisdom, noting that John Grady had in his mind a picture of how his life would be once he freed Magdalena and settled into domestic bliss with her. "What is wrong with this story is that it is not a true story," he says to Billy. "Men have in their minds a picture of how the world will be. How they will be in that world. The world may be many different ways for them but there is one world that will never be and that is the world they dream of" (p. 134). Myths tend to be collective and social, but this final Border Trilogy book also explores a different, more personal kind of myth (which can overlap with those larger myths): the myths we tell ourselves about how our life is or will be.

This is the dark message at the heart of the Border Trilogy, and it is the ethos that drives McCarthy's narrative far from convention and allows him to shatter reader expectations and carve out a distinctly idiosyncratic (many would say pessimistic, or even nihilistic) vision. In the trilogy, there is something that is uncapturable — that cannot be contained by the histories, *corridos*, or stories we tell ourselves: destiny. And if myths are the worlds that we create, collectively or on our own, then in McCarthy's vision destiny is the thing that was created for us long before we or our world existed. Myths don't hold up, but destiny is unwavering — and destiny is the idea that is most deeply deliberated on in *Cities of the Plain*.

What makes the trilogy ultimately such an enigmatic and inconclusive reading experience, however, is that McCarthy forces his characters to deliberate on the very sort of deep ontological notions that he presents as unfathomable. The nature of being, the nature of history, self-perception, even his characters' orientations to God; all get pulled into the vortex of this questioning, and the epilogue of *Cities of the Plain* returns us to the thorny philosophical terrain that characterized large sections of the previous book, *The Crossing*. Here, Billy's encounter with a mysterious, indigent stranger beneath an overpass leads to a dialogue whose full philosophical burden must be weighed against the entire trilogy.

But it is a difficult pill to swallow, as McCarthy doesn't tie things up; rather, he casts the reader into some of the greatest uncertainties yet. He dashes any reassuring certitude and risks undermining the whole reading experience of the trilogy — or at least anything we thought was certain about the characters' lives. "But what is your life? Can you see it?" asks the stranger of Billy. "It vanishes at its own appearance. Moment by moment. Until it vanishes to appear no more ... is there a point in time when the seen becomes the remembered? How are they separate? It is that which we have no way to show" (p. 273). Earlier, Billy wonders aloud to the stranger, "Where do we go when we die?" to which the man replies, "I don't know ... where are we now?" (p. 268).

The metafictional component of the epilogue also renders problematical McCarthy's very idiom: language and narrative. The traveler, telling Billy about his mysterious dream, notes that the ancient figures were communicating in "a language that is older than the spoken word at all. The idiom is another specie and with it there can be no lie or no dissemblance of the truth" (p. 281). We see then the weakness of language and narration, yet this is all we have to make sense of the world and ourselves: "The events of the waking world ... are forced upon us and the narrative is the unguessed axis along which they must be strung," says the mysterious stranger to Billy — who is now tellingly referred to as the "narrator." "It falls to us to weigh and sort and order these events. It is we who assemble them into the story which is us. Each man is the bard of his own existence" (p. 283).

What we witness in the epilogue is not only one of those deeply philosophical exchanges for which the trilogy is known, but the actual narrative of the whole trilogy folding back on itself: "Those stories which speak to us with the greatest resonance have a way of turning upon the teller and erasing him and his motives from all memory," says the stranger (p. 277). But who is this stranger? Is he the embodiment of McCarthy's omniscient narrator, that faceless voice which exerts such power upon the trilogy? Is he an embodiment of McCarthy himself, as creator of the stories? What is the difference between the two? The epilogue pushes us toward the unfathomable, toward a realization that always seems just out of view, beyond our understanding. All that is certain is destiny, a destiny that never unfolds to us in the cohesive shape of a map or narrative that we may view or capture an objective vantage point, but one that we only know by the present moment in which we dwell: "however you may choose to tell it," says the stranger, its "shape was forced in the void at the onset and all talk of what otherwise might have been is senseless for there is no otherwise.... That we may imagine other histories means nothing at all" (p. 285). Destiny, we learn in the *Cities of the Plain*, is the only absolute: "The template for the world and all in it was drawn long ago" (p. 287). The stories of the world, our narratives, our tales, our personal histories, are "all the world we know," but those created worlds don't "exist outside of the instruments of its execution" (p. 287).

Nevertheless, amidst all of McCarthy's narrative deconstructing, one shouldn't mistake this for a novel predominately about "ideas," for the paradoxical capability of the trilogy is that even amidst the loftier ideas there is a "story" here — in fact, there are many stories — with tremendous emotional resonance that grounds the novel at an emotional level. For one, there is the brotherly relationship between Billy and John Grady and the final, crushing image of Billy carrying the just-deceased John Grady through the streets of Juárez. Billy could save John Grady no more than he could have saved his brother Boyd in *The Crossing*. Destiny is absolute, and a group of schoolchildren bear witness to this:

> They could not take their eyes from him. The dead boy in his arms hung with his head back and those partly opened eyes beheld nothing at all out of that passing landscape of street or wall or paling sky or the figures of the children who stood blessing themselves in the gray light. This man and his burden passed on forever out of that nameless crossroads and the woman stepped once more into the street and the children followed and all continued on to their appointed places which as some believe were chosen long ago even to the beginning of the world [p. 261].

It is the relationships, both current and past, that ground the more esoteric elements of *Cities of the Plain*. And at a whole other level — separate from yet parallel to the great philosophical stirrings — this is a story about kindness between people and the loneliness of old cowboys.

In the previous two volumes, the reader constantly witnessed the charity of the Mexican people, as both John Grady and Billy, as complete strangers, were summoned to numerous tables to eat and given numerous places to sleep. As the ranch hands, including Billy and John Grady, sit around a campfire in *Cities of the Plain*, one old cowboy remembers the kindness he too had received in Mexico: "Those people would take you in and put you up and feed you and feed your horse and cry when you left. You could of stayed forever," he recalls. "That plateful of beans they set in front of you was hard to come by. But I was never turned away. Not a time" (p. 90).

Part of the softer, wistful touch of *Cities of the Plain* also comes from several of the cowboys' sense of loss. Billy, of course, still reflects on the death of Boyd (which occurred in *The Crossing*), and his friend and fellow ranch worker Troy also relates the loss of a favorite brother. (Interestingly, the demise of both was precipitated by their love for a woman.) But the most striking passage to take up that theme involves the old cowboy Mr. Johnson, who in his mentally addled grief over the loss of his daughter is bound to fits of sleep-walking about the grounds of the ranch in his night clothes. After one such episode, John Grady has compassionately led him back to the house and helped him get into his clothes. "When John Grady took his plate to the sideboard and went out it was just breaking day. The old man was still sitting at the table in his hat. He'd been born in east Texas in eighteen sixty-seven and come out to this country as a young man," writes McCarthy. "In his time the country had gone from the oil lamp and the horse and buggy to jet planes and the atomic bomb but that wasn't what confused him. It was the fact that his daughter was dead that he couldn't get the hang of" (p. 106).

We find a further example of the meditation on personal relationships and kindness through the family that takes in the aged Billy at the end of the epilogue, giving him a shed room, where he sleeps and cries out from his dreams for his long-deceased brother Boyd. When the woman of the family, Betty, checks on Billy, she comments that he still misses his brother. "Yes I do. All the time," answers Billy. Then, as she pats his hand in reassurance, we get, for the first time in the Border Trilogy, a physical description of Billy, if only his hand: "Gnarled, ropescarred, speckled from the sun and years of it. The ropy veins that bound them to his heart. There was map enough for men to read" (p. 291). In that image we are reminded once and for all what Billy is: he is a cowboy and this is a cowboy story (though a unique one). The final lines of the trilogy are spoken between Billy and Betty:

> I'm not what you think I am. I ain't nothing. I dont know why you put up with me.
> Well, Mr. Parham, I know who you are. And I do know why. You go to sleep now. I'll see you in the morning.
> Yes mam [p. 291].

Billy is an old cowboy, an archetype of an old way of life, and that means something to her and it means something to readers. In 2007, Cormac McCarthy said of American cowboy lore, "It's a story that everyone in the world knows.... You can go to Mongolia and they know about [American] cowboys ... but no one had taken it seriously and as a subject for literary effort" (Kushner). We see then a raison d'être for McCarthy's undertaking of the Border Trilogy which presents a whole different kind of "cowboy story" with layers of meaning and depths of emotional and philosophical resonance that had never been applied to the subject before — but it is a cowboy story, nonetheless.

The finale of the Border Trilogy was met with mixed reviews, perhaps because *Cities of the Plain*, even more than the difficult *The Crossing*, did not have the immediacy of *All the Pretty Horses*. But many reviewers also appreciated the stirring elements of the novel and its relationship to the overall endeavor of the trilogy. The London *Times* review spoke of how, by "[c]rossing and recrossing [the literal and figurative border] in these three fierce, desolate, beautiful novels, [McCarthy] has created a masterpiece, one that engages with the tremendous questions of life and death and has the weight to take them on" (Hughes-Hallett). Another London newspaper, the *Independent*, regarded it as "McCarthy's most laconic and understated book" (Bradfield, "Twilight Cowboy").

The *Washington Post* thought that compared to the previous two volumes the novel was "more contemporary and urban, narrower in focus [and] at times over-emphatic" but pointed out that "its language, especially in the descriptions of men at work, still soars.... One reads such passages as if they were poetry—and they are" (Dirda, "Last Roundup"). The *Boston Globe* declared that "in several ways this is a smaller novel" than the previous two books of the trilogy, noting that the book "lacks the breathtaking inner dimensions of the first two volumes and the wrenching deliverance of *The Crossing* ... at times its trademark prophecies and oratory seem less illuminative than tacked on as rhetorical dressing" (Caldwell, "Unsheltering Sky"). But the same critic admitted that what "the novel does beautifully is capture a way of life so unspoken and deep that most people never knew it existed: the essence of a man's life lived on a horse on the plains" (*ibid.*).

Academic Edwin T. Arnold suggested that some readers "will view *Cities of the Plain* as a lesser work, and certainly it is more constricted than either of the first two volumes." However, he also goes on to claim, "It may, in fact, prove ultimately to be the wisest of the books, and, in its cumulative effect, the one that in retrospect will move us the most deeply" ("Last of the Trilogy," p. 222). Arnold raises a point worth ending on—that, while not as emotionally devastating as *The Crossing* or as immediately gripping as *All the Pretty Horses*, *Cities of the Plain* has a softer, more ruminative focus that is as beguiling and effective by degrees. And a close look at the three Border Trilogy volumes side-by-side reveals that each of the books is distinctly different in perspective and style, despite the many connections that bind them. Perhaps the last word on the entire trilogy is that it amounts to *some* cowboy story.

- *Further reading*

Arnold, Edwin T. "The Last of the Trilogy: First Thoughts on *Cities of the Plain.*" *Perspectives on Cormac McCarthy*, eds. Edwin T. Arnold and Dianne C. Luce. Jackson: University Press of Mississippi, 1999.

Dirda, Michael. "The Last Roundup." *The Washington Post Book World*, May 24, 1998.

Mosle, Sara. "Don't Let Your Babies Grow Up to Be Cowboys." *New York Times Book Review*, May 17, 1998, p. 16.

Cole, John Grady

John Grady Cole cuts an anachronistic figure across the landscape of Cormac McCarthy's fiction as the author's most purely romantic protagonist. An intuitive and ardent horseman, adventurer, dedicated lover of two women (one an aristocrat; another a prostitute), and a figure possessing an almost exaggerated sense of justice, Cole debuted in *All the Pretty Horses* (1992), spearheading McCarthy's popularity with mainstream audiences. Along with Billy Parham, Cole is the author's only other recurring figure, appearing as well in *Cities of the Plain* (1998), the final book of the Border Trilogy.

Prior to *All the Pretty Horses*, McCarthy had peopled his books with protagonists that ran a short gamut from ambivalent to downright troubling (a serial killer/necrophiliac, an incestuous brother). The title figure in *Suttree* (1979) perhaps comes closest to Cole as a conscionable character, but is a haphazardly romantic figure at best (and one prone to bursts of pure degeneracy), while "the kid" from *Blood Meridian* (1985), another runner-up, is still ambivalent despite arguable moral evolution throughout the pages. John Wesley Rattner, from *The Orchard Keeper* (1965), is certainly benevolent, but the reader only witnesses him in a limited scope of stifling formative years and a tiny home community. (By contrast, Cole's adventures into Mexico and back seem boundless.)

The *Irish Times* considered John Grady Cole, in *All the Pretty Horses*, as "not only a romantic hero and idealist ... [but] the moral heart of [a] book in which right and wrong are explored with brutal clarity" and furthermore noted that even if his "aspirations have been narrowed" in *Cities of the Plain*, he is still "very much the young knight in love," though his object here is a doomed young prostitute (Battersby). (This contrasts with the evolution of Billy, a more complicated, older figure whom we encounter bawdily wisecracking at the bar of a bordello in the opening passages of *Cities of the Plain*.)

Newsweek noted that Cole "partakes of violence with the greatest reluctance and wears its memory with genuine remorse," a quality that seemed to set him apart from the wanton violence of the author's previous oeuvre, and termed the "gentle, stubborn and honorable" cowboy among McCarthy's "greatest achievements" (Jones, p. 68). London's *Independent* proclaimed how, in *All the Pretty Horses*, McCarthy attempts "some things he hasn't attempted before, and mostly he succeeds," singling out the rendering of "McCarthy's first certifiably 'good man,' a 16-year-old boy named John Grady Cole" (Bradfield, "Mystery"). The write-up also saw a thematic break from McCarthy's former orientation toward violence: "Refusing to let the bloody world reduce him to meaninglessness, Cole seeks instead to attach some value to it, some formal signature. It is arguable that, by the end of this fine novel, he succeeds" (*ibid.*).

In fact, McCarthy clearly delineates his hero himself when he writes of John Grady Cole, "What he loved in horses was what he loved in men ... all his fondness and all the leanings of his life were for the ardent-hearted and they would always be so and never be otherwise" (*All the Pretty Horses*, p. 6). Here, laid out for the reader, are the two prime drives in Cole: his ardent-heartedness — seen most clearly in his love for both Alejandra and Magdalena — and his simpatico orientation toward horses. (He even runs among horses in his dreams.) And what Cole says of a "good horse" — that it "has justice in [its] heart" (*Cities of the Plain*, p. 53) — sounds like a projection of sorts. The same could be said of Cole himself, who is compelled to flay his conscience before a judge (both in court and at the judge's home) at the end of *All the Pretty Horses* because he killed a would-be assassin in self-defense in a Mexican prison. The judge, in turn, offers a sage observation: "Son ... you strike me as somebody that maybe tends to be a little hard on theirselves" (p. 291).

See also *All the Pretty Horses*; The Dueña Alfonsa; *Cities of the Plain*; Parham, Billy; Rocha, Alejandra

Corridos

The *corridos* are the popular Mexican ballads that are consistently referred to in the Border Trilogy, particularly in *The Crossing* (1994). The sung ballads — composed of four-line verses and relatively simple song structures — typically narrate the legends of Mexican heroes, bandits, and outlaws. The *corrido* has also served as a medium for Mexican workers to "to analyze political events, criticize leaders, lament tragedies in their communities and declare political resistance" (Stacy, p. 231).

These ballads have primarily been the medium of the working classes, who use them as an outlet for cultural galvanization and to express cultural pride. Martha I. Chew Sánchez points out how "the personal stories of the *corridos* become collective stories because of the level of identification with the main protagonists. This strong identification seems to create social consciousness" (Sánchez, p. 71). Scholars have often used the *corridos* as an important historical context through which to view Mexican working-class attitudes over the years (*ibid.*).

These songs can be traced back to the romantic Spanish ballads of the conquistadores in basic form and theme, though they have been distinctly shaped by their Mexican heritage in more recent times. In fact, the modern *corrido* represented in the Border Trilogy is largely a product of "the late nineteenth and early twentieth century, especially of the intense social change occasioned by the Mexican Revolution" (Limón, p. 18). And while the *corrido*'s focus can be on several categories of "events that are of particular significance to the *corridista*'s community and that capture and articulate this community's values and orientations," one theme stands out above others with a "special resonance" — "violent confrontation, between individual men who often represent larger social causes but just as often are concerned with their personal honor" (*ibid.*, p. 16).

It is this class of *corrido* that primarily concerns Cormac McCarthy. In fact, Boyd, Billy Parham's brother in *The Crossing*, evolves from a flesh-and-blood character to a figure that Billy can only trace in the legend of the *corridos*. Boyd becomes pure myth and legend, his existence in Mexico having been absorbed into the *corridos*, which turn him into a folk hero. Billy, on the trail of Boyd (who is dead), encounters accounts of his brother in the songs that he hears — ballads that tell of a brave, fair-haired, pistol-wielding hero from the north ("*Pelo tan rubio. Pistola en mano*" [p. 375]), who is killed in pursuit of honor.

But McCarthy also uses the convergence of Boyd's death and the *corrido* as a wedge into dialectic about history and myth-making. Billy, as brother to Boyd, comes to understand that the mythology constructed in the *corrido* has a tenuous relationship to Boyd's actual life. "He didnt kill the manco in La Boquillo," says Billy in his dialogue with the Yaqui Indian Quijada about Boyd and the nature of *corridos*. "I was there" (p. 384). In addition, the killings Boyd undertook after he left Billy may problematize the *corridos*; they may not have fit the criteria of honor. "He killed two men in Galeana," Quijada tells Billy. "No one knows why. They did not even work for the latifundio [great estate owner]" (*ibid.*). The *corrido*, however, has its own discursive agenda, as Quijada tells Billy: "It tells what it wishes to tell. It tells what makes the story run," regardless of actual events (p. 386).

The *corrido* is a preexisting narrative into which Boyd's actions in Mexico have been fitted to the discursive practices and sustaining cultural "truths" of the Mexican working class. The story itself had shape, form, and life, long before it subsumed Boyd into its structures. "I heard the tale of the güerito [fair-haired man] years ago," says the Yaqui Indian Quijada. Before your brother was even born" (p. 386). And while this is perceived as a question of the *corridos'* veracity in *The Crossing*, seen in another manner it becomes one of the *corrido's* enduring characteristics — one scholar indicates how they "are perceived as cultural artifacts that transcend time and space because the main content of the *corrido* applies to many generations from different regions" (Sánchez, p. 71).

The *corrido* is so enduring, in fact, that it still absorbs and broadcasts distinct takes on the issues of the day. If one visits the media-sharing website YouTube, *corridos* about Barack Obama and even Michael Jackson (upon the occasion of his death) can be located (as of this writing, in late July 2009). In addition, the *corridos'* fascination with outlaw characters has taken a darker turn in recent decades, giving rise to a strain called the *narcocorrido*: ballads that glorify — or at least speak approvingly or sentimentally of— drug smuggling and the narcotics trade.

The Mexican band Los Tigres del Norte popularized the *narcocorrido* in the 1970s, with ballads that became popular hits of the day and possessed such titles as "Contrabando y Traicion" ("Contraband and Betrayal"), "Los Tres Gallos" ("The Three Roosters" or "Three Best Friends"), "La Camioneta Gris" ("The Gray Pick-up"), and "La Mafia Muere" ("The Mob Dies"). In the 1990s and into the new millennium, the popularity of the *narcocorrido* grew considerably, with many popular Mexican groups taking up the form. Many radio stations and government officials in Mexico have banned or spoken out against the *narcocorridos* for fear of their corrupting influence (Edberg, p. 44). Interestingly, however, *No Country for Old Men* (2005), McCarthy's meditation on the evil of border narcotics trade, did not contain any references to the *narcocorridos*.

To turn back to the Border Trilogy, the *corridos* are most prominent in *The Crossing*, but there are also references to the ballads in the first trilogy book, *All the Pretty Horses* (1992). At an old colonial hotel in the ancient city of Zacatecas, in "the courtyard ... an old man knelt among pots of red and white geraniums, singing softly a single verse from an old *corrido* as he tended the flowers" (p. 247). In that same city, Alejandra takes John Grady to a plaza where her grandfather was killed in the revolution and in one statement bursts the spell of romanticism that *corridos* cast across such events: "There was no mother to cry. As in the *corridos*. Nor bird that flew. Just the blood on the stones" (p. 253).

And this seems to largely be the tack that McCarthy takes on the *corridos* in his novels — that is, he acknowledges them as an important cultural component, but questions their tales in the same manner that he questions the construction of other "histories."

See also All the Pretty Horses; *The Crossing*; History; The Mexican Revolution; Parham, Boyd; Quijada

The Crossing

The Crossing, released in 1994, is the powerful middle book of the Border Trilogy, a work that the *New York Times* deemed "a miracle in prose, an American original" (Hass) and a vast, heart-wrenching, complex book that has been described as the "dark center of the trilogy, the profound mystery that gives foundation to the more conventional [novels] that bracket it" (Arnold, "'Go to Sleep,'" p. 58). *The Crossing* has all of the grave power and difficult scope of such great American books as Herman Melville's *Moby-Dick* and William Faulkner's *The Sound and the Fury*, and, like most Cormac McCarthy novels, it is also remarkable for its evocative imagery and rigorously forged prose.

But it is also capable of engaging deep and thorny philosophical themes that question the very nature of existence while still having an astounding emotional impact. Much of the book's bracing mystery comes from this central idea of borders and crossings. There is, of course, the literal border between the U.S. and Mexico, which the young central cowboy figure Billy Parham repeatedly crosses, but there are other figurative borders that are crossed, even blurred and melded, as the novel often seems to occupy a paradoxical hinterland or twilight state between life and death, the dream world and waking, and the old and the new.

A scene that is emblematic of this liminality comes when Billy returns to America in book 2, after his ill-ended quest to return a pregnant she-wolf that he had trapped to the Mexican mountains. He recrosses the border on his way home as a ragged, gaunt, and weathered figure, a shadow of the idealistic boy who had once crossed in the other direction. At the border he meets an amiable guard named Gilchrist. It's a simple encounter on the surface, but like much of *The Crossing*, it is somewhat mystical and esoteric as well, with larger implications. The guard suggests that the teenager had stayed in Mexico "a little longer than what you intended" (p. 162). Billy in response somewhat uncharacteristically asks for the loan of a half dollar coin for something to eat, with the promise that he'll return it. The guard flips a coin through the air to Billy, and there is something stirringly symbolic in the exchange, right down to Billy's observation to Gilchrist, "You aint from around here," which casts the guard in a mysterious, rootless light (*ibid.*).

The encounter evokes a reversal of the Greek myth of Charon, the guardian figure of the Styx, that "flowing boundary between the lands of the living and the dead" (Kastenbaum, p. 315). In mythology, Charon required coin payment before ferrying the dead to the other side, thus the Greek burial custom of placing a coin in the mouth of the dead. Billy pays the coin back when he reenters Mexico with his brother Boyd, both righting the direction of the Charon myth and foreshadowing the death of his younger brother Boyd during that venture to Mexico. Years later, in book 4, when he returns to Mexico to locate his brother, Billy gives the *aduanero* (customs officer) a silver coin. In a ceremonious image, the *aduanero* "saluted him gravely and addressed him as caballero [gentleman]" (p. 355). Here, again, the reader encounters a portal figure granting Billy ceremonial passage to what could be perceived as a world of the dead, and, of course, Billy soon finds out that Boyd has been killed and endures much hardship trying to return Boyd's bones across the border.

The boundary between life and death is not always clearly defined, however. Just before returning to the U.S. the first time, Billy, in a dreamlike episode, sees his father's horse walk down the street in the old desolate Mexican town of Santa Maria, where Billy has stopped over for a night. But when he walks out in the street to confirm the sighting, the street is empty: He "looked east and west and he walked up to the square and looked out along the main road north but horse or rider there was none" (p. 160). Is this a vision? His father has indeed been killed — he will soon discover that when he crosses back into New Mexico — and his father's horse *has* been stolen, and Billy and Boyd will set out on another ill-fated adventure to regain his family's horses.

But the sighting also comes like a dispatch from the land of the dead. Much later in the book, Billy encounters a blind man who, as a captured rebel in the revolution, had literally had his eyeballs sucked from their sockets by a monstrously cruel German captain of the Mexican federal army. An old man now, the blind ex-revolutionary feels his condition has "already halved the distance to death" (p. 280) and conjectures "that the blind had already partly quit the world anyway" (p. 282). He is, as he describes, adrift in a state that is neither life nor death but somewhere in between.

There are many more encounters in the novel that seem to involve some kind of transitional realm or borderlands between life and death. When Billy last sees Boyd, his brother is an image of death in life, as if, like the blind man, he had "already halved the distance to death." He is wrapped in muslin coverings (the material used for death shrouds) and appears "paler than his brother could ever remember and so thin with the rack of his ribs stark against the pale skin" (p. 330). The next time Billy sees his brother, he will be simply skeletal remains.

In *The Crossing* the line between death and life is blurred: The dead resonate in the living world and are pervasive, and the lines of communication to them are open. "Speak with them. Call their names," advises one *sepulturero* (gravedigger) to a mourner after a day of interring victims of a mass execution: "Seize them back" (p. 288). As one critic puts it, McCarthy "uses the border metaphor to create ... a world that is not simply ... life or death, but an oxymoronic melding, an ongoing dialectic between the forces of death and life" as well as "other apparent dualities" (Busby, p. 227). One gypsy rhapsodizes to Billy that it is "imprudent to suppose that the dead have no power to act in the world, for their power is great" (p. 413). This is a central ongoing dialectic in the book: the dead and the past are omnipresent in the living action and exert influence everywhere Billy Parham rides.

The Crossing calls to mind Irish poet William Butler Yeats' final incantation in the poem "Under Ben Bulben" (1938), the very lines that the poet made his own epitaph: "*Cast a cold eye / On life, on death / Horseman pass by!*" In the foreboding lines, the supernatural horseman — simultaneously casting his glance on the alive and the dead — evokes Billy, a restlessly peripatetic horseman wandering purposely through these borderlands, surrounded by life and death and circumstances somewhere in between: a sort of "liminal state of humankind, the border living in a world of between" (Busby, p. 227). In one of many dreamlike passages in the isolated outposts of Mexico, Billy enters the small mining town of Namiquipa to find a wedding and a burial happening nearly simultaneously. A dead man cools on a slab in his best suit while townspeople engage in a celebratory wedding processional. In the evening, they turn from revelers celebrating one of life's new beginnings to mourners bearing the dead man to his final resting place.

This is the paradoxical dreamlike canvas and landscape across which the quest hero, Billy Parham, travels, not in a linear fashion or in pursuit of one goal, but back and forth across the border for various reasons. In book 1, Billy, after much travail, traps the pregnant she-wolf that has been pillaging livestock on his father's ranch. When confronted by the sight of the actual injured wolf, he gets it in his mind to free her across the border; thus this improbable journey begins, with Billy abandoning his brother and parents without word, caring for the wounded wolf, and dragging it in tow behind his horse in a captivatingly obsessive and awkwardly beautiful display of compassion.

In true McCarthy fashion, there is no psychological or emotional elaboration as to why he does this; nevertheless, McCarthy renders the growing intimacy between the teenager and wild animal in gorgeous detail. In book 2, he crosses back into Mexico with his younger brother Boyd as an act of poorly planned but again obsessive redemption regarding the murder and horse thievery inflicted against his family, and in book 4 he crosses back on a fixated quest to find his brother, or at least what remains of him. Billy is at the nexus of the book's liminality, with all of the book's confusing and often contradictory forces acting upon him. He even embodies the very duality of the borderlands — a land interpenetrated by both American and Mexican culture — having descended from a Mexican maternal grandmother and having an easy facility for moving between the English and Spanish tongues.

McCarthy also pits the young, itinerant *vaquero* (cowboy) Billy Parham as a classic quest hero in the lineage of Odysseus, but as a 1930s and 1940s borderlands version of the mythical hero. This is what has been called McCarthy's "Joycean mode," wherein the writer "juxtaposes the breadth and grandeur of classical epic with ... an average man's life" (Ellis, "McCarthy Music," p. 168). James Joyce did this to great effect in *Ulysses* ("Ulysses" being the Roman equivalent of "Odysseus") by mirroring classic myth in the travels throughout Dublin of the central character, Leopold Bloom, during one "normal" day. (McCarthy has said *Ulysses* is on his list of great novels, which "stops at four" and also includes "*The Brothers Karamazov, The Sound and the Fury* and his favorite, *Moby-Dick*" [Kushner].)

Nevertheless, Billy and his experiences do not contain the clear-cut heroic nature of Odysseus or his trials. "Doomed enterprises divide lives forever into the then and now" (p. 129), writes McCarthy in the opening passage of book 2, and "doomed" is exactly what Billy's trials are. Taken up with a grim but unyielding sense of purpose, they inevitably consummate in death and sorrow, and he is left adrift in these dreamlike Southwestern borderlands.

All of these themes seem to contribute to one overriding purpose in *The Crossing*: McCarthy's consistent preoccupation with — and meditations on — the nature of death and violence. The novel points to violence and war as timeless, pervasive, and endlessly repeating historical motifs. The novel expresses this in its mythological resonance: *The Odyssey* is one of the ultimate canonized war tales. But it also emerges in Billy's consistent encounters with the scars and sorrowful legacy of the Mexican Revolution, which had ended decades prior. In addition, in the U.S. he witnesses a country just entering and consumed by World War II, as ranches shut down and young men head abroad. Billy is fixed "both in [a] historical moment and in its aftermath" (Wegner, "Wars and Rumors," p. 76), and this in-between state has much larger implications; McCarthy represents it as the condition of history itself, caught up in an endless cycle of warring. In the borderlands we see the slow, inevitable turn of this cycle, the bloody aftermath of the Mexican Revolution and the newly confronted deaths and mourning of World War II.

The U.S.-Mexico borderland itself was gouged into consciousness after the Mexican-American War (1846–1848), when Mexico lost a great deal of territory to the United States, territory that constitutes the mythologized American Southwest. Roland Romero encapsulated the various ways in which the border has been described as "an open wound," "a scar," "a zipper," "a sore," and a line of "scrimmage" (Romero, p. 36). All of these unsettling metaphors suggest the legacy of bloodshed that established the border and its environs, as well as the continually uneasy co-habitation and co-dependence that characterizes the region.

And this legacy, as *The Crossing* makes implicit, is regenerative. In fact, according to a 2004 *New York Times* piece, about 2,000 migrants died crossing the border ("National Briefing") from 1998 to 2004, demonstrating an ongoing cycle of death arising out the very raison d'être of the border itself. Before the Mexican/American conflict, there were the Comanche and Apache, who were massacred into obsolescence. Blood is in the very soil of these borderlands, and McCarthy's prose wallows in this blood, taking up the reverberations of that legacy. We see that in *Blood Meridian* (1985), which deals with a time immediately following the Mexican-American War. And we see that in a more implicit manner in *The Crossing*.

In fact, in one scene from a historical oral narrative within the larger story, alleged Mexican rebel sympathizers were lined up and executed. Later, the rains drove the blood into the earth, and packs of dogs scooped up "mouthfuls of the bloodsoaked mud and ate it down and snapped and quarreled and slank away again" (p. 288). Here, in a telling image, blood is of the very earth, a sustenance that is battled over by wild dogs. The borderlands are sustained by replenishing layers of blood, and it is no mistake that both this book and its predecessor, *All the Pretty Horses* (1992), begin with disturbing images of Native Americans, reminding us of the full breadth of this history. (Not one to proselytize, McCarthy renders the violence reciprocal, as Indians allegedly kill Billy's parents and steal their horses.)

Dreams also prominently figure in the novel, as both mysterious portents of violence and connections to the dead. On his final trek back toward the U.S. border with his brother Boyd's remains, Billy dreams of his brother while camped out under the stars, while Boyd's emaciated, skeletal corpse is safely lodged in the crook of a nearby tree. In the dream, Billy asks Boyd about death and what it's like, but he "only smiled and looked away and would not answer. They spoke of other things and [Billy] tried not to wake from the dream" (p. 400). Even before Boyd's death, Billy dreams of holding his dead brother in his arms (p. 325), and upon waking he is wracked by even more encompassing and apocalyptic dreamlike visions (p. 326).

In another portentous night visitation, he dreams of his father "lost in the desert," searching the landscape with eyes "that seemed to contemplate with a terrible equanimity the cold and the dark and the silence that moved upon him and then all was dark and all was swallowed up in the silence" (p. 112). Dreams and waking visions, as one critic describes, are often "narrative devices" in McCarthy's work that "provide both insight into characters and experiential possibilities" (Arnold, "'Go to Sleep,'" p. 38).

Even the waking life of Billy Parham is dreamlike, particularly in Mexico, where he experiences a phantasmagoric land of characters and experiences: a carnival where Billy's she-wolf is forced to fight dogs to the death; a group of indigenous miners traveling with the wrapped corpse of a fellow worker; gypsies hauling the wreckage of an antique plane; a traveling opera company; a hermetic Mormon keeping watch over the ruins of an old settlement.

And if there is something unremittingly hopeless and grim in Billy's experiences and trials, there is also something deeply and profoundly philosophical and elevated about many of the exchanges he engages in during these encounters. This also adds to the dreamlike inclination of the novel, as the speeches often have a heightened, antiquarian cast to them that doesn't come off like everyday speech. Through his characters' various voices McCarthy raises probing questions about conditions such as fate, the nature of God, justice, temporality, the very nature of being itself, and even storytelling and historical narrative.

Often the revelations are bleak, even nihilistic, as when the Mormon hermit asserts that "the world itself can have no temporal view of things. It can have no cause to favor certain enterprises over others. The passing of armies and the passing of sands in the desert are one" (p. 148), or when the blind ex-revolutionary tells Billy that "in his blindness he had indeed lost himself and all memory of himself ... in the deepest dark" (p. 291) and that "the picture of the world is all the world men know and this picture of the world is perilous" and bound to disintegrate to "naught but dust" (p. 293). Nevertheless, despite these bleak philosophical assertions, and despite all of the violence and tragedy that Billy encounters, it is important to point out McCarthy's rendering of the consistent kindness and generosity of the Mexican people, particularly the poorer citizens. This is another strange duality: despite the perilous, foreboding qualities of *The Crossing*, Billy is consistently fed, looked after, and given counsel by complete strangers.

In another confusing duality, Billy seems trapped somewhere between the old and the new; there is a timeless, burnished cast to the story itself that doesn't feel like the mid-twentieth century, and when evidence of modernity does materialize — a truck, a radio, a stretch of blacktop road — it can be both surprising and anachronistic. Wolves, during this period in the Southwest, are heading toward obsolescence, despite having once widely ranged over northern Mexico and the U.S. borderlands, and here the wolf represents a vanishing, old order — just as Billy himself, an itinerant cowboy traveling the plains on horse, represents a vanishing presence.

In the book's opening passage, Billy, just a boy, slips from the house at night to bear captivating witness to the wolf pack running antelope in the moonlight, a scene that McCarthy renders in a stream of prose that gathers power in Hemingway-like layers of rhythm and repetition: "Then he saw them coming. Loping and twisting. Dancing. Tunneling their noses in the snow. Loping and running and rising by twos in a standing dance and running on again" (p. 4). In order to capture the she-wolf, Billy turns to another vestige of the past, the skill of trapping, which becomes a kind of black art in *The Crossing*, with Billy turning to a legendary trapper's menacing, ancient implements and murky, talismanic concoctions of scents in an abandoned cabin. He also consults a dying Mexican trapper who casts the wolf in an ancient, supernatural light, as a "being of great order [who] knows what men do not" (p. 45). The wolf, as McCarthy describes, lives by "old ceremonies. Old protocols" (p. 25). Here again, Billy is pitching around in the horse latitudes between the old and the new. He's a *vaquero*, a trapper, a witness to the ravages of the Mexican Revolution — yet an undercurrent pulls him toward the new age, toward the great modern and mechanized war abroad, as he repeatedly attempts to enlist in the U.S. Army to fight in World War II.

We witness a seismic shift in history when comparing the opening scene of Billy watching the wolves to the final passages of the book, wherein Billy is awoken from slumber in an abandoned way station in New Mexico by the blinding flash of the Trinity nuclear test and the wind heaving in the aftermath. The open spaces across which wolves and cowboys once ranged now serve a more modern and world-shaking purpose for the U.S. industrial military complex. The geographically specific violence of McCarthy's Southwest is projected out onto the world.

This dark progression is forecasted by the progression of Billy's dreams, which open up into a larger enterprise, beyond this land. At one point, he dreams vividly of an intimate encounter with a wolf pack in which he can feel their warm breath on his face, which smells of "the heart of the earth" (p. 295). But then his final, apocalyptic dream is of "God's pilgrims ... returning from some deep enterprise," an endeavor beyond even his own concept of war (p. 420). We move from the natural world or the old order, which stimulates Billy's imagination in sensorial detail, to a new faceless and unimaginable atomic order, a world order that his imaginative sleep state cannot even fully wrap itself around. (This dream-vision may presage McCarthy's Pulitzer Prize–winning 2006 post-apocalyptic novel *The Road*.) War itself has undergone a miraculous evolution in *The Crossing*. From the tales of the horseback-fought Mexican Revolution that weave throughout the text to the great mechanized advent of World War II, the conflicts that "form the backdrop of the trilogy represent opposite ends of [a historical] spectrum" (Wegner, "Wars and Rumors," p. 74).

Ultimately, though, within the context of the trilogy, *The Crossing* is a much different, less straightforward, and less accessible book than the first volume of the Border Trilogy, 1992's *All the Pretty Horses*. The ambitious novel can be ungainly for the reader to swallow whole, and it is best to think of it as a difficult and enduring pleasure — but a pleasure nonetheless — like Melville's *Moby-Dick*. (There are even multiple stories within the larger narrative and elements of the classic picaresque.) The ideas are sweeping and profound and the imagery richly layered, and there is as much implicit as explicit in the novel.

The *Washington Post* encapsulated the captivating effect and emotional impact of the work, noting how "despite its occasional longueurs and excesses, *The Crossing* generates an immense and sorrowful power.... By its last page the reader will have suffered a great deal — this is not a happy book" (Dirda, "At the End of His Tether," p. X1). The review also celebrated McCarthy's language and noted its mythical slant: "languorous yet exact, stately, wistful, occasionally humorous, McCarthy's sentences achieve a kind of epic serenity, as if Homer were to sing of cowboys instead of Achilles" (*ibid.*). At the end of the day, the book is quintessential McCarthy. Having just been dragged out into the mass public glare by the commercial success of National Book Award–winning *All the Pretty Horses*, the writer could have easily played it safe with the follow-up volume. But being Cormac McCarthy, he struck out for deeper waters, crafting a grippingly complex, emotionally powerful, "difficult" and timeless novel that seems to take on the entire dark weight of existence through the borderland trials of one young cowboy.

- *Further reading*

Arnold, Edwin T. "'Go to Sleep': Dreams and Visions in the Border Trilogy." *A Cormac McCarthy Companion: The Border Trilogy*, eds. Edwin T. Arnold and Dianne C. Luce. Jackson: University Press of Mississippi, 2001.

Busby, Mark. "Into the Darkening Land, the World to Come: Cormac McCarthy's Border Crossings." *Myth, Legend, Dust: Critical Responses to Cormac McCarthy*, ed. Rick Wallach. Manchester, UK: Manchester University Press, 2000.

Dirda, Michael. "At the End of His Tether." *The Washington Post Book World*, June 5, 1994.

Hass, Robert. Review of *The Crossing. New York Times Book Review*, June 12, 1994.

Wegner, John. "Wars and Rumors of Wars in Cormac McCarthy's Border Trilogy." *A Cormac McCarthy Companion: The Border Trilogy*, eds. Edwin T. Arnold and Dianne C. Luce. Jackson: University Press of Mississippi, 2001.

Dreams

Dreams are an integral component of McCarthy's literary vision, most significantly in the Border Trilogy — though dreams have been an important component of his narratives throughout his career. The characters' dreams resonate at a few different levels in the books. At the simplest level, they often are a means of divination; for example in *All the Pretty Horses* (1992), Alejandra has a vision of John Grady Cole's death in a dream (p. 252) — the very death that will come to pass in *Cities of the Plain* (1998). Also, in *The Crossing* (1994) Billy Parham has a prophetic vision that presages his discovery of his father's death, though it is less literal and he does not see it as portentous at the time. He envisions his father "afoot and lost in the desert," contemplating "with a terrible equanimity the cold and the dark and the silence that moved upon him ... then all was dark and swallowed up and ... he heard somewhere a solitary bell that tolled" (p. 112).

Early in that same novel, Billy's brother Boyd has a recurring and apocalyptic dream-vision, one that he worries may carry over to waking life: "I had this feeling that somethin bad was going to happen," he tells Billy. "It dont mean nothin. Go to sleep," says Billy (p. 35). In addition, in *All the Pretty Horses*, when John Grady asks Alfonsa if she thinks dreams mean anything, she emphatically replies "Oh yes ... Dont you?" (p. 134).

At another level, the dream state becomes a "borderland" between life and death, a place where the dead visit those they have left behind. In *All the Pretty Horses*, Blevins comes to John Grady in his sleep and "they talked of what it was like to be dead" (p. 225). Similarly, in *The Crossing* Boyd comes to Billy in his dreams, but his is a more taciturn visitation: "When finally [Billy] did ask him what it was like to be dead Boyd only smiled and looked away and would not answer" (p. 400). The scene is perhaps best understood through the gypsy's caution to Billy that "[t]he loved ones who visit us in dreams are strangers" and more our own conception of the past than anything else: "the past ... is always this argument between counterclaimants. Memories dim with age" (p. 411).

There is a more sophisticated implication to Cormac McCarthy's conjuring of dreams in his narratives, however. The dream visions both link McCarthy's work to ancient narratives and cultures and underpin his ruminations on the endless ebb and flow of civilizations. One of the earliest known written works of literature is the ancient Sumerian epic poem *Gilgamesh*, which dates from around 2000 bce and which existed in oral versions for hundreds of years before that. In that account, the titular king has dreams that are a driving force in the narrative, visions that he brings to his mother, Ninsun, who untangles them as "both prophecies and directives for action" (Bulkeley, p. 117).

This fascination with dreams is a common thread between disparate civilizations, both ancient and recent, from ancient Greece, where Plato discoursed on dreams, to the figurative twentieth-century borderlands of McCarthy. In this way, dreams become a cultural thread that binds all civilizations, regardless of language and before written history. Therefore, in the McCarthy worldview there are three constants: each civilization is consumed by violence, each comes to an inevitable end, and each dreams — and tries to make sense of those dreams.

This tendency cuts across cultures and faiths. In India, Debendranath Tagore was leader of the Brahmo Samaj reform movement, which sought to reconcile traditional Hinduism and encroaching Western modernity in the nineteenth century. Struggling with this conflict, Tagore found insight in a dream state described as a "borderland" or a condition "between waking and sleeping," what Kelly Bulkeley deems a condition of "transcendent awareness" (Bulkeley, pp. 44–45). This parallels McCarthy's border metaphor, which operates at several levels in the trilogy, including a borderland between waking and sleeping and life and death. Tagore, like McCarthy's characters, is visited by the dead in the dream, in this case his mother. Similarly, the Border Trilogy protagonists often experience their dreams in troubled, fitful states — often sleeping outside, on the hard ground — that are between sleeping and waking, conditions that, like Tagore's, are driven by the "intensity of [their] anxieties" (*ibid.*, p. 45). Even as late as *No Country for Old Men* (2005) McCarthy presents transcendent states that occur somewhere between awake and asleep. "I had this dream," Carla Jean tells Sheriff Bell. "Or it was like a dream. I think I was still about half awake" (pp. 131–132). In this state, she experiences a prophecy about meeting her future husband, Llewelyn Moss.

In addition, throughout history and across cultures individuals have been consumed by "ontologically ambiguous dreams in which the dead return to the living" (Bulkeley, p. 45). In ancient Chinese culture as well — in line with the Confucian notion of ancestor veneration — one find that dreams "of deceased love ones ... play a profound role in shaping people's spiritual beliefs and practices" (*ibid.*, p. 51). The Daoists of ancient China took a different tack, struggling with the ontological issue that McCarthy himself wrestles with in *Cities of the Plain*, by questioning "the underlying idea that waking and dreaming are stable, meaningfully related categories of existence" (*ibid.*, p. 64). To take the historical discussion to even more primordial origins, McCarthy must also find it compelling that going back a million years, archeologists found that Neolithic (*Homo sapiens*) groups typically included at least one shamanic figure "who served as a collective dreamer, healer, ritual specialist, and mediator between the living and the dead" (*ibid.*, p. 52). This certainly calls to mind the stranger's comment to the aged Billy at the end of *Cities of the Plain* that, in certain dreams, "there is a language that is older than the spoken word at all" (pp. 280–281).

Needless to say, this peripatetic sweep through the dream lore of various cultures could yield countless more examples — let us not forget, for example, the deceitful dream Zeus visits upon Agamemnon in *The Iliad* (a dream that determines Agamemnon's course of action). The point is that, much like the endless succession of violence that McCarthy attributes to all of humanity, even going back to primeval roots (remember the introductory news clip of a three-million-year-old scalping from *Blood Meridian*), dreams constitute another point of continuity and universality in his novels. Clearly, though, different cultures attributed different types of significance to dreams; some took a religious view, considering an external or higher power to be the source of dream-visions. This is a sharp contrast to the modern Freudian notion of dreams representing the psychological organization of an individual.

Nevertheless, dreams in literature present one with a whole different dilemma than real-life dream theories, because in literature the dreams are multi-representational. The volume *Dreams and History* (2004) directly confronts this issue, as does McCarthy in his own inimitable way, in *Cities of the Plain*. In the former, the authors note the "complex nesting of speaking subjects" in a literary representation of a dream: "a literary figure recounts a dream, which is recounted by a narrator, who is in turn a function of the implicit author.... Between which of the many minds is the dream work taking place?" (Pick and Roper, p. 57).

On its own, this quandary is enough of an interpretive challenge, but McCarthy ups the ante. The ending of *Cities of the Plain*—the conclusion of the Border Trilogy — offers a mysterious itinerant stranger describing a dream to an aged Billy Parham. This already places us in the dilemma presented by Pick and Roper, but to compound that, the dreamer describes a "traveler" figure in the dream that actually has his own portentous dream, creating what the *Washington Post*'s Michael Dirda describes as "a series of dreams, each embedded within the next like little Russian dolls" ("Last Roundup").

This is more than just a clever dream puzzle, however; in fact, such is the importance of the dream motif that McCarthy uses it to contain all others — ontology, history, reality — and the effect is not to provide answers, but to open up even deeper questions and place the reader on even shakier metaphysical ground. "The world of our fathers resides within us. Ten thousand generations or more," says the stranger to Billy. "At the core of our life is the history of which it is composed and in that core are no idioms but only the act of knowing and it is this we share in dreams and out" (*Cities of the Plain*, p. 281).

This is the "transcendental awareness" that Bulkeley described, and McCarthy attributes to dreams an awareness that transcends and precedes cultural forms ("idioms"), such as language itself (alluding to the stranger's claim that in dreams there is sometimes "a language that is older than the spoken word at all" [pp. 280–281]).

Notice as well that the "act of knowing"— the primitive and transcendental awareness of this inwardly concentric history — is shared "in dreams and out" (*ibid.*). Here we witness McCarthy's representation of dreams not being a fully separate realm from waking life; there is, at times, a blurring of boundaries. "Two worlds touch here," says the stranger to Billy, going so far as to claim that the traveler in the dream has a "history" (p. 285): "[W]hatever he may be or of whatever made he cannot exist without a history. And the ground of that history is not different from yours or mine for it is the predicate life of men that assures us of our own reality" (p. 274). For, in the work of McCarthy, and in the Border Trilogy in particular, "these dreams reveal the world also" (p. 283).

But while McCarthy's most probing deliberations on dreams arise in the trilogy, he has significantly employed the dream motif throughout the entirety of his career. Edwin T. Arnold even traces this tendency back to McCarthy's earliest days, noting the "dream-like quality" in McCarthy's first published story, "Wake for Susan," which appeared in the University of Tennessee student literary publication, *The Phoenix*, in 1959 ("'Go to Sleep,'" p. 41). In addition, in the final scene of McCarthy's debut novel, *The Orchard Keeper* (1965), the writer shows an early tendency to blur dreams and wakefulness in John Wesley Rattner's conjuring of the past, as he touches his mother's headstone, which feels to him "less real than the smell of woodsmoke or the taste of an old man's wine. And he no longer cared to tell which were things done and which dreamt" (p. 245).

In the next novel, *Outer Dark* (1968), an opening nightmare offers a peek into Culla Holmes' tortured psyche long before the reader becomes acquainted with him in waking life; and in the latter stages of *Child of God* (1973), necrophiliac and serial killer Lester Ballard has a wistful, pastoral dream that opens up a whole new dimension to his character and offers a glimpse into portions of his being that the reader never knew existed: "Each leaf that brushed his face deepened his sadness and dread. Each leaf he passed he'd never pass again. They rode over his face like veils, some already yellow, their veins like slender bones where the sun shone through them" (p. 171).

In *Suttree* (1979), McCarthy begins to explore dreams as a meeting place for the dead when the title character walks and talks with his grandfather in a sleep visitation. Suttree is "humbly honored to walk with him," and listening to his grandfather's "incertitude"-filled talk, it occurs to Suttree how "all false things fall from the dead" (p. 14). This scene anticipates the positioning of dreams in the Border Trilogy as conduits through which one accesses "the world of our fathers [that] resides within us"— those "[t]en thousand generations or more" of inwardly concentric existences (*Cities of the Plain*, p. 281).

One would be hard-pressed to find a McCarthy novel that doesn't have significant dream imagery. Even the kid in *Blood Meridian*, the character that is the most psychologically inscrutable of all of McCarthy's central figures, experiences nightmarish sleep visitations from the judge, who appears as a "great shambling mutant, silent and serene" (p. 309). The term "mutant" is important in this description of the judge, for the kid's dream-visions reveal the judge to be a deviation from the human condition revealed in McCarthy's trilogy. The judge is something else, perhaps non-human, likely immortal, and constructed of different stuff: "Whatever his antecedents he was something wholly other than their sum" and "[w]hoever would seek out his history ... must stand at last darkened and dumb at the shore of a void without terminus or origin" (pp. 309–310). The worlds of ancestors, in other words, do *not* reside within him.

Over 20 years after *Blood Meridian* and over a decade since the last book of the trilogy, McCarthy's use of dream imagery was still prominent in his Pulitzer Prize–winning novel *The Road* (2006). In fact, in the very opening scene the father wakes from a dream wherein the boy led him through a deep cave into a large stone room where he witnessed a "black and ancient lake" and on its other shore a "creature that raised its dripping mouth ... and stared into the light with eyes dead white and sightless as the eggs of spiders." The "pale and naked and translucent" thing made "a low moan and turned and lurched away" (pp. 3–4). This dream is like Culla Holmes' in *Outer Dark*, written nearly 40 years before, in that we are introduced to the central character's dream life before we meet the characters themselves. And, like Culla's dream, it is meant to reveal something about the man's psychology.

The dream of the incestuous Culla reveals his anxiety about being a pariah whose moral infirmity is uncorrectable by any means. The father's dream reveals his anxiety about having to protect his son in a dead and dying world. Unlike most dreams in McCarthy's fiction, there is nothing recognizably human in it, only a creature of perhaps distantly human origin. The father's inner dream life reflects his outer existence in an utterly bleak and savage world. And that points to what is most interesting about McCarthy's employment of dreams: For a writer who has made a career of studiously avoiding getting inside his characters' heads, this is the one consistent way in which he delves into their psychology. Instead of cluing us into the thoughts of his characters, he offers us their dreams.

- *Further reading*

Arnold, Edwin T. "'Go to Sleep': Dreams and Visions in the Border Trilogy." *A Cormac McCarthy Companion: The Border Trilogy*, eds. Edwin T. Arnold and Dianne C. Luce. Jackson: University Press of Mississippi, 2001.

Bulkeley, Kelly. *Dreaming in the World's Religions*. New York: NYU Press, 2008.

Pick, Daniel, and Lyndal Roper, eds. *Dreams and History*. London: Psychology Press (Taylor & Francis Group), 2004.

"A Drowning Incident"

Cormac McCarthy's second published story was credited to C.J. McCarthy, the burgeoning fiction writer now having dropped the "Jr." from his appellation. Like its predecessor, "Wake for Susan," the March 1960 story appeared in the University of

Tennessee student literary supplement, *The Phoenix*. (And, like the other story, has come to pretty much be disowned by the writer.)

But the tightly wound, grotesque tale seems a leap ahead of its predecessor and a sharp turn away from sentimentality and toward the kind of imagery and tone that would occupy McCarthy's early, Southern novels. Rick Wallach characterized the story as "darker, more economical," surmising, "During the intervening months McCarthy appears to have banished sentimentalism as well as any hint of casual narrative sprawl, and the voice of the mature author suddenly becomes audible" (p. 18).

Wallach also saw a shift toward the "more detailed" and "more succulent" descriptions that would come to typify *The Orchard Keeper* (1965) and *Outer Dark* (1968). The imagery, Wallach writes, is "no longer ornamental ... or even merely ambient" but is "now woven into intricate synchronies of signs and portents" (*ibid.*)

In the story, a nameless boy, left to look after his infant sister, discovers a sack of drowned puppies after his father has exterminated the litter of the family dog, firing up a rash of resentment in the boy toward both the father and the infant. In this tale, we see more prominently the McCarthy of the first four novels: The dead puppies are described as having protruding viscera and the actions of the narrative pulse with potential malice.

Nevertheless, the story, though large steps beyond his first published effort, is largely unremarkable — and the fact that McCarthy was about to embark on the tightly composed, masterful novel *The Orchard Keeper* showed the sharp artistic ascent of the author in his early years.

The Dueña Alfonsa

"The world is quite ruthless in selecting between the dream and the reality, even when we will not," Alfonsa tells John Grady Cole in *All the Pretty Horses* (1992). "Between the wish and the thing the world lies waiting" (p. 238). In this way, Alfonsa's perspective in the novel can be described as a sort of "anti-*corrido*." As she narrates the events of her life to John Grady, she strips away myth and sentimentality to reveal the stark, brutal realities at the core of events. "In the end we all come to be cured of our sentiments," says Alfonsa in the midst her tale of the Madero family and the Mexican Revolution. "Those whom life does not cure [of sentimentality] death will" (p. 238).

Where the *corrido*, the Spanish narrative folk ballad, chooses to romanticize the revolution, Alfonsa takes a completely unromantic view of the historical epoch and the men who participated in it. She speaks of women in her family that have "suffered disastrous love affairs with men of disreputable character," adding the kicker, "of course the times enabled some of these men to style themselves as revolutionaries" (p. 229). She also revises the historical record, using her personal perspective — having had a near love affair with Gustavo, the brother of doomed president Francisco Madera — to render the events in an implacably empirical manner, describing in thorough, objective detail how the angry mob tortured and killed Gustavo. "He was pronounced dead. A drunk in the crowd pushed forward and shot him again anyway," she relates. "They kicked his dead body and spat upon it. One of them pried out his artificial eye and it was passed among the crowd as a curiosity" (p. 237).

Her lengthy lecture to John Grady seems aimed at questioning idealism itself. "Francisco was the most deluded of all," she says of the president whose political ideals ignited the events of the Mexican Revolution. "He was never suited to be president of Mexico. He was hardly even suited to be Mexican" (p. 238). She chooses to cast this light on decades-old history because she sees the sort of idealism in the young John Grady that she herself once possessed: "I was very idealistic," she says of herself as a young person, "very outspoken" (p. 232). In fact, one critic suggests that Alfonsa's narrated "journey may be seen as a tightly compressed parable of [John Grady Cole's]" (Spurgeon, p. 44). Both are teenagers as their stories commence, as well as "romantic, idealistic, [and] enamored of an imagined code of justice and honor in a world built upon injustice and corruption" (*ibid.*).

The character of the Dueña Alfonsa is also distinguished by the fact that she is a multifaceted, powerful, and intellectual female figure. Cormac McCarthy has consistently been criticized for his portrayals of women in his fiction. London's *Independent* suggested that "McCarthy's world is an existential one in which men face two choices — either to battle or to die; the female characters, meanwhile, cook and sew or sell themselves on the street" (Bradfield, "Mystery"). Alfonsa not only challenges that criticism by her very representation, but espouses a distinctly feminist rhetoric. "I am not a society person," she tells John Grady Cole. "The societies to which I have been exposed seemed to me largely machines for the suppression of women. Society is very important in Mexico. Where women do not even have the vote" (p. 230).

Furthermore, Gail Morrison has deemed Alfonsa to be "both a radical and a reactionary.... [S]he rebels against the suppression of women and paternal authority, refusing marriage and rejecting a conventional marriage for her great-niece" (p. 231). In addition, Morrison points to Alfonsa embracing, as a teenager, "the reformist causes of the Maderos ... although they run counter to the traditional interests of the landed aristocracy of which she and the Maderos are members" (*ibid.*). Alan Bilton sees her very actions toward her great-niece as revolutionary, noting how she "will not allow Alejandra to be tied to the ranch by the patriarchal codes of Mexican society and in this sense her 'freeing' of Alejandra will be her final revolutionary act" (p. 111).

See also All the Pretty Horses; The Mexican Revolution; Rocha, Alejandra; Women

Fathers

If one examines the breadth of Cormac McCarthy's work, a complicated portrait of fatherhood emerges. Particularly in his early, Southern novels, the representation is outright negative, with a string of deplorable fathers leaping from the page.

Kenneth Rattner, the father of the young protagonist in *The Orchard Keeper* (1965), is a slithering, conniving petty thief who abandons his family for long stretches and is occasionally prone to violence. Murdered in self-defense after a foiled attack, Rattner spends most of the novel decomposing in a pit in the titular orchard. Ironically, his son

John Wesley's one father figure in the novel is Marion Sylder, who killed Kenneth Rattner in self-defense. In McCarthy's second novel, *Outer Dark* (1968), the reader is presented with an even worse father in the form of Culla Holme, who abandons his newborn infant — from an incestuous relationship with his sister — in the forest, laying it on a bed of moss, where it "howled redgummed at the pending night" (p. 16). Culla and his sister Rinthy's parents are never mentioned at all.

In *Child of God* (1973), the central character, Lester Ballard, is abandoned by his father when the older man hangs himself. (Lester's mother had already abandoned him.) Lester is actually the one who first comes upon his deceased father, finding him with his "eyes run out on stems like a crawfish and his tongue blacker'n a chow dog's" (p. 21). The father of the title character in *Suttree* (1979) is very much alive but a non-presence in the novel. Cornelius Suttree has abandoned his upper-crust roots and lives a life for which his father has great disdain. Apparently, Suttree's father had married beneath his station, and in Suttree's eyes, "When a man marries beneath him his children are beneath him" (p. 19). As Suttree tells his maternal uncle, "[M]y father is contemptuous of me because I'm related to you" (*ibid.*). Suttree's father, in fact, writes in a letter to his son that Suttree's street life is lived among "the helpless and the impotent" (p. 14).

The portrait of fatherhood only gets slightly better as McCarthy turns his vision to the Southwest. In *Blood Meridian* (1985) the father of "the kid" is only glimpsed briefly on the first page. Apparently he "has been a schoolmaster" but we find him immersed "in drink, he quotes from poets whose names are now lost. The boy crouches by the fire and watches him" (p. 3). In this case we find another absent mother; she has died after "incubat[ing] in her own bosom the creature who would carry her off" (*ibid.*). The kid himself is clearly neglected; he is raggedly dressed and unwashed and never learned to read or write, despite his father's educated bearing. The mentors and father figures that the boy ends up among, the barbaric scalp hunters of the Glanton Gang, are even worse.

All the Pretty Horses (1992) changed a lot of things for McCarthy, as he seemed to soften his vision and make this novel more accessible, bringing him a wider audience. Accordingly, John Grady Cole's father is a somewhat more sympathetic figure — and a devoted horseman, like his son — but still a largely ancillary and impotent character who, suffering deep emotional and physical wounds from World War II, dies while John Grady is on his adventure across the border in Mexico. The other central protagonist of the Border Trilogy, Billy Parham, has what can best be described as an ambivalent relationship with his father in *The Crossing* (1994), but as often happens in McCarthy's novels, Billy leaves home before the reader can ascertain the dimensions of the relationship — and Billy's parents are killed during his first foray into Mexico.

Interestingly, the strongest father-son bond is in *The Road* (2006), a novel in which a father tries to protect his son in a post-apocalyptic world. It is truly the first genuine father and son engagement we see from Cormac McCarthy, as the father instills lessons in his son and helps shape his perspective on the world (or what's left of the world). Interestingly, this novel coincided with McCarthy becoming a father again and raising a young boy, something that undoubtedly shaped the narrative. In fact, McCarthy dedicated the book to his young son, John, who was seven years old at the time of publication.

It's also interesting that McCarthy has alluded to his own rift with his parents, something that likely influenced his early books in particular. This tension calls to mind *Suttree*: McCarthy's father was a Yale-educated attorney who worked for the federally owned Tennessee Valley Authority, while Suttree's father's idea of respectable work is "the law courts" or "government" or "business" (*Suttree*, p. 14). "I felt early on I wasn't going to be a respectable citizen," McCarthy has said. "I hated school from the day I set foot in it" (Woodward, "Venomous Fiction").

Another interesting biographical element is McCarthy's relationship with his oldest son, Cullen, born in the early 1960s, during McCarthy's brief marriage to Lee McCarthy. (Her maiden name was Holleman.) During McCarthy's first interview, at the age of 58, with the *New York Times*, McCarthy revealed that he was thinking of spending a few years in Spain: "His son, with whom he has lately re-established a strong bond, is to be married there this year," the article reported, as well as the fact that Cullen was "now an architecture student at Princeton" (*ibid.*). How heavily McCarthy's own biography (as a son and father) weighed upon his depiction of fatherhood in his novels will always be speculation, but all of these elements certainly add compelling context.

Film Adaptations

To date, three of Cormac McCarthy's novels have been adapted to the big screen, *All the Pretty Horses* (1992; movie version, 2000), *No Country for Old Men* (2005; movie version, 2007), and *The Road* (2006; movie version, 2009).

The first McCarthy novel to make the transition to cinema didn't fare as well as its predecessor, the Oscar-winning *No Country for Old Men*. In fact, the film version of *All the Pretty Horses*, starring Matt Damon in the lead role of John Grady Cole, was openly panned upon release, its final version having been whittled down to two hours (at the behest of the studio) from the original four hours intended by director Billy Bob Thornton. "Unfortunately, in the process," claimed a review in the *Western Daily Press*, "the film's emotional heart has been left on the cutting room floor ... a shame, because the novel from which the story was drawn, by Cormac McCarthy, is a far deeper, more evocative affair" (Smith, p. 37). Reviewer Steven Rea, from the *Philadelphia Inquirer*, claimed that "Billy Bob Thornton's adaptation of Cormac McCarthy's exercise in Lone Star lyricism sure is pretty. Low-angled sun hitting the mesas as mustangs kick up dust ... Matt Damon, sitting high in the saddle." But he went on to lament that "despite the painterly Western scapes [and] the deep meditations about death and the afterlife" the film was "empty at its core."

The *New York Times'* A.O. Scott joined the chorus of dissatisfaction, commending the filmmakers for resisting "the temptation to incorporate Mr. McCarthy's high literary style into the picture or to seek out its visual equivalent" but complaining that "the story, shorn of its philosophical pretensions and fancy writing, turns out to be thin and banal" (Scott, "Lost Souls").

It would be seven years before another McCarthy novel reached the big screen. The taut, fast-paced Southwestern thriller *No Country for Old Men* seemed better suited for movie audiences, and the film stayed remarkably true to McCarthy's book, retaining some of McCarthy's deep ponderings despite the film's economy and pace. Heralded filmmakers Joel and Ethan Coen (*Fargo*; *O, Brother Where Art Thou?*; *The Big Lebowski*) were on board this time, having bought the rights to the novel and adapted it into a screenplay that they would direct.

This time around the critics were highly enthusiastic about a McCarthy project on film. A.O. Scott, the same *New York Times* critic that eviscerated the film version of *All the Pretty Horses*, heralded the screen adaptation of *No Country for Old Men* as "a brutal and meticulous adaptation of Cormac McCarthy's novel." He found it "[f]aithful to both the mood and the language of Mr. McCarthy's book" and "stark, lean ... and plenty mean" (Scott, "Touch of Evil").

The movie, starring Tommy Lee Jones and Josh Brolin, was nominated for eight Academy Awards and won four Oscars: best picture, best director, best supporting actor (Javier Bardem, as Anton Chigurh), and best screenplay adaptation. McCarthy, in his support for the movie, displayed an unprecedented level of accessibility, even submitting to comments in a October 2007 *Time* magazine article (along with the Coens themselves). During the telecast of the Oscars event, the spotlight-shunning author was even filmed in his seat in close-up when producer Scott Rudin thanked him for his "wonderful book" during the acceptance speech for best picture.

After the film success of *No Country for Old Men*, McCarthy's next novel, *The Road*, was quickly snatched up and adapted to a screenplay. John Hillcoat (*The Proposition*), an Australian, directed the movie, while Viggo Mortensen (*Lord of the Rings*) played the father. The film began shooting in February 2008 in and around Pittsburgh, with footage also shot in New Orleans and on Mount St. Helens (in the state of Washington). The locales were chosen for their bleak, post-apocalyptic scenery, with settings such as deserted coalfields, a burned-down amusement park, and an abandoned freeway standing in for the devastated landscape of McCarthy's novel. The movie was released in November 2009. It had initially been planned for release in November 2008.

Also at the time of this writing, there have been reports of other McCarthy works receiving consideration for movies. Director Ridley Scott has had designs on a film version of *Blood Meridian* (1985) for some time, but his comments in November 2008 left some doubt that it would ever happen with him at the helm. He told a reporter, "It's written. I think it's a really tricky one, and maybe it's something that should be left as a novel." His explanation: "If you're going to do *Blood Meridian* you've got to go the whole nine yards into the blood bath, and there's no answer to the blood bath, that's part of the story, just the way it is and the way it was" (O'Hara). In addition, *Variety* reported in June of 2009 that another candidate, Todd Field, had been "booked to write and direct an adaptation of Cormac McCarthy's *Blood Meridian* for producer Scott Rudin," who had also been the producer of *No Country for Old Men* (Fleming).

As of this writing, there have been murmurings about yet another McCarthy adaptation, with the *Los Angeles Times* reporting in August of 2008 that Australian filmmaker Andrew Dominik (*The Assassination of Jesse James by the Coward Robert Ford*) "wants to film *Cities on* [sic] *the Plain* [1998], the last book in McCarthy's border trilogy" (Horn). However, no definitive word regarding production has been released yet.

What is interesting about McCarthy's work suddenly finding vogue with Hollywood is that the writer had previously — and unsuccessfully — aspired to get his work directly to screen by writing screenplays instead of novels, but this was during a period before his break into commercial success in 1992 (with the novel *All the Pretty Horses*). *Cities of the Plain* had actually first been conceived as a screenplay, over a decade before the first Border Trilogy book. *No Country for Old Men* also started out as a screenplay (likely in the early to mid–1980s), and another screenplay that McCarthy penned, *Whales and Men* (also from the 1980s), has never been published or produced.

See also Whales and Men

Foote, Shelby

Much like Saul Bellow, esteemed American novelist and historian Shelby Foote was a champion of McCarthy's work long before the younger writer gained wide recognition. Foote has said, "McCarthy is the one writer younger than myself who has excited me" and he was pivotal in McCarthy's nomination for a MacArthur Fellowship. "I told the MacArthur people that he would be honoring them as much as they were honoring him," he said (Woodward, "Venomous Fiction").

One of the reasons that Foote may have had such a deep affinity for McCarthy is that he, like McCarthy, had distinct Southern roots. Foote, who died in 2005 at the age of 88, was born and raised in the crucible of Mississippi Delta culture. He was a childhood friend of novelist Walker Percy (*The Moviegoer*). Foote attended the University of North Carolina at Chapel Hill and wrote for the campus literary magazine, but like McCarthy dropped out before obtaining a degree.

After entering the United States Army and serving in World War II, Foote, after rewrites and rejections, published his first novel, *Tournament*, in 1946. He followed that tale of a Delta planter and gambler with four more novels about the South, *Follow Me Down* (1950), *Love in a Dry Season* (1951), *Shiloh* (1952), and *Jordan County* (1954). His last significant novel, *September, September*, was released in 1978 and detailed the Little Rock school-integration controversy of 1957.

Foote came to be primarily recognized in later years for his contributions to Civil War history, writing a rigorously researched and conceived three-volume history of the war that took him two decades to complete. He also notably appeared throughout filmmaker Ken Burns' nine-part 1990 documentary series, *The Civil War*, offering extensive commentary.

The documentary itself heavily relied on Foote's work. A *New York Times* obituary described how the writer, in forging a Civil War history, sought "to tell what he considered America's biggest story as a vast, finely detailed, deeply human narrative. He could focus on broad shifts in strategy or on solitary moments of poignancy" (Martin). Ken Burns added, "He made the war real for us" (*ibid.*).

Foote died in a Memphis hospital at the age of 88.

The Gardener's Son

In 1974, director Richard Pearce enlisted McCarthy to produce a screenplay for *The Gardener's Son*, a television drama about a South Carolina mill owner who is murdered in the 1870s by a disturbed young man with a wooden leg (the "gardener's son" of the title), who is hanged for his crime. The teleplay premiered on PBS in 1977 and starred Brad Dourif, Ned Beatty, and Kevin Conway as members of two families who grow to be at odds with each other, the upper-class Greggs and blue-collar McEvoys. The Greggs own the Graniteville Manufacturing Company, while the Irish-Catholic McEvoys have come to Graniteville to work for the mill. The film was based on actual historical events in the mill town of Graniteville, South Carolina, in 1876.

Gell-Mann, Murray

McCarthy has repeatedly expressed his preference for the company of scientists over that of those in the literary establishment, and one of his closest scientist friends has been Nobel Prize–winning physicist Murray Gell-Mann. McCarthy first met Gell-Mann when the author received a MacArthur Fellowship (dubbed the "genius grant"). At the awards event in Chicago in 1981, the author ended up, predictably, avoiding the other writers and forging bonds with some of the scientists, among them Gell-Mann (who served as a director of the J.D. and C.T. MacArthur Foundation from 1979 to 2002).

Through Gell-Mann McCarthy also became acquainted with the Sante Fe Institute in New Mexico, a locale that would become a haven for the writer and a place to absorb and exchange ideas. Gell-Mann, along with a group of scientists from the Los Alamos National Laboratory in New Mexico, founded the Santa Fe Institute in 1984. George Cowan, head of research at Los Alamos, led the group, while Gell-Mann chaired the board. The scientists came from a broad range of specializations and worked in an inter-disciplinary fashion, dubbing the institute's burgeoning form of study "simplicity and complexity."

It is little wonder why McCarthy was drawn to a mind like Gell-Mann's. Theoretical physicists are "the intellectual aristocrats of science," and Gell-Mann has been called "probably the most important living scientist" (Papineau). Interestingly, Gell-Mann was the man who brought the term "quark" into the scientific lexicon, having lifted it from, of all places, *Finnegans Wake* (1939), a novel by one of McCarthy's favorite writers, James Joyce. ("Three quarks for Muster Mark! / Sure he hasn't got much of a bark / And sure any he has it's all beside the mark.") With his California Institute of Technology colleague Richard Feynman, Gell-Mann sought the simplicity behind the seemingly impenetrable behavior of high-energy particles, and Gell-Mann was awarded the Nobel Prize in 1969 for work culminating in the quark theory.

London's *Independent* notes how "Feynman and Gell-Mann were rivals as much as collaborators. In person they cut contrasting figures. Where Feynman was an insistent nonconformist ... Gell-Mann was the model of a modern university professor" (Papineau). Gell-Mann remains one of the leading lights in science as of this writing (summer 2009), and is currently distinguished fellow at the Santa Fe Institute and the Robert Andrews Millikan Professor Emeritus at the California Institute of Technology, where he first became a faculty member in 1955. He is also the author of *The Quark and the Jaguar* (1995), a book that unveils his ideas on simplicity and complexity to a general readership.

See also The Santa Fe Institute

God

In the work of Cormac McCarthy, a very complicated portrait of God emerges, one that could sometimes be termed pessimistic or agnostic (though not atheistic). The author himself has said, "I don't think you have to have a clear idea who or what God is in order to pray," a useful notion to keep in mind while reading his novels (Winfrey).

At the very least, one can clearly trace a rejection of ecclesiastical forms in McCarthy's work. For example, the title character of *Suttree* (1979), having fallen asleep in the Church of the Immaculate Conception, is awoken by a priest, who gently admonishes, "God's house is not exactly a place to take a nap." The force and sharpness of Suttree's response is surprising: "It's not God's house." The priest replies, "I beg your pardon?" and Suttree repeats, "It's not God's house" (p. 255). An old, insightful drunk in a Mexican cantina is equally dismissive of ecclesiastical forms in *Blood Meridian* (1985): "I pray to God for this country," he says. "I say that to you. I pray. I dont go in the church. What I need to talk to them dolls there? I talk here" (p. 103). Or, in another example, the Mormon hermit relates in his tale to Billy Parham in *The Crossing* (1994), "Of the priest what can be said? As with all priests his mind had become clouded by the illusion of its proximity to God" (p. 155).

The Mormon hermit is also one of the many heretics of McCarthy's novels — as is the man he speaks of in his tale to Billy. But like the man of his tale, the hermit's heresy merely lies in his rejection of traditional notions of God — both he and the man whose story he relates are still deep believers in (and deliberators regarding) God. But they reject ecclesiastical parameters. As the hermit relates in his tale of the heretic, "[H]e thought that the church would not be raised again as to do such work requires first that God be in men's hearts for it is there alone that it truly has its being" (p. 147).

And in *The Road* (2006), the father could be considered a heretic as well, yet even after the very world, its order, and all of its ecclesiastical dimensions have fallen away, he believes in God and carries on a dialogue with that entity, even if it is only, at times, to express his rage and heresy: "Are you there? he whispered. Will I see you at last? Have you a neck by which to throttle you? Damn you eternally have you a soul? Oh God, he whispered. Oh, God" (pp. 11–12). In McCarthy's work, God is most often abstracted — even torn free — from canonical perceptions. But this frequently belies a great belief in God that the characters in his novels possess. And it is in people's hearts that God lies: "For what is deeply true is true also in men's hearts and it can therefore never be mistold through all and any tellings" (*The Crossing*, p. 154).

McCarthy's novels also seek to render the entity of God as a predicament or paradox. Who else but Cormac McCarthy would suggest that serial killer and corpse defiler

Lester Ballard is a "child of God much like yourself perhaps" (*Child of God*, p. 4). In *The Crossing*, the Mormon hermit, in his tale to Billy, goes so far to render individual perceptions of God as paradoxical: "He believed in a boundless God without center or circumference. By this very formlessness he's sought to make God manageable" (p. 153). To make God "formless" and thereby "manageable" is a paradoxical notion, or as the hermit elaborates — "To see God everywhere is to see Him nowhere" (p. 153).

And even when McCarthy seems to adopt traditional Christian heterodoxy, as in titling the final Border Trilogy book *Cities of the Plain* (1998) — after the cities of Sodom and Gomorrah — he still subverts things: Instead of the cities being destroyed because of the hopelessly corrupted humanity (as in the biblical telling), the cities El Paso and Juárez thrive, while the hopelessly "good" John Grady Cole is stabbed to death by a pimp in an alleyway in Juárez.

Because of his tendency to deeply meditate upon and ultimately problematize the normative boundaries of Christianity in his texts, McCarthy has often been termed a Gnostic (not to be confused with "agnostic") — a term of controversial and complicated etymology that is in a very general sense meant in this case to connote an "esoteric" stance in which one seeks to understand God through experience and understanding. Sven Birkerts claims, "McCarthy has been, from the start, a writer with strong spiritual leanings. His orientation is Gnostic.... His intuitions are of the most primary sort, never even remotely doctrinaire" (p. 38).

Leo Daugherty takes the Gnosticism reading into even deeper, historical realms in his essay "Gravers False and True," in which he claims that "[G]nostic thought is central to Cormac McCarthy's *Blood Meridian*" (p. 157). Daugherty establishes the roots of formalized Gnosticism (in this case, "Manichean" and of Iranian origins), noting its roots in "a response to the question, How is it that the world is experienced as so very evil and that so many people's central response to it is alienation?" Daugherty also uses the Gnostic view of creation as a context to understanding McCarthy — i.e., that creation was not something planned and carried out as orderly design, but the result of a supernal fall from within an initially divine or perfect state. Daugherty contextualizes *Blood Meridian* as a meditation on "power relations" and a "world-program ... set up by something like a Gnostic grand demiurge and enjoyed by him as proprieter, with earthly power being that of judgment sprung from will" (p. 163).

In *Blood Meridian* and elsewhere the reader also confronts rhetoric regarding an indifferent or uninvolved God. It is as if the more his characters ponder the dimensions of the Almighty, the more remote they seem from a divine presence. "If God meant to interfere in the degeneracy of mankind would he not have done so by now?" asks Judge Holden (p. 146). In *The Crossing*, we get the sense of Billy's disconnectedness from God: "He studied those worlds sprawled in their pale ignitions upon the nameless night and he tried to speak to God about his brother and after a while he slept" (p. 295). The boy in *The Road* finds himself similarly detached: "He tried to talk to God but the best thing was to talk to his father and he did talk to him and he didnt forget" (p. 286).

McCarthy, it seems, is frequently gauging the great distance between his characters and an almighty presence, a remoteness that his characters often deliberate upon. "I always thought when I got older that God would sort of come into my life in some way.

He didnt," Uncle Ellis tells Sheriff Bell in 2005's *No Country for Old Men* (p. 267). Nevertheless, this has not prevented God from being a pervasive subject matter throughout McCarthy's novels, and the author's characters are typically great believers in an almighty entity — even in their heresy.

- *Further reading*

Daugherty, Leo. "Gravers False and True: *Blood Meridian* as Gnostic Tragedy." *Perspectives on Cormac McCarthy*, eds. Edwin T. Arnold and Dianne C. Luce. Jackson: University Press of Mississippi, 1993, pp. 157–172.

Harrogate, Gene

Gene Harrogate, who Cornelius Suttree takes under his wing in the Knoxville, Tennessee, underbelly that constitutes the novel *Suttree* (1979), is Cormac McCarthy's most broadly comic character. But the sociopathic, hillbilly schemer is spurred to life by the grotesquely humorous components of McCarthy's early, Southern Gothic style; in fact, he is arguably the author's most directly Southern Gothic characterization.

According to James Richard Giles, one particular scene involving Harrogate typifies the world of the Southern Gothic, falling "clearly into the tradition of Southern Gothicism, as practiced not only by Faulkner, but by Edgar Allan Poe, Flannery O'Connor, and Carson McCullers" (p. 84). Giles alludes to the scene where the housebound religious fanatic unleashes a verbal assault on Harrogate from a high window: "This viperous evangelist reared up ... goat's eyes smoking, and thrust a bony finger down. Die! he screamed. Perish a terrible death with thy bowels blown open and black blood boiling from thy nether eye." To which Harrogate responds, "Shit fire ... [while] scurrying down the path with one hand over his head" (*Suttree*, p. 106). This convergence of brimstone-stoked violence and outright comedy is fraught with what has been called (while describing the work of Flannery O'Connor) the "strong, unresolved tension and dualities characteristic of the grotesque" (Flora, MacKethan, and Taylor, p. 323).

Right from his auspicious first moments in *Suttree*, copulating with the fruit in a farmer's watermelon patch, Harrogate is at the nexus of this unresolved tension, at that precise location where hilarity meets violence (a Southern Gothic element). Caught while about to mount one of the farmer's watermelons, he appears before the shotgun-wielding farmer, "standing in the middle of the patch facing them, blinking, his overalls about his ankles," and then, sentences later, "lying on the ground with his legs trapped in his overalls screaming Oh God, Oh God ... blood oozing from that tender puckered skin in the gray moonlight" (p. 35).

Harrogate's theft and slaughter of a pig is even more seamless in its melding of brutality and comedy. The scene rapidly evolves from hungry Harrogate's slapstick stalking and chasing of the loose pigs — "admiring them for plumpness, salivating slightly" (p. 138) — to his savagely incompetent attempts to kill the captured swine: "A whitish matter was seeping from its head and one ear hung down half off. He brought the pipe down again over its skull, starting the eye from its socket. The pig had not stopped scream-ing. Die goddamn you, panted Harrogate" (p. 140).

There are also other unresolved tensions at work in the character of Harrogate, who comes off as a peculiar fusion of innocence and criminality, as well as someone who is distinctly wide-eyed and childlike but also clearly debauched. These unsettling tensions make Harrogate a unique, standout figure in the McCarthy canon, but he also antici-pates the peculiar man-child Jimmy Blevins in *All the Pretty Horses* (1992).

The rendering of Blevins possesses the same unsettling blend of the grotesquely comic and potentially violent. Blevins gets drunk and falls off his horse at one point, and in yet another comic scene his phobia of lightning prompts him to strip down to his undershorts and hide out in a hollow beneath a cottonwood tree. But McCarthy takes those unresolved tensions and dualities seen in Harrogate even deeper in the case of Blevins — to even more unsettling extremes — as Blevins ends up dragged into the woods like an animal and shot by Mexican authorities for committing murder. But the char-acterization of Blevins is clearly rooted in *Suttree*'s Harrogate, and both comic charac-ters exit their respective novels under sobering circumstances.

See also Blevins, Jimmy; *Suttree*; Southern Gothic

History

In *No Country for Old Men* (2005), which is set in 1980 in the Texas borderlands — a region where the bloody histories of Mexico, the United States, and indigenous cul-tures converge — Sheriff Bell muses, *"[T]he dead have more claims on you than what you might want to admit or even what you might know about and them claims can be very strong indeed"* (p. 124). Here at a basic level is the historical enterprise of McCarthy's novels, particularly his Southwestern works (though *The Road* [2006] certainly could be seen as a culmination of those lessons).

In 1893, Frederick Jackson Turner wrote what has become one of the — if not the — most influential tracts in U.S. history, "The Significance of the Frontier in American His-tory." A few years before Turner first delivered his treatise, the U.S. Census Bureau heralded the "disappearance of a contiguous frontier line" in the American West and "Turner took this 'closing of the frontier' as an opportunity to reflect upon the influence it had exercised" (*New Perspectives*). Turner saw this historically amorphous and constantly shifting frontier region and all its synchronies as the defining condition of American history.

More than that, he saw it as a functioning ideal of American character: "To the frontier," he proclaimed, "the American intellect owes its striking characteristics" (Turner, p. 37). These included "coarseness and strength combined with acuteness and acquisi-tiveness; that practical inventive turn of mind ... that restless, nervous energy; that dom-inant individualism" (*ibid.*). Turner's thesis kept alive a Western frontier myth long after a literal frontier existed — moreover, his ideas pervaded the country, influencing histor-ical writings, politics, literature, art, film, etc. (Let us not forget that future president John F. Kennedy swept into office on the robust promise of a "New Frontier" nearly 70 years after Turner's ideas first surfaced.) Jackson became the Prometheus of an enduring and seemingly indelible American mythology; the "West" and the "victory" of the frontier could never be lost, "because the spirit of the frontier was embedded in the American personality forever" (Murdoch, p. 79).

The problematical nature of Turner's frontier thesis is now clear to many, but as Bill Brown suggests, its power and seductiveness were of "epic containment — the production of a history of national consolidation so monumental that it diminishes other events" that don't fit its strictures (p. 31). It disregards issues such as the United States' genocide of Native Americans, the influence of Mexico and European countries in settling what is now much of the American West, the cultural hybridity of the frontier in the 1800s (let's not forget the influx of Chinese immigrants), and — most importantly for McCarthy's purposes — the sheer violence and slaughter that constitutes the true bedrock of American frontier history.

"The narration of the West," writes Brown, "aestheticizes the genocidal foundation of the nation, turning conquest into a literary enterprise that screens out other violent episodes in the nation's history" (*ibid.*). This notion Brown raises, of a continuity of violent epochs that extends beyond the historical frontier, is at the heart of the work of McCarthy, whose own rendering of the American Southwest not only takes up, for example, the mid–1800s bounty scalpers of *Blood Meridian* (1985) but also encompasses the 1940s test explosion of the atomic bomb at the end of *The Crossing* (1994).

Leading Southwest historian Karl Jacoby indicates how the "seeming inevitability of the western story ... has long desensitized us to both the region's violence and its other ways of being" (p. 6). This is a conundrum that new Western historians such as Patricia Nelson Limerick took up in the 1980s and beyond, but it is also a strain of mythology that a writer of Cormac McCarthy's formidable talent, rigor, and unflinching authorial worldview is particularly well poised to counteract (keeping in mind that McCarthy does not write morality fiction or push activism agendas). Literary critic Neil Campbell writes, "Behind the images and rhetoric of Turner's historical narrative of the West lies a 'barbarism' in need of telling," something the "imaginative scope of fiction allows McCarthy" (p. 217). Of the vividly detailed "continuous massacres and mutilations" on display in *Blood Meridian*, leading literary critic Harold Bloom has written, "None of its carnage is gratuitous or redundant; it belonged to the Mexico-Texas borderlands in 1849–1850" (p. 255).

But McCarthy not only rights the historical record by using his literary imagination to include the blood-soaked details that historians politely step over. He also undertakes a questioning of historiography itself, providing a running commentary on "the way in which recorded history is a process of selection and control, whilst providing a fictional landscape for acts of imperialism and conquest so often omitted" (Campbell, p. 218). For example, we find this meditation in *Blood Meridian*: "It is not necessary ... that the principals here be in possession of the facts concerning their case," says Judge Holden, "for their acts will ultimately accommodate history with or without their understanding" (p. 85).

And when the kid's moral evolution leads him away from mindless slaughter, the judge accuses him of interfering in the American historical enterprise — the kid is the "principal" in this case, and it is not his job to possess the facts. Let history be "the judge," says "the judge": "You came forward ... to take part in a work. But you were a witness against yourself. You sat in judgement [sic] on your own deeds. You put your own allowances before the judgement of history" (p. 307). This "process of selection and control" that constitutes the historical record omits much — not only violent acts but sometimes whole races and whole lives lived. The old Comanche trail that John Grady Cole rides on at the beginning of *All the Pretty Horses* (1992) conjures the obliterated people who rode it only a hundred years before, a "ghost of nation passing in a soft chorale ... bearing lost to all history and all remembrance" (p. 5).

The entire "sum of their secular and transitory and violent lives" is lost in the historical undertaking that Turner's frontier myth represents (*ibid.*). And "secular" is an important term here, as the collective belief systems of American exceptionalism, Manifest Destiny, and Turner's frontier represent a kind of ecclesiastical institution, one that the Comanche cannot belong to, except as martyrs to the great destiny of expansion. In fact, engaging the historical reality of the Comanche risks a collapse of the institution itself. In *The Crossing* (1994), we again get a sense of McCarthy's feeling about the unreliability of "history," when the Yaqui Indian Quijada tells Billy Parham that the *corrido* — is the "poor man's history" — a historical ballad that "tells all and ... tells nothing.... It tells what it wishes to tell. It tells what makes the story run" (p. 386).

Dianne C. Luce points out yet another way in which McCarthy problematizes traditional histories, claiming that the author "repeatedly suggests the ambiguous function of the historical artifact in its capacity to evoke or displace the thing of which it is a record" ("'They Aint the Thing,'" p. 21). This is clearly evident in *The Crossing* (1994), in the example of the gypsies hauling the old bi-plane wreck, an artifact from the Mexican Revolution. The American pilot's father had contracted for the craft to be recovered and brought to the border, but the problem remained that "this tattered artifact was known to have a sister in the same condition," making it impossible to tell if this were indeed the intended airplane (p. 405). "The reverence attached to the artifacts of history is a thing men feel," the gypsy tells Billy. "One could even say that what endows any thing [sic] with significance is solely the history in which it has participated. Yet wherein does that history lie?" (*ibid.*). McCarthy emphasizes the ephemeral, intangible qualities of history, and, as Luce points out, even when his work points to the "primacy of imagination and memory over mere record" there is always the "paradoxical frailty of memory" ("'They Aint the Thing,'" p. 21).

See also The American Southwest

Holme, Culla and Rinthy

Culla and Rinthy Holme are the incestuous brother and sister protagonists from McCarthy's second novel, *Outer Dark* (1968), a book that comes off at times like a nightmarish fairy tale. Fairy tales often include a set of siblings, male and female, who are pushed out of their familiar environment into the painful experience of separation and journey. It is typically an adventure "fraught with many psychological dangers," but one that leads to self-actualization (Bettelheim, p. 79). For Culla and Rinthy, the seemingly parentless siblings of the novel, this motif results in two very different journeys.

For comparison, Bruno Bettelheim sees the siblings of the Brother's Grimm tale "Brother and Sister" as an "essentially inseparable unity," with the brother representing "the endangered aspect" of that unity (*ibid*). One finds a similar orientation in *Outer Dark*. Culla is the more "endangered" of the two in the novel, and bears the deepest psychological wounds from their incestuous union (which may not have been consensual). This is established in the opening dream, in which Culla is one among a group of beggarly supplicants seeking the healing graces of a prophet. He stands amid a "beggared multitude ... [a] delegation of human ruin" plagued with blindness, "puckered stumps and leprous sores" (p. 5).

Culla is clearly among them because of a moral infirmity, one that is not as visible as the maladies around him. (The prophet is "surprised to see him there amidst such pariahs" [*ibid*.]). But Culla is clearly the most depraved individual in the dream crowd; in fact, the very sun drops from the sky, bringing darkness, when faced with Culla's moral condition, and the rest of the assembled turn on him "with howls of outrage" (p. 6). In this opening dream, McCarthy establishes the degree to which Culla's psyche is tormented by his actions.

Culla's journey entails confronting what can best be described as shadow figures in his psyche that are represented as an ominous trio that seems to always be one step behind or in front of him as he proceeds through the landscape of the novel. The novel's short opening passage uses the word "shadow" three times in the first sentence; the figures are also described as "shapes" and "in silhouette" in that opening page, pointing toward the potency of a Jungian reading of the novel.

Carl Jung's shadow archetype is described as "a dark companion which dogs our steps" (Stevens, p. 64), and the trio, despite the range and unpredictability of Culla's travels, always remains somewhere near his orbit. Jung also described how the shadow figure appears in dreams as a "sinister or threatening figure possessing the same sex as the dreamer" and often as a predator or "evil stranger" (*ibid*.). The leader of the trio, like Culla, is a father — and not coincidentally Culla's greatest moral crimes are in the name of fatherhood, both through the act of incest and his attempts to abandon the baby to presumably die in the woods.

But McCarthy renders the shadow father so malignantly that that he upstages Culla Holme's own dreadful actions, effectively projecting Culla's malevolent qualities onto the evil father. (See the entry on *Outer Dark* in this volume for a more thorough Jungian reading of Culla Holme and for further description of the imagery that supports such a reading.)

Rinthy's fairy tale/psychological journey in *Outer Dark* is quite different because her impulses are altogether maternal and altruistic: She simply seeks to recover her baby from the tinker who found the "chap" abandoned in the forest. Bettelheim discusses the "contrast between the brother's giving in to the proddings of his instinctual desires and the sister's ego- and superego-motivated concern for her obligations" in the Brother's Grimm tale "Brother and Sister." He furthermore notes that "what redeems us as human beings and restores us to our humanity is solicitude for those whom we love" (p. 83).

Thus, when applied to *Outer Dark*, the outer landscape of the journey reflects Rinthy's inner life, as she is taken in by strangers and given food and shelter — and not driven off and persecuted like Culla. Rinthy is not plagued with her brother's sense of denial and repression. Critic Robert L. Jarrett notes how Culla and Rinthy represent "two opposing forms of alienation: alienation created by Culla's repression of his sin and guilt and by Rinthy's acceptance of hers" (p. 19). He also notes how the title *Outer Dark* is "emblematic" of that "psychological alienation" (*ibid.*, p. 20).

See also Outer Dark

Influences

It could be argued that, beginning with *Blood Meridian* in 1985, Cormac McCarthy has reached a stage of transcending all influences and sublimating them into his own distinct vision (while undoubtedly becoming a huge literary influence himself). Nevertheless, he has had four key influences that warrant examination: Ernest Hemingway, Herman Melville, James Joyce, and — particularly early on — William Faulkner.

One sees the influence of Hemingway in McCarthy's use of objective, pared-back descriptions. Usually these involve workman-like tasks in which the characters are involved; for example, John Grady Cole breaking a horse in *All the Pretty Horses* (1992), Billy Parham setting a trap in *The Crossing* (1994), or the father fixing the wheel of a shopping cart in *The Road* (2006). According to Sara Mosle, these seemingly colorless descriptions arouse "suspense by placing us in the middle of the action, and then slowing it down. We experience, as if in real time, what his characters experience, without any hint of where the story is going." These lean, spare, painstakingly meticulous descriptions are also a hallmark of Hemingway, whose "curt, unemotional, factual style" presents, according to D.S. Savage, "an attempt at the objective presentation of experience" (p. 24). McCarthy is, like Hemingway, "impassively recording the objective data of experience" when he engages in this stylistic tendency (*ibid.*).

Writing about McCarthy, Mosle borrowed a description from W.H. Auden, attributing to these objective flights a "beautiful ... eye-on-the-object look" (*ibid.*). Mario Praz, writing Italy's first article on Hemingway in 1929, remarked, "If one can talk of an objective style, it is his" (p. 117). Praz also commented on how Hemingway's work refreshingly cut against the grain of the more "cerebral" writing fashionable in Europe at the time, work that "no sooner contemplates an object than it deforms and judges it, so as to give an artificial, rhetorical vision of the world" (*ibid.*).

On a thematic level, Hemingway's frank confrontation of war, death, and violence also echoes in the work of McCarthy. In fact, when Lionel Trilling writes of the "critical tradition of the Left" seeing in Hemingway's work "only cruelty or violence or a calculated indifference," Trilling could very well be talking about many of the responses to *Blood Meridian* (p. 64). Additionally, Trilling's following comment addressing Hemingway could be applied to much of Cormac McCarthy's work: "[I]t seems to me that what Hemingway wanted first to do was to get rid of the 'feelings,' the comfortable liberal humanitarian feelings: and to replace them with the truth" (p. 65). In both Hemingway and McCarthy, what many see as harsh literary visions are actually a concerted attempt to deal with the violent or messy realities of humanity in an unflinching and frank manner (though Hemingway, at times, can be the more sentimental of the two). Alan Bilton has said of McCarthy, "[i]t's hard to imagine a more quintessentially American writer" — an accusation that has frequently been leveled at Hemingway himself — and noted McCarthy's "formal debt" to Hemingway, whom Bilton termed "the other pole of McCarthy's prose" (the first is Melville), exuding "a flat, pared-down matter-of-factness about physical things" (p. 131).

The novel *All the Pretty Horses* (1992) has weathered the most frequent and consistent comparisons to Hemingway. One write-up of the novel noted how it "echoes the rhythms of good Hemingway, especially the grave, symbol-laden stories like 'Big Two-Hearted River'" (Dirda, "End of His Tether"). In another essay, Gail Moore Morrison remarks that McCarthy not only displays stylistic suggestions of Hemingway in the novel, but his character "John Grady is like a number of Hemingway's young protagonists in that he finds that his destiny is strangely but inevitably linked to war and revolution" (p. 185).

McCarthy's Hemingwayesque tendencies have been noted elsewhere as well. One review of *The Road* noted how the writer "pares things back, almost to self-extinction," summoning "a language cold and clear as water moving over stones. (Hemingway, not Faulkner, is the presiding spirit.) Dialogue is clipped, monosyllabic; moments of tension are recorded in ungrammatical bites, shorn of adjectives" (Williamson).

At another end of a stylistic spectrum is the influence of Herman Melville on Cormac McCarthy. Alan Bilton notes how reviewers "have drawn attention to [McCarthy's] formal debts to Herman Melville (in terms of his crazed, incantatory sermonizing)" (p. 131). Indeed, McCarthy has cited *Moby-Dick* as his favorite book, and expansive tomes such as *Blood Meridian* and *The Crossing* owe a clear debt to the work of Melville. The former's Judge Holden is the most Melvillian of McCarthy's characters, his high oratory calling to mind Ahab and his physicality and supernatural nature, as Harold Bloom has pointed out, calling to mind the white whale itself. In addition, the multiracial Glanton Gang of the same novel reflects the diverse crew that sailed the Nantucket whaleship the *Pequod* in Melville's book.

But if McCarthy has taken stylistic and thematic cues from Ernest Hemingway, he has gained something more insidious from Melville. Writing in September 1851, prior to the release of *Moby-Dick: or; The Whale*, Melville wrote of his book, "a Polar wind blows through it, & birds of prey hover over it. Warn all gentle fastidious people from so much as peeping into the book" (Melville, *Correspondence*). There is more than a little of that spirit in the work of Cormac McCarthy as well, particularly in works such as *Blood Meridian* and *The Road* (2006).

There is another similarity between *Moby-Dick* and *Blood Meridian*, in that both works saw their respective writers stretching themselves in new directions and testing the limits of their prose — McCarthy, like Melville, showing a "drive to break the boundaries of literary form" (as Andrew Delbanco has written of *Moby-Dick*, p. 122). McCarthy turned away from the safe familiarity of the South and to the great canvas of the American Southwest and Mexico, a region that, like Melville's metaphysical watery reaches, has offered a historical and physical scope worthy of his ambition. McCarthy has certainly been shown to possess the reach of Melville.

On a more specific level McCarthy has borrowed tropes from his favorite novel, *Moby-Dick*, such as the aforementioned multicultural makeup of the Glanton Gang and the Ahab-meets-Moby-Dick characteristics of Judge Holden. Harold Bloom, who has called *Blood Meridian* "the strongest imaginative work by any living writer" (p. 237), also points out how the "ragged prophet" Elijah, the biblically inspired character who appears in chapter 19 of *Moby-Dick* to warn Ishmael and Queequeg against sailing with Captain Ahab, echoes in *Blood Meridian*. In chapter 4 of that work, an old Mennonite "warns the [k]id and his comrades not to join Captain Worth's filibuster, a disaster that preludes the greater catastrophe of Glanton's campaign" (Bloom, p. 258). Bloom also writes, "Destroying the Native American nations of the Southwest [and Mexico] is hardly analogous to the hunt to slay Moby-Dick, and yet McCarthy gives us some curious parallels between the two quests" (p. 258).

Elijah reappears 21 years later in *The Road*, in which the man and his son encounter the old man Ely, whose nihilistic and absurdist prophesying befits a world in which everything that had once been known is dead and gone. As Pulitzer Prize–winning author William Kennedy (of the Albany, New York, cycle of novels) noted in his *New York Times* review of the book, "Elijah ... turns up as a destitute straggler who looks like 'a pile of rags fallen off a cart' .... In one of the longest conversations in the novel the father talks to Ely about being the last man on earth." But in *The Road* McCarthy has transmuted Elijah's prophecies into something grimmer and darkly absurd, claiming that "things will be better when everybody's gone" (p. 172), with the kicker that even death himself will face demise: "He'll be out in the road there with nothing to do and nobody to do it to. He'll say: Where did everybody go?" (p. 173). ("Who knew Elijah did stand-up?" cracks Kennedy in his review.)

The influence of James Joyce might not be as profound as that of Melville and Hemingway — or as that of William Faulkner in McCarthy's early career — but the Irish writer is nonetheless important. His impact is most significant in *Suttree* (1979), McCarthy's Knoxville novel, which gives epic resonance to that city's underbelly and its down-and-out denizens, much like Joyce's epic rendering of an ordinary Dublin day in *Ulysses* (1922). The sprawling, effusive, elliptical composition of *Suttree* —as well as the detailed examination of the city — also calls to mind Joyce's Dublin work, though McCarthy's work covers roughly a five-year period and Joyce's only a single day. One can also trace McCarthy's "Joycean mode," wherein the writer "juxtaposes the breadth and grandeur of classical epic with ... an average man's life," in John Grady Cole and Billy Parham's individual travails in the first two books of the Border Trilogy (Ellis, "McCarthy Music," p. 168).

In McCarthy, one also occasionally finds a stream-of-consciousness tendency that recalls Joyce, particularly in its challenging of syntax and tests on the limits of language. In this voice, for example, a training ride on a horse becomes something else entirely — something, frankly, puzzling at first (especially in the use of "who's" rather than "whose"). But the effect is to pose a question ("who is?") that shows the tension of rider's and horse's wills as the horse-in-training evolves from a state of wildness to a condition of submission:

While inside the vaulting of the ribs between his knees the darkly meated heart pumped of who's will and the blood pulsed and the bowels shifted in their massive blue convolutions of who's will and the stout thighbones and knee and cannon and the tendons like flaxen hawsers that drew and flexed at their articulations and of who's will all sheaved and muffled in the flesh and the hooves that stove wells in the morning groundmist [*All the Pretty Horses*, p. 128].

Here, the Joycean outpouring and contortion of language illustrates the tension of wills and suggests the eventual subsuming of will that culminates in the horse becoming an extension of rider.

On another, more mundane level, McCarthy noted in his TV interview with Oprah Winfrey how Joyce influenced, or at least corroborated, his own tendency to be sparing with punctuation. "James Joyce is a good model for punctuation. He keeps it to an absolute minimum," McCarthy noted. "There's no reason to blot the page up with weird little marks. If you write properly you shouldn't have to punctuate" (Winfrey).

The final writer that should be mentioned is William Faulkner, the novelist who was such an important influence on McCarthy's early novels. In fact, so distinct were the strains of Faulkner in Cormac McCarthy's first novel, *The Orchard Keeper* (1965)— published when he was 31— that the *New York Times* review noted that some writers, "although they are highly gifted ... are sorely handicapped by their humble and excessive admiration for William Faulkner. Cormac McCarthy, author of *The Orchard Keeper*, is one of these" (Prescott). (The review itself ran under the title "Still Another Disciple of William Faulkner.") From Faulkner, McCarthy has inherited many capacities, but perhaps the most significant is the capacity for probing, telescoping illumination in seemingly simple moments — illuminations that spill out in a stream of language:

Then I began to smell it again ... that odor in his clothes and beard and flesh too which I believed was the smell of powder and glory, the elected victorious but know better now: know to have been the only will to endure, a sardonic and even humorous declining of self-delusion which is not even kin to that optimism which believes that that which is about to happen to us can possibly be the worst which we can suffer [Faulkner, *The Unvanquished*, p. 10].

This is Faulkner, writing from Bayard's perspective of his father's return from battle, but it is the booming insight that bursts forth in McCarthy as well — a voice that lends a simple moment both universal and mythic resonance.

McCarthy may have abandoned the darkly antiquarian Southern slant of Faulkner as his gaze turned to the West, but he retained this mythically resonant voice, as witnessed here in *All the Pretty Horses*: "They all seemed to be waiting for something. Like passengers in a halted train," writes McCarthy as a Mexican prison official regards Cole and Rawlins. "Yet the captain inhabited another space and it was a space of his own election and outside the common world of men. A space privileged to men of the irreclaimable act which while it contained all lesser worlds within it contained no access to them" (p. 179). What McCarthy has taken from Faulkner is the capacity to deliberate on the familiar — or a small thing or a moment — and push it, through the effort of language, into something transcendentally aware of untapped layers of meaning.

Nevertheless, Cormac McCarthy eventually evolved into such a profoundly singular prose stylist, one beyond influence and one whose own work is so powerful that burgeoning writers who read his work may find it hard to shake McCarthy's meter and find their own voice. Therefore, it is fitting to also mention ways in which McCarthy ultimately diverges from his key influences. Consider first that if McCarthy were to parallel Faulkner's career, he would have continued to try to wring purchase out of the eastern Tennessee environs of his early work, rather than pulling up stakes and moving to El Paso to explore a region to which he was not native. Faulkner is ultimately a renderer of native soil, not an explorer like McCarthy. For Faulkner, the environs of Mississippi "in its smallness and intensity, [would] prove a wonderful source for the imagination of William Faulkner.... Oxford and the surrounding countryside and villages was, it must be said, almost the only source he needed" (*Authors: William Faulkner*). This, of course, makes McCarthy fundamentally different at that level.

To put distance between Cormac McCarthy and Herman Melville, simply contemplate the success, recognition and accolades that, despite his public reticence, came to McCarthy later in life (in his fifties, sixties, and seventies): MacArthur Fellowship, National Book Award, Pulitzer Prize, several bestsellers, an Academy Award for a movie based on *No Country for Old Men* (book: 2005). By contrast, Melville languished in obscurity after a moderately successful career in his twenties as a writer of ocean-bound adventure stories such as *Typee* (1846) and *Omoo* (1847).

Moby-Dick (1851) was hardly noticed in his lifetime and did not reach a broad readership. It was not until the 1920s (Melville died in 1891), with the advent of modernism, that readers were prepared to fully appreciate his probing, experimental tome — making it an overdue classic of American literature. In his final years, Melville did not even live the life of a novelist, as has been afforded Cormac McCarthy, but worked as a U.S. customs inspector on the Manhattan docks, along the Hudson and East rivers. As biographer Andrew Delbanco recounts:

> For the better part of twenty years, beginning in 1866, he took the horse car down Broadway six times a week, then headed west, where he walked the docks along the Hudson down to the Battery. (Later he was assigned to an East River pier uptown at Seventy-ninth street and traveled to work on the new Third Avenue El.) On West Street, wearing a brass-buttoned woolen coat modeled on a naval officer's uniform, he shared an office with other inspectors in what was little more than a dockside shack [p. 291].

Additionally, the manuscript to the celebrated *Billy Budd*, written later in life, languished until decades after Melville's death, when it was published in 1924.

A world of difference also separates McCarthy from Hemingway, and here it is again useful to leave the pages and look at the lives of the men. Hemingway's persona was a big part of his life's work and was deeply intertwined with his books, whereas McCarthy has consistently diverted attention from his own life and has avoided cultivating a public writer's persona. Even in his reclusiveness McCarthy has been outshined by more determined recluses such as J.D. Salinger and Thomas Pynchon, who have in fact become famous for their strict public reticence. McCarthy is not as famous for his reclusiveness, and in fact makes the occasional appearance. His position is not that he is not a public person, but that he doesn't choose to play the media or literary-circles games.

Additionally, Hemingway produced some of his weakest work late in life, including the widely reviled *Across the River and Into the Trees* (1950), though he did manage the short, Nobel Prize–winning masterpiece *The Old Man and the Sea* in 1952. (And both Hemingway and McCarthy have had their work turned into Hollywood films.) Nevertheless, Hemingway committed suicide in 1961, just shy of his 62nd birthday, having suffered greatly from the wages of alcoholism. McCarthy is antithetical to these circumstances, having begun to reach his widest audience and receive some of his greatest accolades as he entered his sixties, and having reportedly quit drinking altogether in his early to mid-forties (as he once told *New York Times*). And, at the time of this writing, in the summer of 2009, the world awaits yet more from the imagination of Cormac McCarthy, who remains on an upward trajectory as he enters his late seventies.

See also Style

Judge Holden

Cormac McCarthy has often presented terrifying scenarios for his readers, but never has one of his characters so embodied the darkest recesses of humankind as Judge Holden from *Blood Meridian* (1985). The judge has been called "among the most unforgettable, appalling figures in American literature" (Bancroft) and "less a man than a metonymn for human depravity" ("The Judge from Blood Meridian"). The London *Times* claimed the judge "recalls Milton's Satan, Dostoyevsky's Grand Inquisitor, Melville's Captain Ahab" and "is the personification of evil" (Miano).

But while Judge Holden is capable of unspeakable acts of sadism, what truly amplifies his terrifying aspect is his sheer refinement. The monstrous and hairless judge is not only terrible, but a paragon of high culture. He is a fine musician and a nimble dancer; he is multilingual and socially gracious; he is a keen historian and naturalist; he is an eloquent orator. In this way, he embodies high-water marks of civilization.

But for McCarthy "civilization" also embodies violence; therefore, the judge is naturally also emblematic of the most brutal aspects of humanity, which in the *Blood Meridian* worldview exist simultaneously with the more "civilized" affairs of culture. Or, as the judge himself phrases it, "in the affairs of men ... the noon of his expression signals the onset of night. His spirit is exhausted at the peak of his achievement. His meridian is at once his darkening and the evening of his day" (p. 147).

The judge is the embodiment of civilizational violence, and therein lies the immortality that the judge claims for himself. So many critics have (rightly) drawn parallels between *Blood Meridian* and *Moby-Dick*, but to understand the judge in terms of that classic work, one would have to posit the judge as not only an equivalent to Ahab — as many have — or to the whale itself (as renowned critic Harold Bloom has), but as Ahab, the whale, and the enterprise itself, all rolled into one character. This is the sheer amplitude of Judge Holden, who gleefully dances and fiddles in the closing lines of the novel, all of the others, including the kid, having been sent to their graves.

"The dance" of which the judge so often speaks is war — the judge, as Vince Brewton would have it, becoming "the living embodiment and oracle of an ontology of war" (p. 131). And in McCarthy's literary worldview, what he represents shall never sleep or perish: "He says that he will never die. He dances in light and shadow and he is a great favorite. He never sleeps, the judge. He is dancing, dancing. He says that he will never die" (p. 335).

• *Further reading*
Bloom, Harold. *How to Read and Why.* New York: Scribner, 2000.

"The Kid"

Of all the central figures in McCarthy's novels, "the kid" from *Blood Meridian* (1985) is perhaps the most inscrutable. Harold Bloom points out, "[T]hough the Kid's moral maturation [later in the novel] is heartening, his personality remains largely a cipher, as anonymous as his lack of a name" (p. 257). (Note that McCarthy lowercases "the kid," despite many critics' tendency to capitalize it.)

Adding to the kid's impenetrable nature is the fact that even though he is positioned as the protagonist — the reader essentially traces the path of the kid's journey and travails — he has a tendency to blend into the background for long stretches, as the narrative turns its attention to a wider picture of the Glanton Gang, with nary a mention of the kid. (Ishmael in *Moby-Dick* pulls the same reappearing/disappearing act, though Ishmael is allowed first person narration; the kid is not.)

Our introduction to the kid is a puzzle as well. In several intriguing opening sentences, McCarthy establishes the character, but takes us in a different direction than one would expect from the opening sentences, which drip with pathos straight out of Charles Dickens: "See the child. He is pale and thin, he wears a thin and ragged linen shirt" (p. 3). We quickly gather in subsequent sentences that his father "lies in drink" and that the child is "pale and unwashed," furthering this pathos (*ibid.*). Then the description takes a surprising turn, cutting against what McCarthy has established: "[I]n him [the kid] already broods a taste for mindless violence" (*ibid.*). Now we are in the world of Cormac McCarthy and far from the canonized, poor-waif-against-the-world motif (Dickens' *Oliver Twist* and *David Copperfield*, for example).

The kid is subsumed (by his very nature) into McCarthy's continuum of human brutality, established on the previous page by the prefatory news clipping of the archeological discovery of a three-million-year-old fossil skull that appears to have been scalped. The kid will join a band of scalpers, in accordance with that ancient epoch and the layers of historical violence that have preceded him.

For, as McCarthy writes, "[all] history" is present in the kid: "the child the father of the man" (*ibid.*). Or, as the stranger tells Billy Parham in the concluding passages of the Border Trilogy, "The world of our fathers resides within us. Ten thousand generations or more" (*Cities of the Plain*, p. 281). These sentiments are pulled from the first page of *Blood Meridian* ("all history") — the book that is the prequel to the Border Trilogy — and the concluding passages of the trilogy itself. This is the beginning; this is the end; and this is McCarthy's consistent meditation: the inevitability of human brutality and war, from civilization to civilization throughout and before recorded history.

The kid embodies the inevitability of this condition. Not only is he naturally drawn toward savagery as a vocation, but his own "progress" shows that there is no way out of this cycle. *Blood Meridian* is a bildungsroman — of sorts. We do see the evolution of the central character, what Bloom has termed the kid's "long, slow development" and "moral maturation" (p. 257), but there is no clear arc. First, because of the telescoping effect of the narrative, wherein the kid often disappears or blends into the scenery for long stretches (in effect becoming an extra in a story where he is often posited as the lead), the reader is not always sure to what extent the kid participates in some of the more brutal and senseless violence, or how committed he is to the enterprise. (Ishmael, from *Moby-Dick*, is similarly swallowed by an omniscient narrator at times.) The judge even accuses the kid of this ambivalence: "You came forward ... to take part in a work. But you were a witness against yourself. You sat in judgment on your own deeds ... and you broke with the body of which you were pledged a part" (p. 307).

More importantly, however, the "morally mature" kid has nowhere to apply his newfound consciousness in this landscape. Years after leaving the Glanton Gang, at the age of 28, the kid whispers words of reassurance to an old woman that he has found kneeling amid slaughtered "pilgrims": "He spoke to her in a low voice.... He told her that he would convey her to a safe place, some party of her countrypeople who would welcome her" (p. 315).

The kid's words are clear signs of his self-development; the woman, however, turns out to be a dried corpse that has been there for years, and his kindness echoes in a void. And when "the kid" becomes a man in his forties, seeming to have moved away from the brutality of his youth, he is nonetheless forced to shoot a boy to death in self-defense (p. 322) — there seems no way out of the cycle of violence, even for the relatively enlightened. But the man who was once the kid has gained something; he now truly understands the stakes of "the game" that Judge Holden illustrated: "You wouldnt of lived anyway, the man said" (p. 322).

See also Blood Meridian; Judge Holden

Loss

Loss is a prominent motif in Cormac McCarthy's novels, particularly in the Border Trilogy, where the protagonists experience layers of loss. This tone is set in the opening pages of the trilogy, when the reader witnesses John Grady Cole's separation from his heritage as the family ranch is sold off to oil interests. It is this rupture with the past that sends Cole adventuring off into Mexico, losing along the way any kind of familial connection: His father dies, his mother remains estranged, and even Abuela, the Cole family servant who had cared for John Grady and his mother, dies by the end of *All the Pretty Horses* (1992). Cole also loses an even more insidious connection after his travails. When Rawlins suggests to Cole that "[t]his is still good country," Cole pronounces, "It aint my country." Pressed as to exactly where his country is, he replies, "I dont know where it is. I dont know what happens to country" (*All the Pretty Horses*, p. 299).

Billy Parham, the other protagonist of the trilogy, is virtually defined by his loss. In fact, he even loses John Grady Cole, whom he had taken under his wing as a brother figure. Cradling the dead she-wolf at the culmination of his travail in book 1 of *The Crossing* (1994), we find that he "reached to hold what cannot be held, what already ran among the mountains" (p. 127). This idea of trying to hold on to that which cannot be held is a hard lesson that Parham learns again and again, most prominently with the deaths of his beloved brother Boyd in *The Crossing* and John Grady Cole in *Cities of the Plain* (1998).

Billy also loses the old ways of cowboy life as the culture in the Southwest changes. In a particularly telling passage, he finds himself working as an extra on the set of a movie, reduced to an old cowboy facsimile. Such are the dimensions of this loss that by the end of the trilogy, as an old man, he sees himself as reduced to naught: "I aint nothing," he proclaims to a woman who has taken him in, a point that she kindly disputes (p. 292).

This notion of loss resonates beyond the trilogy, however. Sheriff Bell's italicized passages in *No Country for Old Men* (2005) often become laments for passing ways of life, for the old spirit of small-town existence in the borderlands. *The Road* (2006), of course, is McCarthy's most cataclysmic representation of loss, as the living world itself and everything in it is swallowed up in this post-apocalyptic vision.

We see this motif in McCarthy's early work as well — in *Outer Dark* (1968) Rinthy Holme loses her baby at the moment of birth and futilely spends the novel trying to recover it. Even the creepy serial killer Lester Ballard in *Child of God* (1973) experiences a soulful moment of profundity in dream that shows his understanding of all that he is about to lose: "Each leaf that brushed his face deepened his sadness and dread. Each leaf he passed he'd never pass again. They rode over his face like veils" (pp. 171–172). The title character of *Suttree* (1979) is also at the center of a series of losses, from the break with his family, to the death of his infant son and young girlfriend, to the loss of members of his adopted "family" (Ab Jones, Billy Ray Callahan).

But it is not just the main characters of McCarthy's novels that endure crushing loss; in fact, the novels are filled with a constellation of characters managing their grief and yearning. Perhaps most emblematic of this is old Mr. Johnson in *Cities of the Plain*, of whom it is revealed that "[i]n his time the country had gone from the oil lamp and the horse and buggy to jet planes and the atomic bomb but that wasnt what confused him. It was the fact that his daughter was dead that he couldnt get the hang of" (*Cities of the Plain*, p. 106).

But, as Jacqueline Scoones indicates, characters in McCarthy's books "who suffer loss" tend to "do so not with operatic grief, but with intensely private pain" (p. 142). Billy Parham becomes an old man himself in the same novel, and the decades have done nothing to abate his pain over the loss of Boyd, whom he still dreams about and misses — "all the time" (p. 291). Billy even has painful dreams of his sister, who died when they both were small children: "in his sleep he called out to her but she did not turn or answer him but only passed on down that empty road in infinite sadness and infinite loss" (p. 266). And that seems to be Cormac McCarthy's message, particularly in the Border Trilogy: All else may disappear, but loss is infinite.

"The Man" (*The Road*)

For the man (a.k.a. the father) in *The Road* (2006) a whole world, an entire universe of existence, has crumbled around him. Everything that was once familiar — loved ones, friends, a morning sunrise, nature, and the very lineaments of life as he knew it — has perished. Even his own identity and the identity of those few that still remain alive have dissolved in this post-apocalyptic oblivion. "Are you a doctor?" he is asked at one point. "I'm not anything," he tellingly responds (p. 64). Later in the novel, both the man and boy are asked, "What are you?"—"They'd no way to answer the question," writes McCarthy (p. 162). In an earlier passage, when the boy asks who could be nearby, the man answers. "I dont know. Who is anybody?" (p. 49).

But the man, unlike his son, is burdened with the memory and recalled sensations of the pre-apocalyptic world. He chides himself to "[m]ake a list. Recite a litany. Remember," so as not to lose the sensations of his previous life (p. 31). In some ways these memories become a source of resolve; for example, the recollection of a boyhood day at the lake with his with his uncle becomes, in a reverie, "the perfect day of his childhood ... the day to shape the days upon" (p. 13). Of the boy's mother, who ended her own life, leaving him with sole charge of the boy, he remembers "everything of her save her scent" (p. 18). And the tangible mnemonic traces of her, such as the feel of her thin summer dress long ago in a theater, give him strength: "Freeze this frame," he commands himself. "Now call down your dark and your cold and be damned," he taunts the heavens (p. 19).

Mostly, however, what defines the man is a sort of personal manifest destiny to protect the child. He knows that this is his duty and moreover the only thing standing between him and death. And like a true "manifest destiny" it is ordained by God: "If [the boy] is not the word of God God never spoke," ruminates the man (p. 5). Whatever identity he once had, whatever life he once experienced, has been swallowed up and replaced by his almighty warrant to protect the boy.

Nevertheless, as that warrant begins to slip away, and as the inevitability of the man dying and leaving the boy alone becomes a closer and closer reality — and as the boy evolves and matures — what little was left of what one would consider "a life" (memories, etc.) slips off into the void as well. Close to his death, he "thought about his life but there was no life to think about" (p. 237). Here is manifested what the man feared earlier in the novel: "The names of things slowly following those things into oblivion. Colors. The names of birds. Things to eat. Finally the names of things one believed to be true.... Drawing down like something trying to preserve heat. In time to wink out forever" (p. 89).

As the boy matures and becomes more cynical, even the bedrock beliefs that drove the two of them come into question and risk the annihilation just described. The boy questions whether they are truly the good guys, whether they truly "carry the fire." He questions the belief system with which his father has inscribed him. "But in the stories we're always helping people and we dont help people," the boy insists (p. 268).

Throughout the novel one could rightly question whether the man himself believes the protective philosophy that he weaves around the boy and himself, but ultimately he does — even if he wavers along the way — and ultimately this is a story of redemption in the utter blackness (unusual for McCarthy). In his final moments, the father displays a belief in things that had seemed doomed to oblivion — "luck" and "goodness" — and he tells the boy the fire is indeed real: "It's inside you. It was always there. I can see it" (p. 279).

The ultimate redemption for the man may come in that beautifully cryptic final passage of the novel that has puzzled so many readers. It is a memory of the world as it once was, the natural world, with mountain trout "standing in the amber current where the white edges of their fins wimpled softly in the flow. They smelled of moss in your hand" (p. 286). This calls to mind the sense memories that the man had relied upon for strength early in the novel, the memories that seemed to leave him as the narrative progressed: reveries of the day at the lake with his uncle; the sensation of the boy's mother, of whom he could recall so much, except for her scent.

The final passage of *The Road* recovers a memory of a lost world, with everything intact, scent and all (the brook trout "smelled of moss"). Whether this is the man's memory or an omniscient memory (or both) is not perfectly clear (the passage suggests it may be a memory older than humanity), but much like the boy's rescue, the memory is a hint of redemption at the end of a harrowing road.

See also "The Boy"; *The Road*

McCarthy, Lee

Lee McCarthy (formerly Lee Holleman), who died at the age of 70 on March 21, 2009, was Cormac McCarthy's first wife and the mother of his eldest son, Cullen (born in 1962). The marriage was short-lived, and Lee McCarthy would go on to make her own reputation as a writer, becoming a poet of some renown over the decades.

In 1975, she was awarded a Stegner Fellowship to Stanford University, and she has also received the Nicholas Roerich prize in poetry (1991) and the Ion Books National Chapbook Competition (1992). She organized a poetry reading series in Bakersfield, California (her home for four decades), that brought in many well-known poets, including onetime United States poet laureate Ted Kooser and Pulitzer Prize winner Philip Levine.

She published three poetry collections: *Desire's Door* (1991), *Combing Hair with a Seashell* (1992), and *Good Girl* (2002). *Desire's Door* is of interest to Cormac McCarthy enthusiasts because Lee McCarthy chronicles the failed marriage in some of the poems of this collection. She also seems to sometimes work a terrain that overlaps in a certain respect with her ex-husband, particularly in this image, from the poem "Santa Paula": "There's a woman kissing a cowboy across the street. / ... She's really planting one on him, his Stetson in danger." Ted Kooser, the onetime laureate, praised "Santa Paula" as of a strain of poetry that "offers us vivid scenes but which lets us draw our own conclusions about the implications of what we're being shown." He added, "Here is something seen from across the street, something quite ordinary yet packed with life" (Kooser). The praise certainly echoes the types of plaudits sent Cormac McCarthy's way over the years.

On March 29, 2009, Lee McCarthy's hometown newspaper, the *Bakersfield Californian*, published an obituary that referred to her as "a poet and writer who taught the school children of Kern County for more than three decades and then spent the latter part of her life bringing world class poetry to Bakersfield" (Lee McCarthy obituary). The article also noted that she was an Arkansas native who had met Cormac McCarthy at the University of Tennessee.

Upon their marriage, "they moved to a shack with no heat and running water in the foothills of the Smoky Mountains outside of Knoxville" (*ibid.*). They separated shortly after, and Lee McCarthy moved to Wyoming, where she first began teaching. In 1966, she moved to the Bakersfield area and continued her profession as a teacher, leaving only to earn a master's degree at San Francisco State University. For over three decades, according to the obituary, she "was a fixture at Wasco Union High School, teaching teenagers and eventually their children about the great works of literature" (*ibid.*). The write-up also noted that she was the recipient of the Arts Council of Kerns Individual Arts Educator Award in 1993, and had been "a single mother raising a child at a time when it was an exception" (*ibid.*).

The Mexican Revolution

While none of the Border Trilogy books actually takes place during the time of the Mexican Revolution (1910–1920), there are strong reverberations of that violent historical epoch throughout the trilogy. Both Billy Parham and John Grady Cole encounter a Mexico that is distinctly marked by the memory of the revolution. John Wegner points out that "accounts of the Mexican Revolution ... become integral parts of the trilogy's narrative" ("Wars and Rumors," p. 74) and that the reflections upon the revolution help "shape the ideas and actions of the Trilogy's protagonists and antagonists alike" ("Mexico para los Mexicanos," p. 249).

The revolution also provides a compelling counterpoint to World War II, a less prevalent but important historical specter in the trilogy, as the revolution was a pre-mechanized conflict, fought largely on horseback, a distinct contrast to the modern world war fought mere decades later.

The devastating legacy of the revolution is also manifest in the *corridos*, the narrative ballads devised and sung by rural revolutionaries that constitute a "poor man's history" (*The Crossing*, p. 386). The *corridos* themselves are fraught with their own kind of history: particularly tales of lives lost during that bloody decade. "Listen to the *corridos* of the country. They will tell you," the primadonna tells Billy and Boyd in *The Crossing*. "Then you will see in your own life what is the cost of things" (p. 230). And while, historically, the *corridos* were also intended to pass along tales of banditry, outlaws, and anti-authoritarian heroism, in the trilogy they tell "one story only"—"for there is only one to tell, and that story is of death" (p. 143).

In *All the Pretty Horses,* Alejandra actually takes John Grady to a plaza where her then-young grandfather was killed in 1914, while Dueña Alfonsa relates to John Grady her own romantic experiences (before the start of the revolution) with the brother of

Francesco I. Madero, the president whose assassination was a key event in the revolution. (Madero was the first freely elected president.) In that same novel, John Grady and Lacey Rawlins also work with an old man, Luis, a veteran of that conflict.

The tales of the revolution that he and others tell are a potent component of the trilogy; in *The Crossing*, for example, Billy listens to the story of how a blind man lost his sight after having his eyeballs literally sucked from his sockets by a sadistic captain of the federal army. In *Cities of the Plain*, old Mr. Johnson remembers being in Mexico during the time of the revolution, and relates to John Grady the nightmarish images he witnessed: "The executions against the mud walls sprayed with new blood over the dried black of the old ... and the corpses stacked in the streets or piled into the woodenwheeled carretas" (p. 64). In *The Crossing*, Billy is told of a mass execution of townspeople during the revolution: "The blood soon soaked into the earth and with fall of dark before the rain packs of dogs arrived and gouged up mouthfuls of the bloodsoaked mud and ate it down" (p. 288).

In the Border Trilogy, the Mexican Revolution resonates McCarthy's ultimate pessimistic conclusion about human civilization: As Alfonsa tells John Grady, "What is constant in history is greed and foolishness and a love of blood and this is a thing that even God — who knows all that can be known — seems powerless to change" (*All the Pretty Horses*, p. 239). She also intones that "those who do not know history are condemned to repeat it. I don't believe knowing can save us" (*ibid.*). The Mexican Revolution, then, becomes a way for McCarthy to point out what he deems the ultimate historical truth about *all* of humanity —"the dead have no nationality," as the Yaqui Indian Quijada tells Billy (*The Crossing*, p. 387)— that is, the inevitability of such violent conflict.

But the revolution is also a device through which McCarthy calls into question the traditional handling of "histories." For one, the author extracts heroic sentimentality from memories of war through his frank, detailed, and objective descriptions of bloodshed. "In the end we all come to be cured of our sentiments," says Alfonsa in the midst of her tale of the Madero family and the revolution. "Those whom life does not cure [of sentimentality] death will" (*All the Pretty Horses*, p. 238). Another way in which McCarthy undermines traditional handlings of history is to present what a gypsy in *The Crossing* reveals as a "third history ... the history that each man makes alone out what is left to him. Bits of wreckage. Some bones. The words of the dead. How make a world of this? How live in that world once made?" (p. 411). The *corridos* of the Mexican Revolution function as a third, individual history, but a history that in its rejection of collective history (in order to favor the individual) becomes, paradoxically, a collective history as well: "It tells the tale of that solitary man who is all men" (p. 386).

But the *corrido*, in its production of history and need for narrative structure, is ultimately unreliable as well; it "tells all and it tells nothing ... it tells what it wishes to tell. It tells what makes the story run. It is the poor man's history" (*ibid.*). In other words, it is the poor man's lie about the past, akin to the academic or societal history in its discursive need to present elevated meaning where there might be none. Travis, in *Cities of the Plain*, takes an ultimately less sentimental stance on the Mexican Revolution, the very view that the Border Trilogy is projecting: "None of it done anybody any good.... Or if it did I never heard of it" (p. 90).

Facts without context are meaningless, but this is a meaninglessness that McCarthy keeps driving home. Ideals or historical narratives provide context, but the context is the "lie" that is born: The *corrido* "believes that where two men meet one of two things can occur and nothing else. In the one case a lie is born and in the other death" (*ibid.*). Alfonsa ultimately believes that "little ... can be truly known" of her country, despite her and others' attempts to find meaning (*All the Pretty Horses*, p. 238). Thus, her telling of the events of the revolution, of the Madero family and their ideals, is boiled down to a microscopic detailing of the senselessly violent event: She relates how Gustavo Madero was struck and burned, how his eye was pried from its socket with a pick. She tells how a man held a revolver to Madero's head to shoot him but someone jostled his arm and the shot went amiss and "tore away [Madero's] jaw" (p. 237).

There is no historical understanding to be extracted from these details of the past. Alfonsa points out how scientists engaging in empirical observation use a "second group," a control group to "judge the significance of what has occurred" (p. 239). The control group is necessary for understanding, but in history "there are no control groups. There is no one to tell us what might have been. We weep over the might have been but there is no might have been" (*ibid.*). Or, as the Mormon hermit claims in *The Crossing*, "Things separate from their story have no meaning. They are only shapes. Of a certain size and color. A certain weight" (p. 142).

If there is any meaning to be extracted from the memories of the Mexican Revolution in the Border Trilogy, it is a meaning that resides on a whole other level of understanding than the intellectual. It is beyond language, story-telling, history or any of the other signifiers or markers that we use to make sense of the world. As Quijada tells Billy, "The world has no name. The names of the cerros and the sierras and the deserts exist only on maps. We name them [so] that we do not lose our way" (p. 387). Billy glimpses this understanding of the Mexican Revolution and what it truly means in the bullet-hole-scarred, drunk veteran of the revolution, in a charged moment before Billy's own potential death:

> What he saw was that the only manifest artifact of the history of this negligible republic where he now seemed about to die that had the least authority or meaning or claim to substance was seated here before him in the sallow light of this cantina and all else from men's lips or men's pens would require that it be beat out hot all over again upon the anvil of its own enactment before it could even qualify as a lie [p. 363].

In this angry, battle-scarred veteran — and in this moment of potential death — Billy sees, for a moment, a kind of historical "truth" and authority that actual histories could never reveal. Perhaps a similar, simpler truth appears in an exchange between Billy and the Yaqui Indian Quijada: "That sounds like death is the truth," says Billy. Quijada replies, "Yes. It sounds like death is the truth" (p. 386).

Nevertheless, despite the fact that the Border Trilogy presents a different kind of "history," it is still necessary for comparison and context to provide a traditional historical account of the revolution. In 1910, the year cited as the start of the revolution, Porfirio Díaz was president and de facto dictator of Mexico. With the exception of one term, Díaz had run the country since 1876, bringing it into the modern era with an iron fist.

He brought great economic prosperity, but the wealth and land was distributed among the prosperous few. Also, as Dan La Botz points out, his governing strategy was encapsulated in the phrase "*pano o palo*," in other words, "a loaf of bread for those who cooperated ... and a beating with a club for those who did not" (p. 44). The *federales*, or federal army, saw to it that his will was forcefully and efficiently carried out. He also strengthened his position by aligning himself closely with the large landholders of the region, rich foreign investors (European, British, American), and the powerful Catholic Church.

His reign was characterized by the concentration of wealth and the exploitation of the poorer rural and working classes. In fact, 95 percent of the citizens lived in poverty, owning no land and often toiling as sharecroppers on the large haciendas throughout the country (*ibid.*). Particularly exploited were the indigenous people of Mexico, who lost what land they had to the expansion of the haciendas. Meanwhile, foreign investors, particularly the United States, controlled much of the Mexican economy.

Francisco I. Madero, an upper-class landlord from the northern state of Coahuila, published *The Presidential Succession of 1910* in 1909. Madero was a Berkeley-educated idealist and liberal, and in this tome he called for reform, criticizing Díaz's absolutist and militaristic grip on the country. Bolstered by the popular reception of his ideas, Madero ran for president against Díaz in 1910, and the rhetoric he espoused at rallies throughout the country — particularly the idea that the seized lands should be given back — ignited the oppressed rural communities of Mexico. Madero, unfortunately, was promptly imprisoned by Díaz. But Madero's call had been heard by revolutionaries such as Pascual Orozco and his general, Francisco "Pancho" Villa, bandits who led forces in the north, and Emiliano Zapata, a leader of a powerful peasant army in southern Mexico. Madero, a slight man with a high-pitched voice (who held such esoteric beliefs as communicating with the dead through a medium), became a catalyst for the uprising of the long oppressed.

While out on bail, Madero disguised himself and escaped on a train to the border, where he slipped into Texas, staying in San Antonio and releasing another political document, the *Plan of San Luis de Potosí*, which called for the overthrow of Díaz's authoritarian regime and the institution of democracy. Bolstered by Madero's proclamations, revolutionary uprisings of forces throughout the country succeeded in driving Díaz out of Mexico in November of 1911, and Madero, who had participated in the fighting, was eventually elected president.

Nevertheless, the Treaty of Ciudad Juárez, which ended the fighting after the rebels had put down the federal army, left a good portion of Díaz's regime intact, as well as the federal army itself. The treaty also disbanded the revolutionary forces (Gonzales, p. 80). Madero's willingness to compromise with the regime, while stalling on sweeping land reform, drove a wedge between him and the very people who had fought to bring him to power.

Zapata and his forces, the Zapatistas, made a swift and decisive break from Madero and "declared themselves in rebellion" of the new presidency (La Botz, p. 48). Zapata also issued his own edict, the Plan of Ayala, which demanded the return of appropriated land to the peasants, "the expropriation of one-third of the haciendas for landless peasants, and the nationalization of the land and property of those who opposed the plan" (*ibid.*). The manifesto also took a harsh tack against Madero, speaking of his treachery and betrayal in not enacting land reform, and encouraged peasants to take up arms against the government. Revolutionary leader Orozco also rallied his own anti–Madero forces. The first freely elected president was now in the unenviable position of ruling in a regime that contained former enemies while having alienated his one-time allies, the revolutionary forces. Moreover, the country was entering the crucible of violence, as regionally based revolutionary movements would continue to sweep "across most of Mexico between 1910 and 1917" (Hart, p. 237).

February 1913 saw what have come to be known as the "Ten Tragic Days" ("*La decena tragica*") in Mexico City. The commander of the federal army, Victoriano Huerta, conspired with U.S. ambassador Henry Lane Wilson to overthrow Madero. Huerta sent troops to storm the National Palace, where Madero was captured and, later, forced to resign in exchange for alleged safe passage out of the country.

Meanwhile, the American ambassador lobbied to make Huerta the interim president. Madero never received the exile he had been promised; he and his vice president, Pino Suárez, were both taken to the federal penitentiary, led to the prison courtyard, and shot in the head (Gonzales, p. 98). The president's brother, Gustavo A. Madero, received an even worse fate, the very fate Alfonsa describes in vivid detail in *All the Pretty Horses*: He was released to troops in a plaza near the restaurant where Huerta had arrested him (under the auspices of a reconciliatory dinner), where he was tortured and killed.

Huerta put in place a counter-revolutionary regime, which "pushed the revolutionary conflict into a renewed phase of violence" (Hamnett, p. 211). He also eventually established what was, for all intents and purposes, a dictatorship. Zapata and Villa refused to recognize the authority of Huerta and pursued aggression toward federal forces. (U.S. president Woodrow Wilson also refused to recognize the regime.)

Venustiano Carranza, the governor of Coahuila (and onetime secretary of war under Madero), formed the Constitutional Army (Ejercito constitucional) in opposition to Huerta's presidency — which he declared illegitimate — and drafted the Plan de Guadalupe, which espoused a more liberal ideology, stressing liberty, judicial power, and equality (Stacy, p. 135). Many revolutionary leaders, including Villa, Zapata, and Alvaro Obregón, fought alongside Carranza, whose forces went head to head with Huerta's for more than a year. After a pitched battle campaign, Carranza's forces seized Mexico City and Huerta was forced to resign.

Nevertheless, the aftermath of that victory showed what a complex and thorny political canvas Mexico was, as opposing factions instantly materialized within the victors, with Carranza and Obregón on the one side and Villa and Zapata on the other, leading to further bloodshed until Carranza, victorious against the now opposing revolutionary leaders as well, assumed the helm of Mexican government in 1915.

But the country remained very much in turmoil. In 1916, Carranza pulled together a constitutional congress out of the ashes of Huerta's absolutist rule and drafted a new constitution. (The previous constitution dated back to 1857.) One of the major components was to strengthen Mexico's position against foreign investors. While the U.S. and European countries had had a great stake in the country's resources and commerce, the new document deemed that natural resources were the property of the state — and foreign industry had to operate under Mexican federal law and endure heavy taxation, something which the U.S. in particular protested.

The constitution, which also favored the working class and farmers, became official in February of 1917 (*ibid.*, p. 136). (The document also undermined the once-dominant state power of the Catholic Church.) Soon after, Carrenza officially became president. He then turned to infrastructure concerns (roads, railways, etc.), quelling the violence in the country and restructuring the military by reducing its numbers (*ibid.*).

All was not harmonious, however. Carranza did not undertake the kind of agricultural reforms that were expected, and Mexico still had an impoverished underclass and ballooning unemployment rates. Those who did work endured remarkably low wages. This provoked protests, which the federal army put down. Meanwhile, the defeated Villa, who had once been backed by the United States, began to make violent bandit raids across the border, incensed by that country's refusal to provide him further weaponry. He murdered Americans and conducted a notorious raid in New Mexico (Suchlicki, p. 116).

McCarthy's *Cities of the Plain* evokes the violence inflicted by Villa's various raids through the accounts of the old ranch hand Travis, who recalls witnessing the aftermath and the piled corpses. "That sobered us up, I can tell you," he says (p. 190). The U.S. enlisted decorated general John Pershing to capture Villa in Mexico, but Villa, notorious for his affinity for the mountains of northern Mexico, succeeded in eluding him. Villa's ability to evade and frustrate the great American military power only enhanced his aura among the rural poor of Mexico, and "Villa became a popular folk hero in *corridos*" (*ibid.*). Villa would be assassinated in his car years later, in 1923, while visiting Parral, Chihuahua.

As testament to the regenerative cycles of violence in Mexico, Carranza soon met his end as well, when he was assassinated in 1920 for not supporting the potential presidency of Alvaro Obregón, his onetime ally (and minister of war), and the man who seemed, to many, to be Carranza's natural predecessor. In supporting Ignacio Bonilla, a Mexican ambassador to Washington, D.C., who had no connection to the revolutionary groups, he sealed his fate. Carranza viewed Obregón as a military man who didn't understand the big picture and complexities of the presidency (Krauze, p. 374).

Carranza had already raised the ire of revolutionary groups by refusing to fully support land reform, and his lack of support for the popular Obregón led to an uprising in Mexico City, led by that candidate and his supporters. Carranza fled to Tlaxcaltongo, Puebla, in central Mexico, only to be shot by one of his own guards while seeking refuge. After Obregón was elected, he adhered to the constitutional principles of agrarian reform, and during the time of his term in office "he distributed 921,627 hectares of land, almost five times more" than what had been distributed under Carranza (*ibid.*, p. 395). (One hectare is the equivalent of about 2.5 acres.)

Because the Mexican Revolution was a condensed period of such pervasive and pitched violence, it's clear why McCarthy would employ it as a background and underpinning to the Border Trilogy. It is interesting, however, that he chooses to meditate on the *legacy* of the revolution, not the time of the revolution itself, placing his books primarily in the 1940s and 1950s. (*The Crossing* takes place earlier than the other two novels, just before and during World War II.) The palpability of the revolution and the descriptions of its effects on the Mexican people — on an individual and community level — are yet another way in which McCarthy subverts the traditional Western. In making the revolution such an integral part of the trilogy, McCarthy also acknowledges the cultural hybridism of the Southwest. He melds the historical myths of the American West and Mexico, while reframing both.

• *Further reading*

Gonzales, Michael J. *The Mexican Revolution: 1910–1940*. Albuquerque: University of New Mexico Press, 2002.

Hamnett, Brian R. *A Concise History of Mexico*. Cambridge, UK: Cambridge University Press, 1999.

Krauze, Enrique. *Mexico: Biography of Power*. New York: HarperCollins, 1998.

La Botz, Dan. *Democracy in Mexico: Peasant Rebellion and Political Reform*. Cambridge, MA: South End Press, 1995.

Stacy, Lee, ed. *Mexico and the United States*. Tarrytown, NY: Marshall Cavendish, 2003.

Suchlicki, Jaime. *Mexico: From Montezuma to the Fall of the PRI*. Washington, D.C.: Brassey's, 2001.

Wegner, John. "'Mexico para los Mexicanos': Revolution, Mexico, and McCarthy's Border Trilogy." *Myth, Legend, Dust: Critical Responses to Cormac McCarthy*, ed. Rick Wallach. Manchester, UK: Manchester University Press, 2000.

The Mexican War

Historically, the Mexican War (sometimes known as the Mexican-American War) has been marked between the years 1846 and 1848, but the roots of the conflict well precede that, and the reverberations continued long after. More significantly for our purposes, *Blood Meridian* (1985) is set immediately in the wake of the main conflict, and the implications of the war and its root issues resonate throughout the novel.

In fact, in the early stages of the novel, the central character, the kid, is encouraged by a recruiter to join Captain White's outfit, with the purpose of heading into Sonora, "whip[ping] up on the Mexicans," and enjoying the spoils of war, primarily land (p. 29). The kid's response is: "The war's over," to which the recruiter tellingly responds, "[Captain White] says it aint over" (*ibid.*). Captain White, a self-presumed (if minor) agent of Manifest Destiny, tells the kid that the Mexicans, a "race of degenerates," are "manifestly incapable of governing themselves. And do you know what happens with people who cannot govern themselves? That's right. Others come in to govern for them" (p. 34).

Blood Meridian makes clear what history also underscores: The Mexican War may have been the official conflict, but the relationship between the two countries during the 1800s, particularly as the United States absorbed former Mexican lands, is one of deep-rooted complexity and often animus. An understanding of the Mexican War, though, is contingent upon a comprehension of events from preceding years, particularly those involving Texas.

By the 1820s, Texas was a northern province of Mexico, but it had allowed Moses Austin and his son Stephen to lead a large number of American settlers into the region. With the constant contention for land in this region, particularly between the United States and Mexico, this may seem like a strange thing to have done, but the reason was twofold: The government had been largely unable to get Mexicans to settle there and "needed to have the area populated as a buffer against both Indian depredations and the ... land hunger of the United States" (McCaffrey, p. 1).

There were terms of residency for the American settlers, however: They had to become Roman Catholics and Mexican citizens. In truth, though, the already unstable Mexican government was unable to monitor these conditions very closely in this far north province. Also, the land in Texas was much cheaper than in the United States, making this an irresistible offer for many.

The offer was so seductive that by 1830 Anglos far outnumbered Mexicans in the region, causing the Mexican government to forbid any further influx of Americans into Texas, a decree that was highly objectionable to the Texas colonists, who demanded a repeal and, furthermore, "statehood status within the Mexican territory" (*ibid.*, p. 2). In 1833, Mexico loosened restrictions on Texas, not wanting the region to achieve independence, but a bloody epoch was around the corner.

When Antonio López de Santa Anna assumed the presidency, he turned out to be a decidedly non-liberal and dictatorial leader, going so far as to abolish the Constitution of 1824, which had called for a federal republic much like the United States. Santa Anna's draconian rule was met with rebellion in the Mexican states of Zacatecas and Coahuila, but he forcefully put down these revolts. By 1835, Texas, led by commander in chief Sam Houston, had risen up in rebellion as well, seeking independence during the six months of violent engagement known as the Texas Revolution. The "Texians," as they were known, displayed much grit early on, winning a decisive battle at San Antonio and pushing Mexican forces back across the Rio Grande.

Santa Anna, incensed, redoubled the effort, the former general personally leading an army back to San Antonio, where they found approximately 150 Texians "standing firm in the old mission known as the Alamo" (*ibid.*, p. 3). While the defenders at the Alamo were able to hold off the Mexicans for a time, within two weeks all of the Texians, as well as the few reinforcement troops that came to their aid, had been killed.

In a separate engagement in Goliad, approximately 400 Texas rebels were captured, but rather than treat them as traditional prisoners of war, the Mexican troops marched the detainees out of Goliad in a few separate attachments, and then, in a surprise execution, halted the Texians and shot them while they stood in ranks.

Nevertheless, the savagery of the events at the Alamo and Goliad ignited the rebels (this is the genesis of the "Remember the Alamo!" battle cry), and Sam Houston led victorious forces at the key Battle of Jacinto, during which Santa Anna was captured and forced to sign a treaty declaring an independent Texas (a treaty he would later disavow).

Sam Houston's hope was that this independence would soon lead to Texas' U.S. statehood, but that was still seven years off. One of the key sticking points was the issue of slavery; as Congress was already struggling with the issue of slavery, northern politicians "opposed the annexation of another slave state" (Ward, p. 107). In addition, many

United States citizens of both the North and South "were no less hostile to incorporating within the United States a large new population of Indians and Hispanics" (*ibid.*). But as president of the Republic of Texas, Houston became a canny statesman, flirting with seeking a guarantee of independence from Britain and encouraging more settlers, from the United States as well as France and Germany. The years of independence were not without further violent border confrontations with Mexico, however.

During a diplomatic expedition to the Mexican town of Santa Fe, 300 Texians were seized and marched to prison in Mexico City, many perishing during the arduous journey. There were two failed raids into Texas by Mexico after the Santa Fe expedition as well, and then a group of Texans attempted to capture Mier, a Mexican village, with disastrous results: They were themselves captured by the much larger Mexican forces and marched toward Mexico City. Deep into the travail, the captured men escaped and scuttled back north. But most of them were overwhelmed by the harsh terrain and soon recaptured.

In a famous incident, the recaptured men were forced to draw beans from a jar. Those who drew white beans were allowed to live; the 17 men who drew black beans were shot. The Mier expedition makes an appearance in *Blood Meridian*, when the kid encounters a fellow Glanton Gang member who had been there: "He'd been at Mier where they fought until the draintiles and the gutters and the spouts ... ran with blood by the gallon and he told them how the brittle old spanish Bells would explode when hit" (p. 76).

Fortunately for Sam Houston and the Republic of Texas, the rabidly expansionist-minded James K. Polk assumed the American presidency, winning the election in 1844. Finally, under this new administration, Texas was admitted to the Union in December of 1845. The flint of the Mexican War was struck only months later, in May 1946, when "a Mexican Army splashed across the Rio Grande and attacked an American patrol" (Ward, p. 109). President Polk saw an opportunity to not only defeat the Mexicans in their northern provinces with a large force, but to then move those troops and the navy on to California to claim that highly coveted area for the Union as well. Suffice to say that the Mexican War perfectly suited the American ideal of expansion.

The war was a "bloody, desperate struggle that cost thousands of Mexican lives," and its end came in early 1848, when American troops swept straight into Mexico City (*ibid.*, p. 111). Geographically, the war represented a huge loss to Mexico, which sacrificed about half of its territory to the rapidly expanding United States. The war officially ended in February of 1848, when Mexico signed the Treaty of Guadalupe Hidalgo. The treaty formally recognized the annexation of Texas and also ceded California and New Mexico.

To understand the impact of this war and its importance to the work of Cormac McCarthy, consider the fact that the war officially carved out the American Southwest. Nevertheless, the war is only a chapter in the succession of claims over the region, the farthest reaching claims belonging to the indigenous people of the region, whose violent encounters with the Spanish (and later the Mexicans) stretched back centuries.

See also The American Southwest; *Blood Meridian*; History; The Mexican Revolution

• *Further reading*

McCaffrey, James M. *Army of Manifest Destiny: The American Soldier in the Mexican War (1846–1848)*. New York: New York University Press, 1992.

Singletary, Otis A. *The Mexican War*. Chicago: University of Chicago Press, 1962.

Ward, Geoffrey C. *The West: An Illustrated History*. New York: Little, Brown and Company, 1996.

Moss, Llewelyn

Llewelyn Moss is the unfortunate Texas everyman who kickstarts the action of *No Country for Old Men* (2005) when he comes upon a drug deal gone bad in the remote borderlands and steals more than two million dollars in drug money.

He is a down-on-his luck 36-year-old, a working-class welder and Vietnam veteran who resides in a trailer with his 19-year-old wife, Carla Jean, whom he met while she was working at the Wal-Mart. But in the parlance of Cormac McCarthy, he is also much more than all of that would suggest.

When we first encounter Moss, he is out hunting antelope in the desert, and as he stalks his quarry he passes by ancient pictographs etched into the rocks, the "men who drew them hunters like himself. Of them there was no trace" (p. 11). Moss, then, is a familiar figure in McCarthy's borderlands, and one who fits on the author's historical continuum of the region: he is a hunter and a man who has witnessed war firsthand. This connects him to the mid–1800s terrain of *Blood Meridian* (1985), as well as to the world of the men who carved those pictographs "perhaps a thousand years [ago]" (*ibid.*).

But McCarthy takes this doomed protagonist into new regions and toward a confrontation with newer manifestations of the same old evil. Moss sets out into the morning to hunt antelope, and in abandoning that quarry for a leather case of narcotics money, he breaks with the past. The violence, the blood, and the evil remain, but the bounty scalpers of *Blood Meridian* have been replaced by drug runners and the monstrous Judge Holden has been supplanted by Anton Chigurh, an "implacable mercenary who takes his job far beyond the limits of his profession, a morbid philosopher of murder for whom there are no exceptions to his errand of extermination" (Brancano, p. 77). These are new manifestations in the same geographical space that McCarthy has explored before, the borderlands — a contested space, a *frontera* space of illicit movements, dark enterprises, and blurred boundaries.

And if the novel yields up a certain connection to *Blood Meridian*, then Moss also links us to McCarthy's other Southwestern works, the Border Trilogy books. Though inhabiting a time (1980) that is a few decades beyond the world of John Grady Cole and Billy Parham, Moss calls to mind those protagonists. The *Washington Post* review saw this connection, noting, "Moss has a moral clarity reminiscent of John Grady Cole from *All the Pretty Horses* ... he knows he's making the worst mistake of his life but can't resist the temptation or the chance to test himself" (Lent). London's *Daily Mail* proclaimed him "a basically good-hearted man" (Ratcliffe), while the *Economist* review surmised,

"One senses that Llewelyn is motivated less by greed than by a determination to pick up what fate has thrown in his path like a gauntlet" ("Not a Pretty Sight").

Moss, however, does not stumble into his demise in the same manner that he stumbled upon the site of the drug massacre; as one academic put it, he is the "willing protagonist of a plot that will eventually overwhelm him, for he is aware ... he is setting in motion machinery that in the end will prove too large and sinister for him to control" (Brancano, p. 76).

But the money represents other things to Moss as well; in it he sees his "whole life ... sitting there in front of him. Day after day from dawn till dark until he was dead. All of it cooked down into forty pounds of paper in a satchel" (p. 18). On one level, he senses the full transpiring of his existence via that satchel ("Moss absolutely knew what was in the case and he was scared in a way that he didnt even understand" [p. 17]), but he also sees all of his lifelong labor and day-after-day existence boiled down to a monetary sum.

Moss's fatal flaw, however, is that "moral clarity" that the *Washington Post* review described. Woken from sleep by a troubled conscience—"[b]ut it wasn't the money that he woke up about" (p. 23)—he returns to the massacre site to aid a mortally wounded Mexican drug runner, an act that connects his identity to the stolen money. We also see evidence of his decency in his treatment of a young runaway girl that he picks up while being pursued. He gives her money and takes a mentor role toward her in their brief time together. Ultimately, of course, these are the very qualities that send Moss to his death, long before the ending of *No Country for Old Men*.

See also Chigurh, Anton; *No Country for Old Men*; Sheriff Bell

Mothers

McCarthy's representation of mothers in his work is ambivalent at best—with a host of cold and absent mothers littering his books. One can trace this tendency to the author's very first novel, *The Orchard Keeper* (1965), in which the central figure, John Wesley Rattner, is reared by a mother who is not only cold toward him but puts undue pressure on the boy to avenge his father: "You goin to hunt him out. When you're old enough," she tells the agonized boy. "Goin to find the man that took away your daddy" (p. 66).

Furthermore, she is deluded about John Wesley's father, who is little more than a drifter and petty criminal, considering him a good Christian and war hero. Such is her remoteness from her son that the central plot involves John Wesley seeking out surrogate parental relationships with bootlegger Marion Sylder and Uncle Ather, the self-ordained orchard keeper of the title. Furthermore, McCarthy renders the mother repellent through his physical descriptions of her: "Eyes ... blink when she swallows like a toad's. Lids wrinkled like walnut hulls. Her grizzled hair gathered, tight, a helmet of zinc wire" (p. 61). (The subsequent novel, *Outer Dark* (1968), presents a set of absent parents and a case of unrequited motherhood, as Rinthy Holme seeks to find her newborn throughout, coming up empty.)

One encounters an aloof mother to John Grady Cole in *All the Pretty Horses* (1992).

The distance between her and her son is made clear in the opening stages of the novel, as she sells off the ranch, and therefore Cole's inherited way of life, something that causes him complete dismay and which he considers utter betrayal. She also is one of McCarthy's frequently absent mothers in the text. The reader does not encounter her firsthand in the narrative — there is only a glimpse of her on stage, as she performs in a play; otherwise, she does not speak for herself and we do not become acquainted with her or her relationship to her son.

This absence deepens in other novels. In *Child of God* (1973) we learn early on that Lester Ballard's "mother had run off" (p. 21), leaving the future necrophiliac/killer alone with a father who will soon hang himself. The kid in *Blood Meridian* (1985) is also left with an insufficient father for the first 14 years of his life after his mother dies giving birth to him. The father, an alcoholic, "never speaks her name, the child does not know it," illustrating a striking absence (p. 3).

There is an alarming consistency to McCarthy's portrayals of absent or insufficient mothers. In fact, one can trace these representations all the way to 2006's *The Road*, in which the mother chooses to take her own life and leave behind the man and the boy rather than face the horrors that a post-apocalyptic world would serve up. Her break with her family is utterly cold: she refuses to say goodbye to the boy, says that she has "taken a new lover" (death), and repeatedly proclaims "I cant help you" to the man amid his pleadings and protestations (pp. 57–58). She exists only in memory in the book: "She was gone and the coldness of it was her final gift" (p. 58).

See also Fathers; Women

National Book Award

Cormac McCarthy's receipt of the National Book Award for fiction for his sixth novel, *All the Pretty Horses* (1992), coincided with his becoming a widely recognized, best-selling author after decades of critical acclaim but relative obscurity. Around this same time, McCarthy also won the National Book Critics Circle Award for fiction.

McCarthy, as is his fashion, did not attend the awards ceremony, but Knopf editor and publisher Sonny Mehta, speaking for the author, noted how "[g]iven what Cormac has accomplished over the last 27 years ... these books were not afforded wide success until lately." In this way, Mehta compared him to William Faulkner: "*The Sound and the Fury* was issued on the 7th of October, 1929, and despite its immediate claims on the literary conscience, this book enjoyed a sale of some 3,000 copies over a 15 year period." He added, "Awards and bestsellerdom come two ways, to paraphrase Hemingway.... Gradually, and then suddenly, if at all." He concluded his remarks by saying, "People have never doubted that with Cormac McCarthy, we were in the most vivid presence of a man whose books were made to last, so thank you all very much indeed" (Mehta).

The National Book Awards go back to 1950, when writers, editors, publishers and critics gathered for the inaugural event. The goal of the awards is to "recognize the best of American literature, raising the cultural appreciation of great writing in the country while advancing the careers of both established and emerging writers" (National Book Foundation). Since 1996, independent panels of five writers have bestowed awards in the categories of fiction, nonfiction, poetry, and young people's literature. In 1992, the year Cormac McCarthy was honored, awards were given in three categories, fiction, nonfiction, and poetry. The National Book Foundation organizes the awards.

See also All the Pretty Horses; Pulitzer Prize

Nature

When critics deliberate upon Cormac McCarthy's themes, the first thing typically addressed is the brutality and grimness of his vision; nevertheless, the author's keen sensitivity toward nature and the originality of his natural descriptions rival his penchant for rendering the more dreadful aspects of humanity (and sometimes the two motifs even intersect).

In a lengthy and insightful essay on McCarthy in a 2005 edition of the *New Yorker* James Wood described how the writer has been "a wonderfully delicate noticer of nature" throughout his career. Even in the epic historical bloodbath of *Blood Meridian* (1985) "nature is almost always precisely caught and weighed: in the desert, the stars 'fall all night in bitter arcs,' and the wolves trot 'neat of foot' alongside the horsemen," writes Wood. "[A]nd the lizards, 'their leather chins flat to the cooling rocks,' fend off the world 'with thin smiles and eyes like cracked stone plates'" (Wood). McCarthy's work contains what Gail Caldwell has termed "a near-mystical regard for the natural world" ("What Bond").

As a child growing up in eastern Tennessee, the author was highly attuned to the surrounding natural landscape and spent much time exploring it. "When I was a kid, I was very interested in the natural world," McCarthy told an interviewer in 2007. "To this day, during casual conversations, little-known facts about the natural world will just crop up" (*ibid.*). Malcom Jones, Jr., writing in *Newsweek*, noted that "in all his books, McCarthy delights in the natural world" and the "fatalistic harshness of the desert fits his temperament like handmade boots" (Jones, p. 68).

Long before he turned to the desert, though, one could trace the bold prominence of the natural world in his books. In his first novel, the eastern Tennessee–located *The Orchard Keeper* (1965), the central figures John Wesley Rattner and Arthur Ownby are characterized by their tendency to be "acutely at one with the natural world" (Arnold, "'Go to Sleep'"). The novel explores this connection, as well as the corrupting encounters between the forces of commerce and bureaucracy on the one hand and the natural environment on the other. In the novel the two seem like unruly wills at odds with each other.

This idea is put in place in the preface to *The Orchard Keeper*, when workers discover a wrought iron gate embedded in an elm tree. One man observes that the gate has in fact "growed all through the tree" (p. 1) (not that the tree — the living thing — has grown up around the iron object). Nature is not passive to these intrusions in the novel, though, and is an invasive force itself. When worker shacks are constructed (a harbinger of industry and commerce), green molds immediately grow over the structures: "Some terrible plague seemed to overtake them one by one" (p. 11). The natural ecosystem and the civilizational ecosystem exist simultaneously; as Georg Guillemin indicates, oftentimes "civilization represents but one ecosystem among many" in Cormac McCarthy's novels (p. 15).

Nature continues to be predominant in McCarthy's subsequent Southern novels. In *Outer Dark* (1968), one is presented with richly detailed, dark forests and vivid rural landscapes that seem straight out of fable or folklore — representing a psychological dreamscape (human "nature") that is much like a folk or fairy tale but even darker and much more unrelenting.

Lester Ballard, in *Child of God* (1973), retreats deeper and deeper into nature as he is expunged from society. But nature in *Child of God* is not always a bucolic place, and his movement deeper and deeper into the natural world, until he eventually resides in a cave, parallels his descent into the furthest, murkiest reaches of human nature. And the environment can be unruly and disordered in this novel; a shack that he takes up residence in is overrun by animals and penned in by lush overgrowth. The book overtly makes this connection between human nature and the natural world: "Disorder in the woods, trees down, new paths needed. Given charge Ballard would have made things more orderly in the woods and in men's souls" (p. 136).

In *Suttree* (1979) the life-sustaining natural resource of the Tennessee River is blighted and corrupted to a remarkable degree, with oil, human waste, condoms, and all sorts of detritus — even dead bodies — bubbling up out of the river and bobbing in its watery stretches. Again, though, nature is far from passive or bucolic. Cornelius Suttree's forays into the mountain wilderness force him to stand on the edge of death's chasm: In one instance an overhanging cliff collapses onto a young girlfriend; in another, his own mystic solo journey into the winter mountains brings him nearly to the point of death.

In fact, humans, nature, and industry often seem locked in some "paradoxical harmony of destruction" — what Guillemin regards as an egalitarian, "nonhierarchical" structure in McCarthy's work that is established by his aesthetic vision. Guillemin uses the example from *Suttree* of the burning train coursing through the snowy mountains to illustrate this point, an image that suggests a "shared tendency to entropy while integrating it into the dominant theme of natural beauty" (p. 15). As the old railroader remembers it, "That was in nineteen and thirty-one and if I live to be a hunnerd year old I don't think I'll ever see anything as pretty as that train on fire ... lightin up the snow and trees and the night" (*Suttree*, p. 182).

If one looks ahead to *The Crossing* (1994), that "paradoxical harmony of destruction" is evident in the she-wolf episode, which is so often read only for its natural pathos; but the wolf gives as good as it gets, ravaging livestock — destroying the humans' livelihood in order to sustain its own life (and the life of the unborn pups). Billy's attempt to save the she-wolf disrupts this destructive "harmony." (Destruction/harmony: We are often in the world of paradox when discussing Cormac McCarthy.) And this rupture leads to disastrous circumstances: Both the wolf and Billy's parents, whom he has abandoned to save the wolf, die terribly.

The "egalitarianism" that Guillemin alludes to in McCarthy's aesthetic vision might also be translated as such: His descriptions sometimes ascribe "natural" beauty to terrible things and "terribleness" to a natural world that is traditionally rendered as beautiful. (In the latter, he once again harkens back to Herman Melville.) This is embodied in the she-wolf, which is "at once terrible and of a great beauty" (*The Crossing*, p. 127).

This same terrible beauty appears again and again in the natural landscape of *Blood Meridian*, in which night falls "like a thunderclap," shooting stars drop "in bitter arcs," and weeds set to "gnashing" (p. 15). Mountain vistas appear "stark and black and livid like a land of some other order out there whose true geology was not stone but fear" (p. 47). Even a potentially beautiful sunset becomes "the red demise of day ... the distant pandemonium of the sun," an image that resonates the novel's titular emblem (p. 185). The natural, isolated, edenic La Purísima of *All the Pretty Horses* (1992), which contains "natural springs and clear streams" and "species of fish not known elsewhere on earth" (p. 97), as well as John Grady's true love and more wild horses than he could ever dream of, also becomes a place of dread and fear.

In *No Country for Old Men* (2005), set in 1980, the ancient tradition of the antelope hunt is intruded upon by the terrible new, new order: drug trafficking. Llewelyn Moss hunts in a landscape of "raw mountains," river breaks, and "baked terracotta terrain" (p. 8), surrounded by rock-carved pictographs "perhaps a thousand years old. The men who drew them hunters like himself" (p. 11). The sustenance he returns with from that natural landscape is drug money, though, not antelope—and it initiates devastation upon his life.

But the apotheosis of this view comes in *The Road* (2006), in which nature is not just described or envisioned in grim, corrupt, or sinister ways, but is in fact *dead*. The natural world has been rendered "barren, silent, godless" (p. 4), "[c]harred and limbless trunks of trees stretching away on every side" (p. 8). The empty hope of the sea, which the man and boy resolutely struggle toward, in anticipation of signs of life, is dead as well: "the ocean ... shifting heavily like a slowly heaving vat of slag and then the gray squall line of ash" (p. 215). "I'm sorry it's not blue, he said. / That's okay, said the boy" (*ibid.*). But, conversely, sometimes McCarthy attributes natural beauty to the unnatural: "the lights of the cities burning on the plain like stars pooled in a lake" (*Cities of the Plain*, p. 221).

All of this is not to undermine those moments when the beauty of the natural world is just that, though. For instance, when a young Billy Parham observes these balletic movements on the nighttime plain: "the wolves twisted and turned and leapt in a silence.... Loping and twisting. Dancing. Tunneling their noses in the snow. Loping and running and rising by twos in a standing dance and running on again" (*The Crossing*, p. 4). Or the last horse ride between father and son on an early March day (in *All the Pretty Horses*) "when the weather had already warmed and the yellow mexicanhat bloomed by the roadside" and the "creek was clear and green with trailing moss braided over the gravel bars." The snowy "thin blue ranges" marked distant points—that on this day at least seemed not so sinister at all (pp. 22–23).

See also Style; *The Orchard Keeper*

- *Further reading*

Guillemin, Georg. *The Pastoral Vision of Cormac McCarthy*. College Station: Texas A&M University Press, 2004.

No Country for Old Men

McCarthy's taut, intense crime thriller *No Country for Old Men* (2005) might seem like a departure or even a dalliance in genre for an author of such a literary pedigree, and in truth it is a pared-down version of McCarthy, cut back to a laser-sharp, fast-moving plot fraught with intrigue, narcotics, gunplay, police investigation, and lots and lots of bloodshed. One will also find less of the philosophizing and weighty ideas that crop up in the preceding Border Trilogy, and when the ruminations do crop up, they run more along the lines of "philosophy-lite" compared to previous novels.

Much of the ruminating comes from Sheriff Bell, during his italicized soliloquy chapters, which break from the main action to reveal Bell's inner thoughts. This stylistic flourish represents a major shift for McCarthy, who has consistently avoided getting inside his characters' heads and looking too deeply into their psychological motivations. Therefore, despite what appear on the surface to be the leaner, less lofty ambitions of *No Country for Old Men*—particularly when compared to baroque works such as *Blood Meridian* (1985) and *The Crossing* (1994)—this device represents a significant development and shift in McCarthy's rendering of his protagonists.

But *No Country for Old Men*, despite being a fast-paced action-thriller, also picks up a thread of continuity that, originating in *Blood Meridian*, ran straight through the Border Trilogy novels. In fact, the action of this novel takes place along such border towns of Texas as Sanderson and Del Rio and the city of El Paso—and even slips off into Mexico for a stretch, recalling the final Border Trilogy novel *Cities of the Plain* (1998), whose action also hewed closely to municipalities right up against the border.

In *Blood Meridian* and the Border Trilogy McCarthy used the geographical locale of the borderlands to delve into universal themes such as destiny and the very nature of being, but more specifically he found rich purchase in both the savage histories that opened the West and the layers of existences of the inhabitants (Native American, mercenary, settler, ranch cowboy), which crested and then sank toward oblivion.

No Country for Old Men takes place in 1980 and comes in the wake of all that, as the borderlands witness the rise of a new culture, one just as pervasive and significant as the scalp hunters of *Blood Meridian* or the cowboys of the Border Trilogy: dope dealers. And in McCarthy's worldview, the narcotics trade is just as malevolent as the motley band of murderers and scalp hunters who ran amok across the plains and deserts of *Blood Meridian*. Sheriff Ed Tom Bell, an old-timer nearing retirement and one of two central protagonists in the novel, including the doomed Llewelyn Moss, makes this observation about the new marauders of the plains, an observation that reverberates with Cormac McCarthy's own grim worldview:

> I think if you were Satan and you were settin around tryin to think up something that would just bring the human race to its knees what you would probably come up with was narcotics.

Maybe he did. I told that to somebody at breakfast the other mornin and they asked me if I believed in Satan... I had to think about that. I guess as a boy I did. Come the middle years my belief I reckon had waned somewhat. Now I'm starting to lean back the other way [*No Country for Old Men*, p. 218].

As the *Wall Street Journal* review put it, the novel "is rooted in the corruptions of the modern-day border — the world of human trafficking, drug smuggling ... against which Bell fights his losing battle" ("Not a Pretty Sight"). And in *No Country for Old Men*, the narcotics trade in these borderlands picks up a dark and continuous thread that goes back to Judge Holden in *Blood Meridian* and runs through the bloody memories of the Mexican Revolution that haunt *All the Pretty Horses* (1992) and *The Crossing* and the Sodom and Gomorrah-evoking *Cities of the Plain*, in which the just and noble John Grady Cole is knifed to death by, of all people, a Juárez pimp.

Narcotics is McCarthy's new evil, one just as pervasive and unharnessed as past evils — and one ultimately rooted in human nature. For Bell knows that where there's supply, there's also demand: "They sell that shit to schoolkids," says a fellow sheriff to Bell. "It's worse than that," responds Bell. "Schoolkids buy it" (p. 194). But for McCarthy, this is also the legacy and continuity of the land: "I thought about my family and about [*Uncle Ellis*]," ponders Bell, "and it just seemed to me that this country has got a strange kind of history and a damned bloody one too" (p. 284).

Another way in which *No Country for Old Men* picks up the thread of the previous four borderlands books is through the very characters of the two protagonists, Sheriff Bell and Llewelyn Moss. Wars are an important historical earmark for McCarthy, and reverberations of wars — the Mexican-American War, the Mexican Revolution, World War II — pulse through *Blood Meridian* and the Border Trilogy. Here, we have Bell, a veteran and alleged hero of World War II, and Moss, a 36-year-old Vietnam veteran.

The two, from different generations, have each witnessed firsthand the violence of two very different wars, but they are unequipped to deal with the kind of homefront battle being waged along the border. And for Cormac McCarthy the borderlands are a nerve center and hotspot for his universal themes of violence. In the final passages of the novel, Bell asserts that this part of the country "had not had a time of peace much of any length at all that I knew of" (p. 307).

But one of the ways in which *No Country for Old Men* deviates from both McCarthy's previous border books and typical crime thrillers is in the structure of the novel. Short, italicized chapters that are essentially Bell's inner monologues are interspersed between the action. In the monologues — which come off like lamentations — Bell meditates on aging, his own flaws, and how everything around him is changing for the worse. In these lamentations we find the basis for the book's title, which is from the first lines of Irish poet William Butler Yeats' "Sailing to Byzantium." In that poem, the aged speaker, much like McCarthy's sheriff, finds himself painfully out of step with the world around him: "That is no country for old men. The young / In one another's arms, birds in the trees / — Those dying generations — at their song."

The pessimistic slant in the lines also fits the worldview that McCarthy has carved out in his novels — that is, this idea that generations, even at their peak, are soon bound to pass and sink toward extinction, ushering in a new culture fated to do the same.

(Interestingly, another Western novel, Larry McMurtry's debut, *Horseman, Pass By*, released in 1961—which was adapted into the Paul Newman movie *Hud*—also takes its title from a Yeats poem.)

That theme is consistent with McCarthy's previous four books, as in his borderlands work he consistently gazes into that brief window of time between a culture's existence and obliteration. An apt title for the book might have been "No Country for Old Cowboys"; in fact, Bell's heritage is similar to that of John Grady Cole and Billy Parham from the Border Trilogy. Bell's father, like John Grady Cole, was a keen trainer of horses who spoke to the animals in an intuitive manner. His Uncle Ellis has a "clouded eye" from being thrown from a horse years ago, and Ellis had turned to law enforcement decades before, knowing that it paid "about the same as cowboyin" (p. 267). Bell's history will be familiar to those who have read *All the Pretty Horses*; just as John Grady's ancestors died in all sorts of mishaps that can be attributed to the hard ways of the West, so too did Bell's great uncle Mac get "shot down on his own porch" by a group of Indians in 1879 (p. 269).

Bell is also descended from another lawman, his grandfather, but the type of traditional Texas lawman that Bell represents, with his old moral codes, is not sufficient to this modern age. As Bell laments: "[T]he worst of it is knowin that probably the only reason I'm even still alive is that they have no respect for me. And that's very painful" (p. 217). These wistful soliloquies regarding his failings — interspersed between gunplay, lightning-paced action, and death — provide a compelling contrast, a softer, elegiac focus that cuts against the grain of the manhunt. And as is often the case in McCarthy's novels, things simply don't work out for the better or resolve themselves — Bell, despite great effort, keeps running up against his own insufficiencies, and he is ultimately unable to protect anyone. In fact, Llewelyn Moss, the unfortunate everyman protagonist on the run — with millions of dollars that he recovered from a drug exchange gone wrong in the desert — dies well before the book ends.

But it is Anton Chigurh, McCarthy's most distinct villain since *Blood Meridian*'s Judge Holden, who truly proves to be a force beyond Bell's or anyone else's control. Chigurh is not rendered as sensationally as Judge Holden — and is quite different — but he has that special sense of strangeness that McCarthy invests in his darkest characters. This strangeness often comes from paradox: for example, Judge Holden's simultaneous savagery and refinement. Chigurh, paradoxically, is a cold-blooded killer with a strangely unshakable moral code. Long after Moss is dead, Chigurh seeks out Moss' wife, Carla Jean, to kill her as well. Chigurh has recovered the money and killed Moss; therefore, there seems no tangible reason for it:

> She sat slumped forward, holding her hat in her arms.
> You've got no cause to hurt me, she said.
> I know. But I gave my word.
> Your word?
> Yes. We're at the mercy of the dead here. In this case your husband.
>
> .   .   .
>
> I don't have the money. You know I ain't got it.
> I know.

You give your word to my husband to kill me?
Yes.
He's dead. My husband is dead.
Yes. But I'm not [p. 255].

Chigurh not only strictly adheres to his own code of honor — making him a yin to Bell's yang — but he's an ascetic, somehow beyond the greed that drives so many. As he puts it to Wells, a fellow bounty hunter, before he kills him: "You think I'm like you. That it's just greed. But I'm not like you. I live a simple life" (p. 177).

All of these qualities make Chigurh a psychopath, and, moreover, a zealot who acts out of unwavering adherence to principle. Before he kills Carla Jean, he tells her, "All followed to this. The accounting is scrupulous. The shape is drawn. No line can be erased.... And the shape of your path was visible from the beginning" (p. 259). This kind of rationale, under the banner of an unwavering grand design, makes Chigurh, in his own mind, no longer a killer but an agent of a divine destiny. The drug trade at the core of the novel's darkness subsists on greed and human weakness, but in Chigurh we see something more insidious: A man of strict principle, as deranged as those principles may be. However, to all but Bell and those whom he has killed Chigurh remains a phantasm; even to Bell, who knows that he exists, he is a cipher. As Bell tells a judge:

He's pretty much a ghost.
Is he pretty much or is he one?
No, he's out there. I wish he wasn't. But he is [p. 299].

And through Chigurh, Bell comes to the kind of final realization that one rarely encounters in a crime thriller: "the answer," he thinks, "is that when you encounter certain things in the world ... you realize that you have come upon somethin that you may very well not be equal to and I think that this is one of them things" (*ibid.*). Even in this genre, resolution is a messy business for McCarthy; the novel concludes by returning to the elements and nature, by slipping back into a primordial reverie. First, Bell contemplates a water trough carved out of stone at his family home, noting how it had been there for perhaps 200 years, and how it stood to "last ten thousand years" (p. 307).

No Country for Old Men was well received upon its release, though most reviewers acknowledged that the book was to be taken for what it was: an easily consumable crime thriller, and not one of McCarthy's more weighty parables. The *New York Times* noted:

After the critical and popular triumphs of *All the Pretty Horses* and its sequels ... McCarthy found himself so thoroughly trussed in garlands and draped in medals that it's a wonder he could breathe ... [so] he decided to have some nasty fun and write like a fellow who was still alive, shedding the murky, grand German philosophizing that bogged down the last two installments of his trilogy for a sleeker, slimmer linguistic manner and a darting movie-ready narrative that rips along like hell on wheels because it has no desire to break new ground [Kirn].

The *Washington Post* proclaimed, "This is an entertaining novel from one of our best writers. Often seen as a fabulist and an engineer of dark morality tales, McCarthy is first a storyteller." But the review ultimately asserted that "*No Country for Old Men* is a minor addition to his work" (Lent). The *Boston Globe* noted that the novel was suspenseful, but "at its best ... is a simple, heartsore story: one of an old Army salt with a daughter he misses and a wife he loves, and a mean-eyed killer who moves with the force of Robo-Cop" (Caldwell, "Lone Star Cauldron," p. D6).

The 2007 movie version of McCarthy's novel, directed by Joel and Ethan Coen, garnered much more excitement, while staying true to the novel, and won an Academy Award for Best Picture. In fact, McCarthy's novel had begun its life as a screenplay in 1984, and he later adapted that effort into a book. This, perhaps, goes a long way to describing the pared-down, gripping, and entertaining nature of *No Country for Old Men*.

- *Further reading*

Kirn, Walter. "Texas Noir." *The New York Times Book Review*, July 24, 2005.
Lent, Jeffrey. "Blood Money." *The Washington Post*. July 17, 2005.

The Orchard Keeper

Cormac McCarthy's first novel, *The Orchard Keeper* (1965), has a Southern Gothic atmosphere and descriptive energy clearly reminiscent of William Faulkner. One can sense Faulkner's influence in the supernatural light McCarthy casts on rural life, in the shifting narrative perspectives, and in the heightened language that infuses seemingly discrete actions with universally mythic resonance. But it is also often deemed a difficult work, and not as immediately appealing as much of McCarthy's canon. (The same could be said of the book's successor, *Outer Dark* [1968].) One critic summed it up as "Cormac McCarthy's demanding first novel" (Ragan, p. 17).

Upon the book's publication, the *New York Times* was openly critical of it, deeming it notable for the "traditional folkways and folk speech, sounds and smells of the natural world, and the violent behavior of men not yet truly civilized" but declaring the "highly gifted" Cormac McCarthy (then 32 years of age) to be "handicapped ... by excessive admiration for William Faulkner" (Prescott). Nevertheless, in this grotesquely descriptive and unremittingly dark novel McCarthy is already engaging in stylistic flourishes and themes that he will use and develop throughout his career, and the knotty, but finely crafted narrative has found plenty of admirers as the decades have worn on.

The most prominent of these themes is the natural world and human beings' connections to it. Few writers describe landscapes like McCarthy; in fact, nature is invested with so much life in *The Orchard Keeper* that it becomes less a canvas or backdrop and more a driving force—even an omniscient and lurking character. People "are not privileged as subjects" (Phillips, p. 443) and humans and nature become equals, "parts of the same continuum" (*ibid.*, p. 446). In *The Orchard Keeper*, trees even speak, murmuring "low admonitions" and shushing to sleep John Wesley Rattner, the boy at the nexus of the narrative (p. 65).

McCarthy truly exults in his vivid landscape descriptions, and he artistically crests in his first novel when he focuses his stylistic firepower on natural scenes. He invests the forested hills of eastern Tennessee with a primordial and mysterious resonance, like "some steamy and carboniferous swamp where ancient saurians lurk in feigned sleep" (p. 11).

Nature consistently rises up against the novel's action as something ancient and resistant to order; it is pre-bureaucracy, pre-commerce, pre–Christian.

But these descriptions of the natural world also have a significant plot function. For one, McCarthy's narrative blurs the line between nature and "human nature," to show that despite an often harsh relationship, they are on that same continuum mentioned earlier. Plant life is invested with human qualities; therefore, "clutching" tree roots "brace themselves against" a slope (p. 11) and "hot winds" are akin to "rancid breath" (p. 10). Conversely, Rattner's doomed, criminal-minded father, Kenneth, slithers like a reptile through a store (p. 8), while laborers are compared to "migratory birds" (p. 12) and old men in the general store are compared to vultures. When Kenneth Rattner's lips touch a beer glass they fasten "on it white and fat as leeches" (p. 22). McCarthy uses the descriptive strategy of the grotesque — a creative flourish often attributed to the Southern Gothic style of Faulkner, Carson McCullers and others — to fuse humans and the natural world in an unsettling manner.

The line between people and nature isn't the only muddled delineation in *The Orchard Keeper*; the natural world and industry also become intertwined — *interpenetrated*, in fact. In an evocative and mysterious preface (a short, italicized passage before the start of book 1), two anonymous men, one white and one black, as well as a boy, struggle to cut an old elm tree into sections with a large saw. When they finally spy the source of their trouble, it turns out to be a wrought iron gate that is embedded in the trunk. The white man exclaims, "It's growed all through the tree" (p. 1). This is a very significant and portentous idea for the reader to have in mind when entering the novel proper. It is not the tree that has grown up around the fence; it is the iron that has "growed" through the tree.

The man, in one observation, invests the metal with natural life and sets up an image of industry fully encroaching on nature, permeating "all through" it in fact. Thus, the crudely constructed shack houses of itinerant workers are like wildlife, squatting "like great brooding animals" (p. 11), and thus the orchard of the title has a giant steel tower in its center, invading and looming over the natural domain that is central to the novel. (The tower has some unexplained and mysterious government purpose.)

Nevertheless, if the blurred line between *humans* and nature exists on the same continuum, the intermingling of domestic industry and the natural world is toxic and corrupting. The aforementioned worker shacks are invaded and rotted by "gangrenous molds" before they are even fully constructed: "Some terrible plague seemed to overtake them one by one" (p. 11). In another foreboding image, a litter of kittens stumbles around unsteadily and blindly, with eyes "festered with mucus, as if they might have been struck simultaneously by some biblical blight" (p. 180). The kittens are a domesticated feline, a clear symbolic contrast to the fabled mountain lion or panther ("painter" in the book's phonetic dialect) that roams the forest around the community and which is spoken of in reverent, mythical tones by the characters in *The Orchard Keeper*.

The modern way of life has a corrupting effect of biblical proportions on the old, more natural relationship between people and nature: plagues and blight and a corrosion of nature — and "human nature." Those who resist the inevitable encroachment of modernity are in for trouble in *The Orchard Keeper*, for at the center of the novel is an attrition of rural traditions and value systems in the face of commerce and bureaucracy. As critic David Paul Ragan puts it, "McCarthy depicts a world in which traditional embodiments of value — religion, community, relationships, agrarian connections with the earth — have deteriorated as a result of ... commercial interests and governmental intrusions" (Ragan, p. 17). At a very basic level, *The Orchard Keeper*, primarily set in the 1930s, is an elegy to a more pastoral and basic way of life.

Young John Wesley Rattner is at the intersection of this conflict. He is coming of age in the community with the opposing pressures of tradition and modernization upon him. The boy's "literal" father, Kenneth Rattner, is a thief and wanderer who only returns to the community of Red Branch long enough to steal money before he is off again. Further complicating things, Marion Sylder, another Red Branch resident and charismatic bootlegger, murders Kenneth in an act of self-defense and pitches his body into an abandoned concrete pit (once used for pesticides) in the orchard.

Sylder befriends the orphaned John Wesley and the two bond over the ancient traditions of bloodhounds, hunting, and trapping, neither knowing that Sylder is the murderer of John's father. Meanwhile, Rattner Senior's body lies decomposing in the concrete pit. To complicate things, John's mother has made him pledge to one day track down his father's killer and vindicate his father. (She is deluded about Kenneth's lifestyle and speaks of him as a war hero.)

The other mentor figure to young John is Arthur Ownby, identified in the earlier stages of the novel as only "the old man." (He is also known as "Uncle Ather" — i.e., "Arthur" in the book's vernacular.) Ownby is the orchard keeper of the title, a de facto overseer of the natural landscape who discovers Kenneth Rattner's body in the pit in a shocking revelation, the "green face leering" up out of the "rotting water" at him and the "hair dark and ebbing like seaweed" (p. 54). Notice how this horrific image picks up on the central imagistic themes: the green skull and seaweed hair blurring the line between human and nature and the "rotting" water and decomposing body suggesting a corruption of both the natural and human worlds.

Ownby, more overtly than the bootlegger Sylder, represents the traditional relationship to the land, a dying way of life. Ragan points out Ownby's "mystical connection to the cycles of nature" (Ragan, p. 18), and one of the reader's first glimpses finds him perched on the branch of a peach tree in the orchard, as if he is an organic part of the landscape. As a keeper of the orchard, he also feels compelled to keep watch over the body in the spray pit, and he ritualistically lays cut cedars over the makeshift grave for a period of seven years, based on the ancient folklore that if people haven't been given a proper burial "their soul takes up in a cat for a spell" (p. 227). Ownby lives an existence that is not tied to money or commerce but is sharply attuned to the seasons, folklore, the weather, and the landscape.

When mysterious government bureaucrats build a large metal tank with a fence around it in the orchard, Ownby spends much time pondering it, and then without explanation takes a shotgun and shoots a crude "X" on the sinister invader, as if inscribing it with a talismanic code to ward off the intrusion. (McCarthy rarely tips his hand to his characters' psychology or motivations, and Ownby's actions are never explained.) Ownby's resistance to the new — or, rather, his simple desire to maintain his pastoral mode of existence — becomes his undoing, and he ends up on the wrong side of the law, incarcerated in a mental institution after a shootout with the authorities and a period hiding out as a fugitive deep in the remote woods. Sylder, the boy's other mentor and his only "true" parental figure — i.e., one that shows genuine concern for him — also runs afoul when he is caught bootlegging and imprisoned in Brushy Mountain.

Much of *The Orchard Keeper*'s fascination also lies in McCarthy's grotesque rendering of the community of Red Branch. With an unflinching hand, he weaves an often phantasmagoric landscape where everything seems misshapen, odd, and fantastical. Even Ownby's old dog seems blighted, with its missing patches of fur and stitched belly. Sylder suffers from deformity as well, with part of his big toe missing. The boy is fascinated by it, and notices that it looks "sort of like a nose" (p. 111). The old men who gather in the roach-infested general store are a strange crew as well, with "a vulturous look about them, their faces wasted and thin, their skin dry and papery as a lizard's" (p. 115). In the market, one witnesses "old women with faces like dried fruit set deep in their hooded bonnets, shaggy striated and hooktoothed as coconut carvings" (p. 82).

In McCarthy's painstakingly and vividly rendered Red Branch, the bizarre is the commonplace: A boy flies a gross-looking pet buzzard like a kite, a string attached to the fowl's leg; a flimsy tavern deck suspended over a gully pitches off into the chasm, and the men crawl from the pit angry and brawling, like some ancient warrior race; a seedy town official labors in the spray pit for days, scavenging in the ashes of Kenneth Rattner's body based on a rumor that Rattner had a valuable platinum plate in his head.

These grotesque, corrupted details are a sharp contrast to the descriptions of Ownby's mystical connection to nature, the genuine paternal affection Sylder shows for John, and John's own formless desperation and the heightened language with which McCarthy renders it. In one passage regarding the latter, the boy runs aimlessly through the country night in a fit of formless pique and anxiety, only to stagger back home emotionally spent: "The morning is yet to the nether end of the earth, and he is weary," writes McCarthy. "Bowing the grass in like sadness the dew followed him home and sealed his door" (p. 67).

This archaic, romantic language is reserved for figures such as John and Ownby, casting them in a different, more stylized light than the more depraved elements of the community — i.e., those that have surrendered to the influence of commerce, bureaucracy and the new order. Sylder, despite being a bootlegger, is also akin to John and Ownby, both for his paternal care of John and because his very vocation resists the corrupted laws and bureaucracy of the community.

McCarthy puts the final flourish on this elegy in the final pages, which leap ahead several years to John returning home to visit Red Branch as an adult. "They are gone now," McCarthy writes in the final passage of this elegy to a way of life, "no vestige of that people remains. On the lips of the strange race that now dwells there their names are myth, legend, dust" (p. 246). During this visit, John visits the grave of his mother, who had died in the intervening years. (In typical, mysterious McCarthy fashion, we are not sure where he is returning from. War? Has he become the actual war hero that his mother falsely claimed Kenneth Rattner was? The mother's date of death on the tombstone is 1945.) In a conciliatory gesture, John simply pats the tombstone, an act that speaks to the ambivalent relationship with his mother.

The final scene also returns us to the book's opening image of the elm tree that had been invaded by wrought iron. First, John hears the click of a stoplight on the street next to the cemetery, a touch of modernization that creates even more distance from the traditional way of life. A man and a woman are in the car at the stoplight. John, in neighborly fashion, waves to them once, and then when they simply stare at him and at each other, he waves again. They stare and pull away.

This is one of those seemingly simple scenes that speak to so much more, and *The Orchard Keeper* is filled with such objective, unexplained, but resounding passages. As John winds his way out of the graveyard, he passes by a stump littered with wood dust and chips and passes through "a gap in the fence, pas the torn iron palings and out to the western road" (p. 246). McCarthy doesn't highlight it, but this seems to be the elm and wrought-iron gate that the anonymous workers had struggled with in the opening passage, the elm with iron "growing" through it that evoked the penetration of industry into rural traditions. John, "the boy," now grown up, steps through opening created by this rupture and heads west, leaving it all behind.

With McCarthy's subsequent fame, including his career-defining Border Trilogy, *The Orchard Keeper* risks getting overshadowed, but in this first published novel, we witness a writer who is already a master stylist and engaging themes he would take up later. *The Orchard Keeper* is rich and packed with startlingly impressionistic moments and heightened description. The 1965 novel has aged well, and it still stands up as relevant, insightful, and timeless — if difficult.

• *Further reading*

Berry, K. Wesley. "The Lay of the Land in Cormac McCarthy's *The Orchard Keeper* and *Child of God*." *The Southern Quarterly* 38, no. 4 (2000), pp. 61–77.

Brickman, Barbara Jane. "Imposition and Resistance in Cormac McCarthy's *The Orchard Keeper*." *The Southern Quarterly* 38, no. 2 (2000), pp. 123–134.

Ragan, David Paul. "Values and Structure in *The Orchard Keeper*." *Perspectives on Cormac McCarthy*, eds. Edwin T. Arnold and Dianne C. Luce. Jackson: University Press of Mississippi, 1999.

Outer Dark

Because Cormac McCarthy has a tendency to imbue his novels with such a distinct sense of time and place, *Outer Dark* (1968) represents a wholly different kind of challenge for the reader. Throughout his career, McCarthy has been very specific regarding the settings of novels, whether it is the 1950s Knoxville, Tennessee, of *Suttree*; the late 1940s and 1950s American Southwest and Mexico of the Border Trilogy; the 1980 Texas borderlands of *No Country for Old Men*; or even the pre–World War II Tennessee setting of his first novel, *The Orchard Keeper*. One gets a vague sense of setting — most likely Appalachia — in *Outer Dark* simply on the basis of vernacular, but McCarthy offers few specifics. The main characters, brother and sister Culla and Rinthy Holme, are from a "Johnson County," which one could assume to be in eastern Tennessee (but there are numerous other counties of that name in different states, including several in the South).

In addition, the time of *Outer Dark* appears to be archaic and pre-mechanized, but again there are few particulars offered that would pin it down. Women wear bonnets, people travel by mule-drawn wagons, and the guilty hang by their necks from trees — that much *Outer Dark* offers us; the rest is left to supposition. There is also a folklorish or even fairy tale–like pall that hangs over the novel — for example, the main characters often travel by foot on a path through the nighttime forest, encountering many sorts of peculiar characters.

Taking into account all of these elements, *Outer Dark* stacks up to be as much a psychological as literal landscape, and this perspective is the best means to get a wedge into this darkly evocative tale. For one, the novel has the unmistakable psychological force of a fairy tale, though the subject matter — incest between brother and sister, as well as infanticide — is certainly extreme for that genre. Nevertheless, the parentless siblings and their respective voyages, as well as the various characters (including a tinker who steals away a baby), the hyper-natural setting, and the archaic temporality certainly place *Outer Dark* in a mode much like a fairy tale.

Distinguished psychologist Bruno Bettelheim, who famously gauged the psychological implications of the fairy tale world in *The Uses of Enchantment* (1976), described how "on an overt level fairy tales teach little about the conditions of life in modern mass society.... But more can be learned from them about the inner problems of human beings" (p. 5). This begins to place us in the world of McCarthy's novel, which makes little sense when the rules of waking reality are applied to it. For example, there is a confusing sense of temporality. At one point, a doctor notes that six months have elapsed since Rinthy gave birth, yet in the narrative structure mere days seemed to have elapsed since that time. Jay Ellis notes how *Outer Dark*'s "indeterminate spatial and temporal qualities round it like a dream" (*No Place for Home*, p. 292). When one examines the novel for its psychological implications, it yields up much more than a more literal reading would.

In fact, *Outer Dark* often comes off like a turgid dreamscape. Edwin T. Arnold, writing on the Cormac McCarthy Society website, noted how the novel "seems derived from the world of folklore or dream, peopled as it often is by mysterious denizens and ruled by some nightmare logic which makes one question at what level of reality the story operates" (Arnold, *Outer Dark* synopsis). Fairy tales often present a close set of siblings, male and female, who are pushed out of the safe orbit of familiarity and set off on the "excruciatingly painful experience" of separation and journey, one that is "fraught with many psychological dangers" and leads to self-actualization (Bettelheim, p. 79).

For Culla and Rinthy this manifests itself in two very different journeys. In the Brother's Grimm story "Brother and Sister," the siblings represent an "essentially inseparable unity," with the brother manifesting "the endangered aspect" of that unity (*ibid*). One finds that same resonance in *Outer Dark*, though the incestuous union between the siblings and Culla's abandonment of the child of that union in the woods adds a whole different level of malevolence. (Additionally, it should be noted that the union between brother and sister may not have been consensual.)

But psychologically, Culla certainly is the more "endangered" of the two, something that is revealed almost immediately in the novel. In their insular, wooded cabin — with no other family to speak of — Rinthy bears the physical burden of childbirth, but Culla bears the deepest psychological wounds from their incestuous union. In the book's opening Rinthy wakes him from a dream after hearing him "hollerin" in his sleep. It is a dream in which Culla is one among a group of ragged supplicants seeking the healing powers of a prophet, a "beggared multitude ... [a] delegation of human ruin" plagued with blindness, "puckered stumps and leprous sores" (p. 5). But Culla, among them because of his own moral infirmity, nevertheless stands apart as different in the crowd.

For one, his infirmity is not physically visible — indeed, the prophet is "surprised to see him there amidst such pariahs" when Culla cries out to be cured (*ibid.*). In addition, the very sun drops from the sky, bringing darkness, when confronted by Culla's malady, causing the rest of the assembled to turn on him "with howls of outrage" (p. 6). In this opening scene, McCarthy establishes the degree to which Culla's psyche is tormented by his actions.

Culla's psychological journey entails confronting this embittered psyche. This is allegorized in the form of shadow figures that appear in the form of the ominous trio that is always one step behind or in front of him, despite the randomness of his flight (an ongoing coincidence clearly best explained by a psychological reading). The reader is clued into this in the novel's short opening passage, which describes the movements of the trio and employs the word "shadow" three times in the lengthy first sentence. (They are also described as "shapes" and "in silhouette" in that opening page.) This is Culla's "outer dark" of the title, which is a manifestation and projection of his inner dark.

Interestingly, Carl Jung's shadow archetype is described as "a dark companion which dogs our steps" (Stevens, p. 64), much like the trio, which always remains somewhere in Culla's orbit. Jung also described how the shadow figure appears in dreams as a "sinister or threatening figure possessing the same sex as the dreamer" and often as a predator or "evil stranger" (*ibid.*). The leader of the trio is the most potent shadow representation, particularly because, like Culla, he is a father — and Culla's greatest crimes are in the name of fatherhood. In fact, the greatest sleight of hand in *Outer Dark* is to render the father of the trio in such malignant terms that he, in effect, upstages Culla Holme's own dreadful actions. Consider the campfire infanticide committed by the shadow father:

> Holme saw the blade wink in the light like a long cat's eye slant and malevolent and a dark smile erupted on the child's throat and went all broken down the front of it. The child made no sound. It hung there with its one eye glazing over like a wet stone and the black blood pumping down its naked belly [p. 236].

Such is the abject, gut-wrenching dread of the description that one might forget for a moment that Culla had left the baby to die much earlier in the novel; the shadow figure is in fact finishing the task that Culla so cowardly botched much earlier when he abandoned the baby, laying it on a bed of moss deep in the forest to howl "redgummed at the pending night," as Culla "lumbered away through the brush without looking back" (p. 16). McCarthy effectively projects Culla's malevolent qualities onto the evil father;

moreover, Culla wallows in self-delusion and denial, and the father of the trio represents a shadow projection of Culla's own repressed shortcomings.

Throughout the novel, this idea carries itself out through Culla's apparent persecution — he is constantly being held accountable for crimes in which he appears to have had no hand, such as grave robbery and the plunging death of a swine herder. Jung details how "man is, as a whole, less good than he imagines himself" and "how the less [the shadow] is embodied in the individual's conscious life, the blacker and denser it is" (Stevens, p. 93). Hence the degree of evil with which McCarthy invests the shadow father in the novel.

Furthermore, such is the degree of Culla's self-delusion and apparent persecution in the novel — he is in constant flight throughout — that the reader falls into the same perspective, viewing Culla through the character's own psychological lens, causing Culla's own detrimental actions toward his sister and child fade into the background. This idea of the shadow nature is also figuratively expressed when Culla peers into an exhumed coffin and witnesses the peculiar sight of two entwined figures, one black and one white: "Across the desiccated chest lay a black arm ... the old man shared his resting place with a negro sexton ... who clasped him in an embrace of lazarous depravity" (p. 88). More specifically, there is this image of Culla early in the novel, when he and Rinthy are still holed up in the cabin (and when Culla is still referred to as only "the man"): "In the yard the man's shadow pooled at his feet, a dark stain in which he stood. In which he moved" (p. 13). At another point Culla is described as "manacled to a shadow that struggled grossly in the dust," a stirring image that is fully emblematic of his psychological torment and looming Jungian shadow (p. 131).

Because, by contrast, Rinthy's intentions and actions are altruistic, her psychological journey in *Outer Dark* is quite different. Rinthy's impulses are purely maternal; her goal is to recover her baby from the tinker, who found the "chap" abandoned in the forest. And, again, there is a parallel to the Brother's Grimm fairy tale "Brother and Sister" — though, as one would suspect, in McCarthy's novel there is no living happily ever after.

In *The Uses of Enchantment* Bettelheim discusses the "contrast between the brother's giving in to the proddings of his instinctual desires and the sister's ego- and superego-motivated concern for her obligations" and declares that "what redeems us as human beings and restores us to our humanity is solicitude for those whom we love" (p. 83). Thus, we see the outer world reflecting her inner drive, as she is taken in by strangers and given food and shelter (though some of the strangers are quite sketchy in and of themselves).

Rinthy's journey also differs from Culla's because she is not plagued with her brother's sense of denial and repression regarding their union. Robert L. Jarrett notes how the differing orientations of Culla and Rinthy lead to "two opposing forms of alienation: alienation created by Culla's repression of his sin and guilt and by Rinthy's acceptance of hers" (p. 19). Jarrett also describes how the book's title is "emblematic" of this "psychological alienation" (p. 20).

Nevertheless, despite the psychological implications manifest in *Outer Dark*, it has received the most scant critical attention of all of McCarthy's novels. Perhaps this can be ascribed to the novel being, as one reviewer put it, "the strangest and most formally challenging of all [McCarthy's] novels," and a work that combines "tortuous prose rhythms and a recondite vocabulary with disjointed plotting, tight suspense and unreasoning terror" (Hill). The novel certainly breaks from the more accessible structure and style of its predecessor, *The Orchard Keeper* (1965), and has none of the histrionic grossness of the novel that followed it, *Child of God* (1973). In fact, McCarthy has not produced any other work that could even be loosely compared, in intent and style, to *Outer Dark*.

- *Further reading*

Bettelheim, Bruno. *The Uses of Enchantment*. New York: Alfred A. Knopf, 1976.

Guillemin, Georg. "'Beyond the World of Men': Emergent Ecopastorialism in the Southern Novels." *The Pastoral Vision of Cormac McCarthy*. College Station: Texas A&M University Press, 2004, pp. 18–72.

Jarrett, Robert L. "*Outer Dark*: Alienation and Isolation, the Exile and the Outcast." *Cormac McCarthy: Twayne's United States Author Series*. New York: Twayne Publishers, 1997, pp. 18–20.

_____. "*Outer Dark*: Parodic Families." *Cormac McCarthy: Twayne's United States Author Series*. New York: Twayne Publishers, 1997, pp. 16–17.

Sullivan, Nell. "The Evolution of the Dead Girlfriend Motif in *Child of God* and *Outer Dark*." *Myth, Legend, Dust: Critical Responses to Cormac McCarthy*, ed. Rick Wallach. Manchester, UK: Manchester University Press, 2000, pp. 68–77.

Ownby, Arthur

Arthur Ownby, identified in the earlier stages of *The Orchard Keeper* as "the old man," and later as "Uncle Ather" (i.e., "Arthur" in the book's vernacular), is the orchard keeper of the title, a de facto overseer of the natural landscape. He discovers Kenneth Rattner's body in the old orchard spray pit in a shocking revelation, the "green face leering" up out of the "rotting water" at him and the "hair dark and ebbing like seaweed" (p. 54), a horrific image that picks up on the central imagistic themes of the novel: the green skull and seaweed hair blurring the line between human and nature and the "rotting" water and decomposing body suggesting a corruption of both the natural and human worlds.

Ownby represents the traditional relationship to the land, a dying way of life. Ownby has what critic David Paul Ragan calls a "mystical connection to the cycles of nature" (p. 18). In fact, an early glimpse finds him perched on the branch of a peach tree in the orchard, as if he is an organic part of the landscape. As a keeper of the orchard, he also feels compelled to keep watch over the body in the spray pit, and he ritualistically lays cut cedars over the makeshift grave for a period of seven years, based on the ancient folklore that if a person hasn't been given a proper burial his "soul takes up in a cat for a spell" (p. 227).

Ownby lives a nearly obsolete existence that is not tied to money or commerce, but is sharply attuned to the seasons, folklore, the weather, and the landscape. When mysterious government bureaucrats build a large metal tank with a fence around it in the orchard, Ownby spends much time pondering it, and then without explanation takes a shotgun and shoots a crude "X" on the sinister invader, as if inscribing it with a talismanic code.

But Ownby's resistance to the intrusive order — the bureaucratic and industrial way of life that is impinging upon human beings' connection to the natural world — becomes his undoing, and he ends up on the wrong side of the law, incarcerated in a mental institution after a shootout with the authorities and a period hiding out as a fugitive deep in the remote woods. McCarthy's novel, it seems, holds out bleak hope for the traditional, natural connection that Ownby represents.

See also Nature; *The Orchard Keeper*; Rattner, John Wesley; Sylder, Marion

Parham, Billy

Billy Parham, central protagonist in the Border Trilogy, is more complex and inscrutable than his trilogy cohort John Grady Cole. John Grady is a clearer-cut romantic figure, defined by his affinity for horses, his loves, and his overwhelming sense of justice. Yet it is Billy, and Billy alone, that the reader is left with in the final pages of the Border Trilogy, the character having reached a ripe old age that was simply unattainable for the doomed John Grady.

What is fascinating about Billy Parham is that he seems to possess both a negative capability (as outlined by Romantic poet John Keats) and a negative capacity, in that he is virtually defined by all that he has lost: "I aint nothin,'" he insists on the final page of the trilogy (*Cities of the Plain*, p. 292). Billy's losses have been profound and many: the she-wolf, his family, his brother Boyd, and John Grady Cole, with whom he had formed a fraternal bond. But for whatever reason, McCarthy has chosen to leave Billy the sole standing figure and chronicler at the end of the trilogy, one who tells children "about horses and cattle and the old days. Sometimes he'd tell them about Mexico" (*ibid.*, p. 290).

In the early nineteenth century, John Keats described negative capability as when a person "is capable of being in uncertainties, mysteries, doubts without any irritable reaching after fact and reason" (quoted in Willey, p. 41). Throughout *The Crossing* (1994) and at the end of *Cities of the Plain* (1998) Billy has much philosophy and esoteric wisdom poured in his ear, yet the reader is never quite certain of the impact upon him. In fact, in one of the more probing and cryptic encounters — when the stranger discourses on the dream within his dream at the end of *Cities of the Plain*—Billy has a telling retort: "I think you got a habit of makin things a bit more complicated than what they need to be" (p. 278). As a younger man, listening to the Mormon hermit unfurl a tale that dwells upon the nature of God, Billy seems to pull a disappearing act akin to the kid in *Blood Meridian* (1985). He is present, but we have no sense of him or his reaction to what he is hearing. This detachment, for lack of a better word, often renders Billy inscrutable, and one is never sure of his orientation to fact or reason. One of the great mysteries of the trilogy is whether the experience and knowledge he has come in contact with has caused him to evolve any way.

Adding to the puzzle of Billy's characterization are his unclear motivations at times. His compulsion to return the pregnant she-wolf to the mountains of Mexico, abandoning his family, is peculiar, and many of those he encounters along the way consider him crazy. And whereas John Grady Cole is motivated by romantic notions and ideals, Billy comes at us in the opening pages of *Cities of the Plain* as a devout bachelor, bawdily assessing a gathering of prostitutes in a bordello barroom. His only close bonds are with fleeting beings — the wolf, his brother Boyd, John Grady. Billy's tale is one of constant loss, of compunction to reach out "to hold what cannot be held," making him the resolute, tragic, but ultimately inscrutable center of the Border Trilogy (p. 127).

See also Cities of the Plain; The Crossing; Cole, John Grady; Loss

Parham, Boyd

There is a hard lesson that Billy Parham keeps learning again and again in the Border Trilogy, a lesson most harrowingly and deeply expressed in the loss of his brother Boyd in *The Crossing* (1994). It involves the "transitory and violent" nature of things, to borrow a phrase applied to the lost ghost nation of Comanche in 1992's *All the Pretty Horses* (p. 5). The loss of Boyd is prefigured by an earlier referent in *The Crossing*, the death of the pregnant she-wolf, when Billy "took up her stiff head out of the leaves and held it or he reached to hold what cannot be held" (p. 217). Like the wolf, Boyd emerges as something onto which Billy cannot hold, no matter how desperately hard he tries.

In fact, Boyd only exists as a tangible figure for a portion of *The Crossing*; after that he becomes McCarthy's most ethereal character — at first an elusive figure that Billy tracks through Mexico, and later a figure that appears only in wordless dream visitations and the legends of the *corridos*. Billy Parham is a protagonist practically defined by his sense of loss in the Border Trilogy, left alone to mourn so many others as an old man at the conclusion of *Cities of the Plain* (1998). But the deepest, most sorrowful absence is that of Boyd; it is a loss that wracks him in the final passage of the trilogy, when, over 50 years after Boyd's death, "he dreamt that Boyd was in the room with him but [Boyd] would not speak for all that he called out to him" (*Cities of the Plain*, pp. 290–291).

The deeply philosophical, multifarious Border Trilogy contains many themes, but on an overt level it is a tale of accumulative sorrow. And Boyd becomes the allegorical vortex of that sorrow, pulling everything else into its emotional wound — even the other primary Border Trilogy protagonist, John Grady Cole, who takes the role of a surrogate Boyd in Billy's life: "More and more you remind me of Boyd," Billy tells John Grady (p. 146). The comment is prescient, as John Grady's fate is to also end up being killed in Mexico — and to become something else close to Billy that he ultimately cannot save or hold on to.

Even in life, though, one gets the sense of Boyd slipping through Billy's fingers, of existing in a twilight state between life and death in which the novel itself often dwells. This idea is most directly allegorized in *The Crossing* through the wounded, blind ex-revolutionary, whose affliction, it is surmised, has caused him to have "partly quit the world anyway" (p. 282) and to have "already halved the distance to death" (p. 280).

We see a corollary to this when Billy last sees Boyd; here, Boyd, is an ethereal image of living death, as if, like the blind man, he was in a twilight state, having "already halved the distance to death." He is wrapped in muslin coverings (the material used for death shrouds) and appears "paler than his brother could ever remember and so thin with the rack of his ribs stark against the pale skin" (p. 330). The desperation that we see in Billy in this scene is a precursor to the urgency with which he will later call out to Boyd in dreams. "I need for you to talk to me," Billy urges:

It's okay. Everything's okay.
No it aint.
You just worry about stuff. I'm all right.
I know you are, said Billy. But I aint [p. 330].

Billy, as well as the reader, has a sense of Boyd's increasing ethereality, as if his corporal being is dissipating before our and Billy's eyes. After this last encounter Boyd becomes increasingly less tangible; first Billy encounters him only as "shadow and rumor" (p. 331), a stage that posits Boyd somewhere between a real person and a myth, and then finally he becomes purely myth, legend, dream figure, and bones — his breathing existence having been appropriated into the *corridos*, the ballads that mythologize and romanticize acts of heroism. Therefore, Billy, on the trail of Boyd, begins to encounter traces of his brother only in the song, which tells of a fearless blonde-haired hero from the north, pistol in hand ("*Pelo tan rubio. Pistola en mano*" [p. 375]), who is killed.

As such, Boyd becomes an allegory for myth-making in *The Crossing*, for that hazy convergence between legend, history, and an actual person's existence. Billy, as one who was close to Boyd, comes to understand that the historical myth constructed in the *corrido* has only a tangential relationship to Boyd's life. "He didnt kill the manco in La Boquillo," says Billy, questioning the rendering of Boyd in the *corrido*. "I was there" (p. 384). The men Boyd killed after he left Billy may problematize the *corridos'* paradigm even more; perhaps they were senseless acts of murder, not heroic killings: "He killed two men in Galeana," the Yaqui Indian Quijada tells Billy. "No one knows why. They did not even work for the latifundio [great estate owner]" (*ibid.*). The *corrido*, however, has its own discursive agenda: "It tells what it wishes to tell. It tells what makes the story run" (p. 386).

The *corrido* is a preexisting narrative into which Boyd's life has been reassembled and fitted to meet its discursive specifications, and furthermore to satisfy the cultural "truths" that sustain the existence of the rural and mountain people of Mexico; the story has its own shape, form, and breathing life beyond those which it subsumes. "I heard the tale of the güerito [fair-haired man] years ago," says Quijada. Before your brother was even born" (p. 386).

See also Corridos; *The Crossing*; History; Loss; Parham, Billy; Quijada

Pulitzer Prize

Cormac McCarthy was awarded the Pulitzer Prize for achievement in fiction in 2007 for his tenth novel, *The Road* (2006). The awards were established in 1911 under terms set up by their namesake, legendary newspaper publisher Joseph Pulitzer. The first prizes were awarded in 1917.

See also The Road

Quest Literature

From Rinthy Holme's journey to recover her baby in *Outer Dark* (1979) to Suttree's *Ulysses*-like wanderings through the Knoxville underbelly to Billy Parham's border traversings in *The Crossing* (1994), many of Cormac McCarthy's works can be categorized as quest literature. Jeffrey Jay Folks and James A. Perkins talk about McCarthy's continual fascination with the "mythos of the pilgrimage" and declare that "[o]ne of the fascinating things about McCarthy is that the quest continues but each new book slightly shifts the grounds traversed by its predecessors" (pp. 165–166).

Most cultures have a variation on quest literature, and the heroes of such narratives typically strive to obtain something (or perhaps someone). The Western canon is fraught with variations on the quest theme, from the ancient tales of Homer to such classics of literature as *Sir Gawain and the Green Knight*, Chaucer's *Canterbury Tales*, Malory's *Le Morte d'Arthur*, Cervantes' *Don Quixote*, and Goethe's *Faust* (part 1). In the twentieth century, James Joyce — an important influence on McCarthy — re-envisioned the hero's journey in *Ulysses* (1922).

But McCarthy, like Joyce, complicates this paradigm in his own way. As Folks and Perkins point out, it is "often difficult to tell whether McCarthy's seekers are mainly driven by something they flee or drawn by something they seek" (*ibid.*, p. 165). And more often than not the outcomes of the quests are less than happy. As the omniscient narrator declares in *The Crossing*, "Doomed enterprises divide lives forever into the then and now" (p. 129). McCarthy offers readers a grim variation on the quest theme, one in which the redemption, identity, and purpose that is so often traditionally sought in these types of narratives remains hopelessly out of reach. We witness this in *All the Pretty Horses* (1992), in which John Grady Cole not only comes up romantically empty after his journey but even loses whatever sort of national identity he had at the outset ("I don't know where [my country] is," he declares. "I don't know what happens to country" [p. 299].) Billy Parham comes up similarly empty in *The Crossing*, and the arduous travels on the titular road in *The Road* (2006) lead not to redemption but a looming question mark — such is the unresolved nature of the quest in McCarthy's novels.

See also All the Pretty Horses; The Crossing; Outer Dark; The Road; Suttree

Quijada

In *The Crossing*, the Yaqui Indian Quijada, despite his brief appearances, plays an important and dual function in the narrative. Many of the individuals that Billy encounters in *The Crossing* have a primarily philosophical role in the text — the Mormon hermit, for example, who encounters Billy Parham once, bends his ear for a long time (unfolding deeply metaphysical notions), and then disappears. Quijada, however, performs both a philosophical and plot-driving function.

His first appears as the *gerente* (manager) of the Nahuerichic division of the Babícora who orders Billy and Boyd's stolen horses to be cut loose and returned to them. Therefore, his initial appearance is as a completely unexpected bureaucratic voice of reason and intuition in the high plains of Mexico — one who gives them the horses, Billy explains to Boyd, "cause he knowed they was ours.... He just knew it" (*The Crossing*, p. 255).

Later in the novel Billy has an encounter of a more philosophical vein with Quijada. By chance, Billy ends up a houseguest in Quijada's small, lone dwelling on a plain. Here the conversation turns to deeper concerns, regarding Boyd and the *corridos*. Through Quijada, McCarthy seeks not only to demystify Boyd and the *corridos* themselves, but the very enterprise of "history" itself.

The *corriodos* have eulogized Boyd as a hero of the working people in the face of arbitrary power and oppression, but Quijada — who has been established as a solid and credible individual through his actions with the Parham horses — relates how Boyd's acts of "heroism" may have been more senseless than the *corridos* — a "poor man's history" (p. 386) — would have it. "He killed two men in Galeana," Quijada tells Billy. "No one knows why. They did not even work for the latifundio [estate owner]" (*ibid.*). The *corrido*, however, has its own history to tell, despite the actual nature of its adopted subject. As Quijada tells Billy: "It tells what it wishes to tell. It tells what makes the story run," regardless of events (*ibid.*).

Quijada reveals the *corrido* as a preexisting tale into which Boyd's actions in Mexico have been fitted to sustain the cultural "truths" of the people who seek their histories in these ballads. The story itself had shape, form, and life, long before it subsumed Boyd into its structures. "I heard the tale of the güerito [fair-haired man] years ago," says the Yaqui Indian Quijada. Before your brother was even born" (*ibid.*). Quijada's revelations have a larger implication as well, for through this character's dialogue with Billy, McCarthy questions history, myth and the hazy nexus where the two meet.

See also Corridos; The Crossing; Parham, Boyd

Race

Particularly in his early, Southern novels, Cormac McCarthy offers frank depictions of racist attitudes. In his very first novel, *The Orchard Keeper* (1965), the following exchange occurs between two boys, Warn and Boog: "You said niggers was as good as whites," says Warn, to which Boog replies, "I never. What I said was *some* niggers is good as *some* whites is what I said" (p. 140). Another boy, Johnny Romines, chimes in, "I had a uncle.... You ought to hear him on niggers. He claims they're kin to monkeys" (*ibid.*). The racial epithet also appears several times in his next two novels, *Outer Dark* (1968) and *Child of God* (1973), but issues of race are not a prime focus in those books; rather, the use of the derogatory term is illustrative of the offhand, matter-of-fact way in which racism appears in everyday vernacular.

McCarthy's most significant meditations on race come in his fourth novel, *Suttree*

(1979), which is set in Knoxville, Tennessee, in the early to mid–1950s, a time and place in which Jim Crow laws were still in effect. One gets an incidental sense of this from details such as "the drinking fountain marked White" (p. 101) at which Harrogate washes some discarded vegetables, but issues of race come at the reader more explicitly through the character of Ab Jones, a black man in a war of attrition with the local police, particularly the police chief, Tarzan Quinn. His open resistance to white authority leads to savage jail beatings and eventually his demise at the hands of Quinn. Frank awareness of racial attitudes also appears in the characters' banter, such as in Jabbo's comment, "Suttree aint too proud to drink after a nigger. Is you, Suttree?"

Nevertheless, we see in the character of Cornelius Suttree — who, as flawed as he is, represents an intellectual and moral center rare to McCarthy's work — a certain egalitarianism when it comes to issues of race; in fact, besides his comedic acolyte, Harrogate, Ab Jones seems the person to whom Suttree, who is from an upper-class white background, is most dedicated. In fact, in his rejection of his genteel roots, Suttree has surrounded himself with a de facto family from the underbelly of Knoxville, one that is a clear representation of miscegenation. The novel suggests that at the level of hardship faced by the characters, race is less of an issue than it is in "legitimate" society; the struggle to survive creates a more level playing field.

Nevertheless, Ab Jones is evidence that even the most down-and-out of white folks will never experience the degree of societal malice inflicted upon blacks: "Bein a nigger is a interesting life," notes Ab to Suttree after a particularly brutal beating at the hands of the local authorities. "They don't like no nigger walkin around like a man" (p. 203). Perhaps because he himself is a person of the margins, Suttree doesn't seem to possess the embedded racist views of the culture in which he was raised; to him, people are people, as we witness when he befriends and assists the Native American character in the novel, who tells Suttree that people call him "Tonto or Wahoo or Chief. But my name is Michael" (p. 225). Nevertheless, even Michael refers to Ab as "a great big nigger," without any trace of malice (p. 229); such is the bracingly matter-of-fact and pervasive usage of the term in McCarthy's representation of 1950s Knoxville.

Suttree, though, seems to have developed a way of calmly sidestepping the racism that is endemic to his surroundings. "You ever get so drunk you kissed a nigger?" asks Harrogate, a caricatured white rural "hick" known for engaging in sexual acts with watermelons. "Suttree looked at him. Harrogate with one eye narrowed on him to tell the truth. I've been a whole lot drunker than that, he said" (p. 144). Suttree subtly adopts a manner that neither affirms nor disputes racist rhetoric. McCarthy seems to carefully choose Suttree's words for him in those circumstances, creating an air of stoic acceptance but clearly not an air of affirmation. We see that tendency in another exchange, with a derelict dubbed Smokehouse.

When push comes to shove, though, Suttree demonstrates his own sense of justice. In the final standoff between Ab and the white authorities, Suttree takes a profound stand by stealing the patrol car while the police are chasing down Ab and sinking it in the Tennessee River. This is not to say that Suttree is making a statement against racial worldviews; he is seeking vindication for a friend. But in dedication to friends, he displays a clear color blindness.

Never one to preach or use his medium as an agent for social justice, the racial picture becomes more complicated in the 1850s borderlands of *Blood Meridian* (1985). In this novel, the scalp-hunting, debased Glanton Gang is a multicultural stew, consisting of whites, blacks, and Native Americans. Here, McCarthy suggests a "degeneracy of mankind" that transcends racial boundaries (p. 146).

In the Old West of Cormac McCarthy, all races are implicated in the violent conditions of the frontier, an idea figuratively expressed in the two Glanton members with identical names: "[T]here rode two men named Jackson, one black, one white, both forenamed John. Bad blood lay between them" (p. 81). Despite the animus between the two John Jacksons — and obviously one must kill the other, as both can't coexist — the cross-racial doppelgangers are brothers in arms when it comes to the savagery that the gang inflicts upon the landscape.

Nevertheless, *Blood Meridian* (1985), McCarthy's first novel about the American Southwest, did have some more overt racial overtures. For one, he sidestepped popular histories and narrations to display "the real extent of ethnic diversity in the West, such as the fact that there were many black, Mexican, Indian, and even Chinese cowboys" (Eaton, p. 157).

As McCarthy delved deeper into his more famous work based in the borderlands and turned his attention away from the American Southeast, black-and-white issues of race became less of a focus, and the cultural milieu of Tennessee was replaced by the intercrossed cultural concerns of the Mexican-American borderlands (expressed most obviously in McCarthy's use of Spanish dialogue).

Perhaps McCarthy's most significant deliberations on race came in a much lesser-known work, *The Stonemason: A Play in Five Acts*. In that play (written in the 1970s and published in the 1990s), he tells of the bond between a young black stonemason, Ben Telfair, and his grandfather, who is the vaunted stonemason of the title and of a dying age. The Telfair family lives together in a house in Louisville, Kentucky, in the early 1970s, and the play deals with issues such as racism, infidelity, drug abuse, and suicide.

See also Jones, Ab; *The Stonemason*

Rattner, John Wesley

Young John Wesley Rattner is at the intersection of so much of *The Orchard Keeper* (1965). For one, he is at a nexus between three fathers: one dead, ne'er-do-well father, Kenneth Rattner, and two surrogates: Arthur Ownby and Marion Sylder. But he is also at the intersection of the conflict between the old and the new in the novel. He is coming of age in the community with the opposing pressures of tradition and modernization upon him.

The boy's "literal" father, Kenneth Rattner, is a thief and wanderer who only returns to the community of Red Branch long enough to steal money before he is off again. Further complicating things, Marion Sylder, another Red Branch resident and charismatic bootlegger, murders Kenneth in an act of self-defense and pitches his body into an abandoned concrete pit once used for pesticides in the orchard.

Sylder befriends the orphaned John Wesley (both unaware he has killed the boy's father) and the two bond over the ancient traditions of bloodhounds, hunting, and trapping, neither knowing that Sylder is the murderer of John's father. Meanwhile, the elder Rattner's body lies decomposing in the concrete pit. To complicate things, John's mother has made him pledge to one day track down his father's killer and vindicate his father. (She is deluded about Kenneth's lifestyle and speaks of him as a war hero.)

The old man Arthur Ownby is another mentor to John Wesley, one who represents the traditional relationship to the land, a dying way of life. Ownby has what critic David Paul Ragan calls a "mystical connection to the cycles of nature" (p. 18). As a keeper of the orchard, he also feels compelled to keep watch over the body in the spray pit, and he ritualistically lays cut cedars over the makeshift grave for a period of seven years, based on the ancient folklore if a person hasn't been given a proper burial his "soul takes up in a cat for a spell" (p. 227). Ownby lives a nearly obsolete existence that is not tied to money or commerce but is sharply attuned to the seasons, the weather, the landscape, and folklore. It is this gauntlet of influences and these conflicting pressures that John Wesley must negotiate.

See also Sylder, Marion; *The Orchard Keeper*; Ownby, Arthur

The Road

With his Pulitzer Prize–winning novel *The Road* (2006), Cormac McCarthy finally realized the dark premonition scattered throughout his previous works. Here is what he had only suggested before: "the end of the civilized world, the dying of life on the planet and the spectacle of it all," as writer William Kennedy put it in his *New York Times* review. *The Road* presents a world that, in the wake of some unnamed, apocalyptic catastrophe, has dissolved into a primordial condition devoid of nature, culture, law, personal identity, government, economics, territorial borders, agriculture, literature, commerce, art — or any recognizable feature of the world in which we live.

For a father and son trudging day by day through a barren, scorched landscape of gray, endlessly foraging in wasted buildings for food and supplies — while trying to avoid rogue tribes of cannibals — there is only good and evil, survival, and God, whom the father sometimes addresses in desperation and anger, lifting his face to the heavens: "Are you there? he whispered. Will I see you at last? Have you a neck by which to throttle you? Damn you eternally have you a soul? Oh God, he whispered. Oh, God" (pp. 11–12). As the *Philadelphia Inquirer* put it, "*The Road* is about the bleakest book [McCarthy] has ever written, and that's saying something" (Barra).

Cormac McCarthy has consistently dwelled on the impermanence of—and what he sees as the inevitable violent end to—the human condition. And post-apocalyptic imagery has been a constant in his novels, from a foreboding and sickly looking litter of kittens in his very first novel, *The Orchard Keeper* (1965), who appear "as if they might have been struck simultaneously by some biblical blight" (p. 180), to the turgid, prophetic dreamworld of Billy Parham in *The Crossing* (1994), where he envisions "God's pilgrims laboring upon a darkened verge ... returning from some dark enterprise" (p. 420). Even

All the Pretty Horses (1992), one of McCarthy's most accessible and popular books, ended with the dire image of a lone bull rolling in the dust "against the bloodred sunset like an animal in sacrificial torment" while the shadows of horse and horseman merged and slipped off into "the darkening land, the world to come" (p. 301). The title of the last book of the Border Trilogy, *Cities of the Plain* (1998), makes a direct reference to the biblical cities of Sodom and Gomorrah, which God destroyed by consuming them in fire and brimstone because of the hopelessly corrupted nature of the humanity that inhabited them. This also calls to mind the ashy, incinerated world of *The Road*, which looks like it could have been consumed in such fire and brimstone.

In *The Road*, though, McCarthy moves beyond suggestion and imagery to finally present the post-apocalyptic world itself in all of its horrible magnitude—the landscape littered with corpses, the sun blotted out, flora and fauna dead, the seas poisoned. Though the novel is not explicit about the cause of the world's destruction, McCarthy did tell *Rolling Stone* magazine in 2007 that he didn't believe that climate change or environmental disaster would be the end for humanity; it would be the violent nature of the human race itself: "We're going to do ourselves in first," he claimed (Kushner).

In presenting to the reader a post-apocalyptic world, *The Road* takes up a theme that has been explored countless times before by other authors, many of them genre writers (primarily in the area of science fiction). But this dystopian idea has been tackled by everyone from Stephen King, in *The Stand* (1978); to Richard Matheson, in *I Am Legend* (1954); to Margaret Atwood, in *Oryx and Crake* (2003). Author Michael Chabon said that McCarthy's "excellent" novel "presented a very pure example of post-apocalyptic literature, pared down to the essentials of a post-apocalyptic vision" (Timberg, p. F9).

However, just as McCarthy took the notion of a "Western" and created something new in the Border Trilogy, so too does his post-apocalyptic novel, funneled through his distinct prose sensibilities, move beyond a genre exercise and bear the markings of a striking original. "What propels *The Road* far beyond its progenitors are the diverted poetic heights of McCarthy's late–English prose," claimed London's *Guardian*: "the simple declamation and plainsong of his rendered dialect, as perfect as early Hemingway; and the adamantine surety and utter aptness of every chiseled description" (Warner).

What also makes *The Road* stand out from other post-apocalyptic renderings is the father and son relationship, which is detailed with heart-crushing pathos. Janet Maslin, writing in the *New York Times*, noted how the turgid, turbulent "narrative is also illuminated by extraordinary tenderness.... The father's loving efforts to shepherd his son are made that much more wrenching by the unavailability of food, shelter, safety, companionship or hope in most places where they scavenge to subsist" (Maslin, p. 8).

The very first lines of the novel let us know that this relationship is the novel's center and that all of the themes radiate outward from the bond between father and boy: "When he woke in the woods in the dark of the night he'd reach out to touch the child sleeping beside him," McCarthy writes as *The Road* opens. "His hand rose and fell softly with each precious breath" (p. 3). McCarthy doesn't meditate on the cause of the devastation and reduces the scope of the novel to this insular tale of survival, this world between a father and son who are never named. The narrative is built around the man and boy's endless trudge down the titular road—heading southward to the ocean and hopefully warmer climes — and their never-ending foraging for food, shelter, and supplies.

But the mind-numbing repetition of their travel and foraging and the succession of bleak, gray days are always charged with the potential of unspeakable violence, keeping the action taut. The father and son must be constantly vigilant against savage elements of post-apocalyptic humanity, including people who will go so far as to consume "a charred human infant headless and gutted and blackening on [a] spit" (p. 198) or keep fellow humans hostage in a cellar, harvesting chunks of their living flesh as food.

Nevertheless, while it is easy to become mesmerized by McCarthy's vivid renderings of unthinkable horror and the phantasmagoria of corpses frozen in all kinds of poses of antic death, *The Road* also takes up some of McCarthy's most compelling questions yet, such as, what wills one to live when every shred of humanity, culture, and society has been obliterated? Or even, what does one live for when the recognizable features of your own life have slipped off into a void? "The slow surf crawled and seethed in the dark and he thought about his life," writes McCarthy of the father, "but there was no life to think about and after a while he walked back" (p. 237).

For the man, the only thread binding him to this barely living world is his son, who was born around the time of the apocalypse and knows no other world. (The boy's mother chose to end her own life rather than try to exist in the dead and dying landscape.) The entire circumference of life is protecting the boy and sustaining him. This is his Ahab-like obsession; existence has been swallowed in the void, and there only remains this mission, a sort of Manifest Destiny handed down to him from above: "My job is to take care of you," he tells the boy. "I was appointed to do that by God. I will kill anyone who touches you" (p. 77).

This mandate from God has also instilled in the father a strict moral compass, an anachronistic quality in a world devoid of humanity, structure, and law. Anointing themselves as chosen ones who "carry the fire," the father and son have a strict, if simple, moral code by which to live. "We're still the good guys," he tells his son. "And we will always be," the son replies. "Yes. We will always be," says the man (*ibid.*). This is the figurative "fire" they talk about; the two decide to lay fierce claim to the last vestiges of goodness in world beyond despair.

It is compelling that the man holds on to a notion of God in the wake of an apocalypse that has taken hope, most of life, and certainly all organized religion with it. And this actually makes *The Road*—the novel that, paradoxically, finally brought to bear McCarthy's end of the world — much less nihilistic and pessimistic than most of his other works. There is even something like hope in the novel's final pages, when the boy is taken in by strangers, strangers who also appear to be rare "good guys," and when the woman says to the boy that "the breath of God was his breath yet through it pass from man to man through all of time" (p. 286). What, specifically, can emerge from this lift at the end is unclear, though, and more a suggestion than a resolution.

Nevertheless, in this book of unrelenting blackness, we see a sea change from the ultimately triumphant evil in books such as *Blood Meridian* (1985). We experienced similar relentless visions of horror in that novel, set in the Old West of the 1800s, such as a tree with the bodies of infants hanging from it, but, as William Kennedy notes, "Evil victorious is not [*The Road's*] theme. McCarthy changes the odds to favor the man and boy, who for a decade have survived death."

There is a flirtation with McCarthy's old brand of nihilism, though, in the form of Ely, an aged and starving man reduced to filth and rags, whose reaction to the desiccated world they inhabit is summed up in the paradoxical assertion: "There is no God and we are his prophets," which casts him for a moment like a character in a Samuel Beckett play (p. 170). But the father, despite his bleak vision for their future, clings to his God and his morality and considers himself a final agent of His will, even if his mission exists in a void, the larger design of the world having been annihilated: "On this road there are no godspoke men," ruminates the man. "They are gone and I am left and they have taken with them the world" (p. 32). *Slate* magazine described the conundrum as a "desire to be good although it serves no purpose" (Egan).

Obviously, all of this points to the biblical overtones in the novel. There are even suggestions that the son of the man is actually a Son of Man and that this road has all of the gravity and importance of the biblical roads to Damascus and Emmaus. Nevertheless, a clear parallel with biblical themes is difficult in a novel where all of culture and the religions within it have dissolved (possibly in the wake of a holy war).

Some McCarthy fanatics on the Internet have debated the significance of the clocks having frozen at 1:17 during the catastrophic impact. If one were to draw a biblical connection, this would place us in Genesis, where God is creating the world and all of life. In 1:17 God places the sun and the stars in the firmament, to light the earth and divide day from night. McCarthy often cuts against the grain of canonical themes and stories and converts them into something that is his own; therefore, it would be just like the author to actually blot out that light in the firmament at 1:17, so that "by day the banished sun circles the earth like a grieving mother with a lamp" (p. 32).

This inversion calls to mind the final border volume *Cities of the Plain*, the title of which alludes to Sodom and Gomorrah. In the Bible, the cities are destroyed by God because they are evil and corrupt, but in McCarthy's narrative, the corrupted cities of Juárez and El Paso flourish while the just and good John Grady Cole is killed by a Juárez pimp, truly a victory for depravity. William Kennedy, himself a Pulitzer Prize winner for *Ironweed*, noted the biblical overtones running through the work and contended that *The Road* "is as biblical as it is ultimate" and even termed it a "messianic parable."

Kennedy also noted the clear parallel between the previously mentioned ragged old man they encounter, named "Ely," and the prophet Elijah. That bent and blighted naysayer from *The Road* also has a corollary in the character Elijah from *Moby-Dick*, McCarthy's self-professed favorite novel. Melville's biblical Elijah is also physically decrepit, sporting a withered arm and deep smallpox scars and speaking in a similarly cryptic and foreboding manner regarding Ahab, whom Ishmael has yet to lay eyes upon.

One of the messianic qualities of the boy — and another bit of redemptive light in the blackness — is his overwhelming sense of compassion for all he encounters: the ragged old man, a boy he briefly glimpses in an abandoned town, one of the last dogs in existence, even a robber whom they overtake after he steals all of their life-sustaining supplies. He is a sort of pure boy and a blank slate. Born after the devastation, he has no sense of the pop culture and structures that preceded this life. He even gets confused by common sayings like "as the crow flies," an expression that has no meaning in a world where all of the birds have died and no one asks for directions anymore.

The Road is dedicated to McCarthy's son, John Francis McCarthy, who was still quite young around the time of the book's release, so certainly McCarthy's own boy and parenting were at the forefront of his mind as he composed the novel. He admitted — in an interview with Oprah Winfrey — that his son inspired *The Road*. In another of his rare interviews, with *Rolling Stone* in December 2007, a year after the release of the novel, McCarthy presented this dismal outlook on raising children in contemporary times, pointing a finger at the growing violence in American society and pop culture: "If kids are unstable, they may very well be cranked up by the violence they see, and might do things that they wouldn't have done or would have taken them longer to get around to," McCarthy said. "But the real culprit is violence against children. A lot of children don't grow up well.... We know how to make serial killers. You just take a Type A kid who's fairly bright and just beat the crap out of him day after day" (Kushner).

McCarthy presents in *The Road* a child who is never exposed to contemporary, violent popular culture and who is under the care of a fiercely protective parent, basically resolving the two issues he speaks of here (though surely this boy is exposed to unspeakable visions in this post-apocalyptic world).

The novel was almost universally well received upon its release in 2006 and won the Pulitzer Prize in 2007. Stylistically, though, it was a bit pared back, especially when compared to the Border Trilogy or *Blood Meridian*. Kennedy noted in his review that it was "a dynamic tale, offered in the often exalted prose that is McCarthy's signature, but this time in restrained doses — short, vivid sentences, episodes only a few paragraphs or a few lines long, which is yet another departure for him." He also pointed out how McCarthy had

> put aside the linguistic excesses and the philosophizing for which he has been both venerated and mocked — those Faulknerian convolutions, the Melvillean sermonizing — and opted for terse dialogue and spartan narrative, a style he inherited from another of his ancestors, Hemingway, and long ago made his own.

Nevertheless, that big, profound stentorian voice for which McCarthy is known does ring out in its omniscient way from the mountaintop occasionally, particularly in the final passage of the novel, a short epilogue that leaves the characters and action to present a brief and final statement, one that is simultaneously filled with hope and hopelessness — as well as downright ambiguity:

> Once there were brook trout in the streams in the mountains. You could see them standing in the amber current where the white edges of their fins wimpled softly in the flow. They smelled of moss in your hand. Polished and muscular and torsional. On their backs were vermiculate patterns that were maps of the world in its becoming. Maps and Mazes. Of a thing which could not be put back. Not be made right again. In the deep glens where they lived all things were older than man and they hummed of mystery [*The Road*, pp. 286–287].

That mysterious hum is often at the heart of McCarthy's novels. Mystery burst free from human strictures and ecclesiast is in fact his very idiom. Here he presents the idea that there is a natural order that can never be restored, yet he also presents us, just before this, with hope for humanity — the boy and the father did keep the course of their moral compass, they did remain the "good guys." And though the father does die, the boy still has "the fire." He still carries that flame of humanity, and he is taken in by others who are "good" as well.

But the lines make it clear that if there is to be a new world, then it will be nothing like the old natural order. There is also a sense of the fleeting condition of the human race: "In the deep glens where they lived all things were older than man and they hummed of mystery" (p. 287). There are no words for that mystery, McCarthy seems to be telling us; it is a mystery that existed long before humans and before the language, philosophy, or religion that we use to explain the world. In fact, in *The Road* McCarthy describes a world that is withdrawing to a pre-language, pre-belief, pre-cultural condition: "The world shrinking down around a raw core of parsible entities. The names of things slowly following those things into oblivion. Colors. The names of birds. Things to eat. Finally the names of things one believed to be true" (p. 88).

That old mysterious hum is something that McCarthy keeps bringing us as close to as he can, but it necessarily remains just beyond our periphery. For it is just that: a hum beyond language and human understanding. As one academic suggested of those final lines in *The Road*: "These evocations of nature function primarily as points of inaccessibility. Not merely because they refer to the past or to that which is dead but because they are intimations of a nature that exceeds the human." The critic added, "They are points of numinosity that signal to the present reader a not-yet-achieved consciousness" (Ryan, p. 11).

Nevertheless, McCarthy's insistence on keeping the mystery just that, a mystery, has frustrated many readers of *The Road*. William Kennedy saw the concluding evocation as too "austere" for such a vividly rendered, post-apocalyptic pilgrimage and furthermore lamented how the "scarcity of thought in the novel's mystical infrastructure [left] the boy a designated but unsubstantiated messiah" with an uncertain future. "It makes us wish that that old humming mystery had a lyric," he concluded in his *New York Times* review. The work of Cormac McCarthy, however, has consistently been to take the reader to the mouth of the allegorical cave or to the edge of those figurative glens — and no further. Just close enough to ponder that ageless hum. Perhaps the final word is best left to McCarthy himself, who said in his TV interview with Oprah Winfrey, "I don't think you have to have a clear idea who or what God is in order to pray."

• *Further reading*
Kennedy, William. "Left Behind." *New York Times Book Review*, October 8, 2006.
Kushner, David. "Cormac McCarthy's Apocalypse." *Rolling Stone*, December 27, 2007.
Maslin, Janet. "The Road through Hell, Paved with Desperation." *The New York Times*, p. E1.

Rocha, Alejandra

The romance between John Grady Cole and Alejandra in *All the Pretty Horses* (1992) represents a complicated interplay of forces, most prominently those of nation and class.

In fact, everything that John Grady does not understand about Mexico, and everything about the country that is beyond his locus of control, is bound up in the relationship with Alejandra; and for his romantic idealism, he is bought, sold, imprisoned, stabbed, freed—all of it beyond his agency.

At the Hacienda de Nuestra Señora de la Purisma Concepción (Hacienda of Our Lady of the Immaculate Conception), the "conception" that actually occurs at the ranch, owned by Alejandra's father, Hector Rocha y Villareal, is the creative crossbreeding of horses of disparate stock from disparate lands. But the hacendado takes a less liberal approach to the idea of interbreeding his own family bloodline, particularly that which runs through his daughter.

Nevertheless, Alejandra's ultimate decision to turn her back on John Grady is still somewhat of a puzzle. "Although her true motivations are never made wholly clear to us," writes Alan Bilton, "her ultimate abandonment of Grady only makes sense if we assume that she chooses the love of her father over the attractions of her lover" (p. 111). Otherwise, she becomes "another [of McCarthy's] example[s] of capricious womanhood.... Indeed, the text makes a number of implicit connections between Alejandra and John Grady Cole's mother, for ultimately both leave their cowboy lover for an ambiguous sense of modern emancipation" (*ibid.*).

But the novel also suggests that the relationship is about the larger forces of Mexico—not personal motivations. And this is what John Grady Cole keeps running up against. "Mexico is not an unwritten, lawless land, but rather possesses a complex history and class structure which McCarthy's naïve hero is unable to comprehend," notes Bilton (*ibid.*, p. 109). This is why the Dueña Alfonsa's meeting with John Grady about her grand-niece Alejandra is mostly saturated with tales of the Mexican Revolution rather than thoughts about the love between the two young people, which she strictly forbids.

This is also why, during the lovers' last encounter, Alejandra chooses to bring John Grady to the spot where her maternal grandfather was killed during the revolution. Her narration of the event and the decidedly non-romantic sheen she lends it serves to further widen the gulf between her and John Grady. She is at once proclaiming her heritage and illustrating the chasm between her sense of heritage and John Grady's. She is also defusing romantic idealism and sentimentality—the very kind of idealism that fueled the romance between John Grady and Alejandra at the hacienda and that was expressed through McCarthy's hazy romantic descriptions. (To wit: "She was so pale in the lake she seemed to be burning. Like foxfire in a darkened wood. That burned cold. Her black hair floating on the water about her, falling and floating on the water. She put her other arm about his shoulder ... and then she turned her face up to him" [p. 141].)

Through Alejandra we witness the paradoxical capability that is the novel's strength—that is, there are boilerplate Western elements and romantic tendencies, yet there is also a thread in McCarthy's rendering that questions and even undermines those modes. The steamy, fantastical descriptions of Alejandra and John Grady at the hacienda—riding horses, mingling with the natural world—are undercut by bedrock realities of McCarthy's Mexico, not just the revolution and its heritage, but the cruel and shifting economic realities. John Grady's own life is bought with Alejandra's family's money, and ironically his next Mexican love interest, the prostitute Magdalena in

Cities of the Plain (1998) cannot be bought and rescued from her harsh life — and his attempts to do so will end his life (as Alejandra sees in a dream prophecy).

In "Romancing the Empire: The Embodiment of American Masculinity in the Popular Historical Novel of the 1890s," Amy Kaplan demonstrates the classic Western and frontier hero archetype: "The subject position of the heroes in these novels ... lies at the conjunction of violent demonstrations of brute strength and a chivalric dedication to women" (p. 671). In *All the Pretty Horses*, we can see how John Grady embodies this description through both his trials in the prison and his "chivalric dedication" to Alejandra, but in McCarthy's borderlands these attributes often echo in a vacuum.

Thus, John Grady endures an essentially emasculating ordeal through his romance with Alejandra; in fact, the romance itself fades and dissipates into the "realities" of McCarthy's Mexico — the economic realities, bureaucratic realities, caste-system realities, and the confusing realities of nationhood. No wonder John Grady, when asked about his country, is left at the end to exclaim, "I dont know where it is. I dont know what happens to country" (p. 299).

See also All the Pretty Horses; Cole, John Grady; The Dueña Alfonsa

The Santa Fe Institute

Located high in the hills outside of the city of Santa Fe, New Mexico, the institute is an independent, non-profit education and research center that was founded in 1984. Cormac McCarthy remains the only fiction writer to have become associated with the institute.

The Santa Fe Institute serves as a point of convergence for nationally and globally renowned scholars in the areas of physical, biological, computational, and social sciences; these great minds come together and collaborate in order to "uncover the mechanisms that underlie the deep simplicity present in our complex world" (Santa Fe Institute website). For example, as described in *The Medici Effect*, "Biologists ... can be found working together with economists and stock market analysts to generate new ideas about how markets behave" (Johansson, p. 28).

Despite this interdisciplinary milieu, however, it is still peculiar to find that McCarthy has a close association with the institute and has in fact used it as a working home base for long stretches of time. It is especially an odd match, as Richard B. Woodward points out, because McCarthy's "grisly, male-dominated literary universe can hardly be said to overlap much with the hygienic concerns of scientists, especially not this international, predominantly liberal group, with whom the novelist, a quiet 72-year-old southern conservative, shares little in either background or education" ("Cormac Country").

But, as Woodward also wrote (in 2005), "He has been a mainstay among the rotating researchers for more than four years, and during that time if you strolled through the terraced-style headquarters ... you were likely to hear him tapping away in his office on a blue Olivetti Lettera 32 portable typewriter" (*ibid.*). Geoffrey West, a British scientist serving as interim president at the time of Woodward's article, told the interviewer, "Even though we have no formal artist-in-residence program, [Cormac] functions in this way. He interacts with everyone" (*ibid.*).

McCarthy's association with the Santa Fe Institute can be traced back to the early 1980s, when the author received a MacArthur Fellowship (dubbed the "genius grant"). At the awards event in Chicago in 1981, McCarthy steered clear of the other writers and, as a matter of preference, ended up forging a bond with some of the scientists, among them Nobel Prize–winning physicist Murray Gell-Mann. Gell-Mann's interests extend way beyond physics, however, and he, along with a similarly catholic-minded group of scientists from the Los Alamos National Laboratory in New Mexico, founded the Santa Fe Institute in 1984. George Cowan, head of research at Los Alamos, led the group, while Gell-Mann chaired the board. They called their burgeoning discipline "complexity."

McCarthy apparently began making routine pilgrimages from his then-home in El Paso to the institute while he was still writing *All the Pretty Horses* (1992), the novel that would bring him to a much larger public (Kushner). One of the benefits that McCarthy has enjoyed over the years is the anonymity. "A lot of people here have no idea who I am," McCarthy told an interviewer from *Rolling Stone* magazine in 2007 (*ibid.*). McCarthy has also enjoyed the exchange of ideas at the sit-down meals, and has said that he only has "two responsibilities.... To eat lunch and attend afternoon tea" (Woodward, "Cormac Country"). McCarthy claimed that during lunch "you just don't know who's going to be there.... People drift in from all over the world — Nobel-winning chemists and biologists." He added, "You ask them something and they'll just stop what they're doing and sit down and tell you all about it. And that's rather remarkable" (Kushner).

McCarthy has consistently praised the rigors of scientific inquiry and in many ways has adapted some of its methods into his work (especially in terms of the accuracy and exactness of situations). "It's sobering how investigations into physical phenomenon are done," McCarthy has said. "It makes you more responsible about the way you think. You come to have a lot less tolerance for things that are not rigorous" (Woodward, "Cormac Country").

McCarthy has even been known to proofread work at the institute. A physicist from Harvard named Lisa Randall told *Rolling Stone* that McCarthy expressed an interest in reading a draft of her book, and she had the rare opportunity for a literary giant to critique her writing. "I got the manuscript back in the mail, and it was marked up on every page," she exclaimed (Kushner).

• *Further reading*

Kushner, David. "Cormac McCarthy's Apocalypse." *Rolling Stone*, December 27, 2007.
Santa Fe Institute website. "An Introduction." http://www.santafe.edu/about/index.php.
Woodward, Richard B. "Cormac Country." *Vanity Fair*, August 2005.

Sheriff Bell

Prior to *No Country for Old Men* (2005), the title character of *Suttree* (1979) was considered McCarthy's only "intellectual focal character" (Giles, p. 86). Sheriff Bell, the old-school lawman of *No Country for Old Men*, might not be an "intellectual" in the obvious sense of the term, but the novel is constructed in such a way that the reader is privy to his ruminations on the changing world of the borderlands.

This showcasing of his thoughts does, in a sense, make him a more "intellectual" character than most of McCarthy's protagonists. These italicized chapters, which break from the action to reveal Bell's inner monologues, also represent a major shift for McCarthy, who has consistently avoided getting inside his characters' heads and presenting their psychological motivations.

Therefore, despite the leaner, less lofty ambitions of *No Country for Old Men*— particularly when compared to densely aspiring, sometimes abstruse works such as *Blood Meridian* and *The Crossing*—Sheriff Bell represents a significant development in McCarthy's rendering of his protagonists. The father in *The Road* will continue in this vein, in that we are also somewhat exposed to his inner life.

Not everyone was so enamored with Sheriff Bell's contemplations, however. Michiko Kakutani, reviewing *No Country for Old Men* for the *New York Times*, considered the monologue chapters to be "tedious" and "long-winded," adding that Bell's "portentous meditations on life and fate and the decline and fall of Western civilization ... weigh down the quicksilver suspense of the larger story." Bell's reflective chapters certainly do shift sharply from the driving action of the narrative, but they are also intrinsic to the very raison d'être of the novel, the title of which is taken from the opening lines of William Butler Yeats' "Sailing to Byzantium."

Bell, echoing the sentiments in the Yeats work, finds himself painfully out of step with the times, and even worse, insufficient to the task of protecting his citizens in this burgeoning era of borderlands drug trade. He laments of the drug traffickers he is chasing, "[T]he worst of it is knowin that probably the only reason I'm even still alive is that they have no respect for me. And that's very painful" (p. 217). As one critic noted of the author's Southwestern novels, "McCarthy is concerned not just with the history of the American Southwest but with ... [t]hat brief moment between a culture's existence and extinction — this is the border that McCarthy's characters keep crossing and recrossing" (Mosle, p. 16). Bell embodies that "brief moment," and many of his monologues lament the passing age and confront the changing world.

In fact, Bell's roots will be familiar to anyone who has read about John Grady Cole and Billy Parham in McCarthy's Border Trilogy. Bell's father was an intuitive trainer of horses, cut from the same cloth as Cole, and Bell's Uncle Ellis has a "clouded eye" from being thrown by a horse into a cholla cactus patch. (Ellis had gone into law enforcement decades before, knowing that it paid "about the same as cowboyin" [p. 267].)

Just as John Grady's ancestors died in all sorts of mishaps that can be attributed to the hard ways of the West, so too did Bell's great-uncle Mac get "shot down on his own porch" by a group of Indians in 1879 (*All the Pretty Horses*, p. 269). Bell is a descendant of other law officers, but the traditional type of Texas lawman that Bell represents — with its old codes — is impotent in this modern age. This is no country for an old man such as Bell.

On another level, Bell's struggles show that the borderlands is no country for old men simply because it takes too many men too early, either by death or physical and emotional attrition. Bell thinks about his "family and about [Uncle Ellis] out there in his wheelchair in the old house" and asserts, "[T]his country has got a strange kind of history and a damned bloody one too" (p. 284). Through Bell's perceptions we also get a highly pessimistic view of aging: "I agreed with [Uncle Ellis] that there wasnt a whole lot of good you could say about old age and he said he knew one thing ... It dont last long. I waited for him to smile but he didnt" (p. 281). Or, as Uncle Ellis puts it, "I dont know what I'm doing here still knocking around. All them young people. We dont know where half of em is even buried at" (p. 271).

This is a book that is as much about regret as it is about the manhunt; the more contemplative elegiac focus on Bell provides the counterpoint, balance, and oppositional tension necessary to make *No Country for Old Men* a thematically and emotionally complete novel. This push and pull between the propulsive action and Bell's deliberations is intrinsic to McCarthy's vision, and the *New York Times* review's assertion that the Sheriff Bell passages "weigh down the quicksilver suspense" of the book is ill-aimed. This is really a suggestion that the book would be better as a one-dimensional (if well-written) pulp thriller — rather than a distinctive Cormac McCarthy work. Sheriff Bell is an updated manifestation of themes that McCarthy has been engaging for decades — borderlands violence and the bloody succession of Southwestern civilizations — and his perspective makes *No Country for Old Men* (note the "old men" of the title) the novel that it is and places it firmly within the lineage of his works.

In fact, the *Economist* magazine review suggested that "in the main his entries are some of the most mournful, moving sections of the book" ("Not a Pretty Sight"). And despite the folksy, no-frills light in which Sheriff Bell is represented, some of the shrewdest insights in the novel are left to him, not some omniscient narrator or verbosely intellectual character: "We're bein bought with our own money. And it aint just the drugs. There is fortunes bein accumulated out there that they dont nobody even know about.... Money that can buy whole countries," he surmises. "But people dont just up and decide to dope theirselves for no reason. By the millions" (p. 303).

See also The American Southwest; Chigurh, Anton; Moss, Llewellyn; *No Country for Old Men*

Southern Gothic

During his early career, when his work was still closely associated with Tennessee and its environs, Cormac McCarthy was often described as a "Southern Gothic" writer. The term — while sometimes employed under a hazy set of parameters — most often refers to Southern literature that explores grotesque, fantastical, and macabre dimensions and that plumbs the societal underbelly, often with strains of black humor. Critics frequently apply the term to such Southern predecessors of McCarthy as William Faulkner, Flannery O'Connor, and Carson McCullers.

The Southern Gothic novel is a descendant of the Gothic novels of England, the pervading darkness of those books transferred to Southern locales and the ruins of antebellum mansions often standing in for the ancient, moldering castles and estates of

England. In fact, the title character of *Suttree* (1979) explores a grand, decaying mansion whose florid description fits the gothic mode, the home "a great empire relic that sat shelled and stripped and rotting in its copse of trees above the river and brooded on the passing world with stark and stoned out window lights" (p. 118). Its "cracked urns ... bedight with concrete flora, broad steps, [and] tall fluted columns with their shattered paint" conjuring Gothic imagery (pp. 134–135).

Horace Walpole's *The Castle of Otranto* (1764) is frequently cited as the first English Gothic (Markman Ellis, p. 27), but Mary Shelley's *Frankenstein* (1818) is perhaps the most well-known novel in that style. Early American novelist Charles Brockden Brown, writing at the end of the eighteenth century, was also known for employing Gothic themes during an age when American literature was still considered more of an outcrop of English letters (not having yet undergone the transformation that such distinctly "American" writers such as James Fenimore Cooper, Nathaniel Hawthorne, and Herman Melville would spur on in the 1800s). Edgar Allan Poe also used the classic elements of the Gothic literature to create his own turgid universe, and despite his relative lack of regionalism he can be seen as a precursor to the Southern Gothic writers of the twentieth century. Gothic elements also permeate such mainstream classics of English literature as Charlotte Brontë's *Jane Eyre* (1847) and Emily Brontë's *Wuthering Heights* (1847).

The Southern Gothic, while having traceable roots to the English form, is nonetheless distinct in its reliance upon the bizarre, violent, grotesque, and often comic. This is evident in McCarthy's first four novels, which are arguably most influenced by such regionalist masters as William Faulkner and Flannery O'Connor. Additionally, McCarthy has directly linked his own vivid explorations of violence — explorations that would also saturate his Western novels — to his Tennessee roots. "If you grow up in the South, you're going to see violence," he has stated, defending the more grisly aspects of his work. "And violence is pretty ugly" (Kushner).

The defining Southern Gothic feature of the grotesque is also on prominent display in his early works. In his very first novel, *The Orchard Keeper* (1965), McCarthy conjures a bizarre, phantasmagoric community in which many elements are fantastical and abnormal, even small particulars such as the missing patches of fur and stitched belly on Arthur Ownby's old dog or Marion Sylder's chopped-off big toe, which looks "sort of like a nose" (p. 111). In the town's general store, roaches crawl about and old men gather — "a vulturous look about them, their faces wasted and thin, their skin dry and papery as a lizard's" (p. 115). In the marketplace, one witnesses "old women with faces like dried fruit set deep in their hooded bonnets, shaggy striated and hooktoothed as coconut carvings" (p. 82). Here, the comically bizarre is commonplace: A boy attaches a string to a buzzard and flies his "pet" like a kite; the back deck of a dive bar collapses, pitching all of the drinkers into a gully; a seedy and corrupt town official scavenges in the ashes of a body based on a rumor that the corpse had a valuable platinum plate in his head.

Grotesque flourishes — strokes that sometimes tend toward caricature — would go on to constitute an important part of McCarthy's next three novels, *Outer Dark* (1968), *Child of God* (1973), and *Suttree* (1979). And even as the author shifts his regional focus to the American Southwest and Mexico in *Blood Meridian* (1985), one can still trace distinct use of the grotesque.

See also Ballard, Lester; *Child of God*; Harrogate, Gene; *The Orchard Keeper*; *Outer Dark*

• *Further reading*

Ellis, Markman. *The History of Gothic Fiction*. Edinburgh, Scotland: Edinburgh University Press, 2000.

Palmer, Louis H., III. "Southern Gothic and Appalachian Gothic: A Comparative Look at Flannery O'Connor and Cormac McCarthy." *Journal of the Appalachian Studies Association* 3 (1991), pp. 166–76.

The Stonemason: A Play in Five Acts

Cormac McCarthy's first staged and published play, *The Stonemason*, bears witness to the fact that the writer's mastery of the novel did not so easily translate to theater. (It was staged — in dramatically revised form — in 2001 and published years earlier, in 1994. The Arena Stage had planned a production in 1992, but it fell through.) There are small impracticalities in the proposed stage directions — a dog that lifts its head on cue, men doing stonework, wind — and moments that come off melodramatic or clichéd, but the central structure of the work is compelling, using two performance spaces: a traditional set where the action takes place, most of it surrounding the Telfair family, and a podium at which Ben Telfair delivers monologues, meditating on his family (in particular his 101-year-old grandfather) and stonemasonry. McCarthy also imbues the drama with enough rich ideas that it operates on several levels.

In the stage directions, Cormac McCarthy indicates that Ben has an agenda in his monologues, that of seeking "his own exoneration, his own salvation" (p. 6). It is this twist in the proceedings that saves the play from simply becoming a sustained celebration of the mysticism of stonemasonry and a rote family tragedy; for what Ben seeks exoneration from is placing faith in stonemasonry above all else. This is something that he has inherited from his grandfather, who sees his chosen trade as part of a grand, God-driven design.

Through Ben's monologues, we get a sense of this worldview. God has laid the stones in the earth for masons to use, he tells us, and the stone arches are held in place by "the thumb of God" (p. 10). The masons place stones "in accordance with the laws of God" and the work itself, which is the oldest of all trades, possesses a "secret nature" (p. 32).

McCarthy seems to draw a parallel between the strictures of ecclesiastical forms and stonemasonry, and within this model, Ben and his grandfather are posited as zealots: "We kept it close to our hearts and it was like a power," says Ben of the stonemason's trade, "and we knew it would not fail us" (p. 33). Ben's grandfather even bases the precepts of his trade on scripture, noting that he will not handle "hewn stone" because of a biblical passage that commands this (p. 63).

The danger of this worldview is the danger of all religious extremism; it is full of conceits and self-delusion — Ben tells how the "beauty of the stonework is simply a reflection of the purity of the mason's intention" (p. 91). Ben and his grandfather's view positions them as custodians of God, as somehow purer for their trade and more closely connected to the divine. Ben's conceit causes him to decide for his sister whether she should know of her son Soldier's existence or not. And while Ben collapses all of his attention and devotion to stonemasonry, the world falls all around him; in fact, three generations of Telfair men die during the course of the drama, leaving Ben the sole living generation of Telfair man.

In the end, however, Stonemasonry becomes less of a mystical connection to the divine, and more of a blunt contrast to the fleeting nature of life: "The big elm tree died. The old dog died. Things that you can touch go away forever.... Trees. Dogs. People" (p. 104). Masonry is not the salvation Ben thought it was, but something that had actually separated him from what was truly divine: "we cannot save ourselves unless we save all ourselves," Ben realizes. "I had this dream but did not heed it. And so I lost my way" (p. 113).

Ben's realizations present the drama, at a very implicit level, as a critique on zealotry and strict ecclesiastical forms. He comes to realize that the stones and the work were merely totems, and that it is qualities such as "charity" and "small acts of valor" that must be held above all (p. 131). The play can also be appreciated on an explicit level as a family tragedy, with meditations on stonemasonry, death, and racism.

Style

For lovers of language and appreciators of master literary stylists, there are few writers to be savored more than Cormac McCarthy. Early in his career, before he turned his attention to the American West, it was easier to spot his influences: William Faulkner, Ernest Hemingway, James Joyce. But starting with *Blood Meridian*, he developed a prose style that was strikingly his own, and he came to be lauded for what Saul Bellow has called an "absolutely overpowering use of language, his life-giving and death-dealing sentences" (Woodward, "Venomous Fiction").

Novelist Madison Smartt Bell has rightfully asserted that "the beauty of the language, the sheer pleasure of washing around in McCarthy's sentences and paragraphs, is a large part of the attraction" ("A Writer's View," p. 7). While it is difficult to pin down an artist such as McCarthy, he does have recognizable tendencies that repeatedly show up in his novels.

One of his less appreciated techniques — one that doesn't garner as much attention as his more elevated prose — is the use of extremely detailed objectivity. He will lower his microscope on a workmanlike scene and painstakingly describe each step in a task such as setting a trap, packing a mount, or breaking a horse. At these times, as a *Washington Post* critic pointed out, "McCarthy's language exemplifies the careful precision of a craftsman" (Dirda, "At the End of His Tether").

This is language utterly devoid of emotion or psychology, a tendency that, claims

New York Times critic Sara Mosle, "lends his work an immediacy often lacking from historical fiction. What would be mind-numbing description in less competent hands is here completely riveting" (Mosle). She adds that it is what W.H. Auden had termed that "beautiful ... eye-on-the-object look" (*ibid.*). For example, in a scene from *The Crossing* (1994), Billy Parham sets a trap for the pregnant she-wolf that has been plundering livestock:

> At the heart of the fire there were live coals yet and he raked them aside to cool and dug a hole in the ground beneath the fire and then got a trap from the basket.... He screwed down the springs with the clamps and opened the jaws and set the trigger in the notch and eyed the clearance while he backed off the clampscrew. Then he removed both clamps and dropped the draghook and chain into the hole and set the trap in the fire.... He drifted ash over the trap with the screenbox and scattered back the charcoal and the charred bits of wood and he put back the bones and rinds of blackened skin and drifted more ashes over the set and then rose and stepped away and stood looking at the cold fire [p. 50].

McCarthy is concerned with absolute, empirical accuracy in these descriptions, and one can be sure that the writer himself has deliberated firsthand over such an animal trap and sought complete technical precision for his rendering of the scene. It is this element of the author's writing that Alan Bilton calls the "relentless attention to detail of McCarthy's prose," adding that the "proof of utility and the practical know-how, the repeated descriptions of how to loop a rope, set a trap, fix a saddle, break in a colt ... [suggest] a pragmatic knowledge which is free from ... duplicity" (p. 109).

In this pursuit of accurate detail, McCarthy has also said that he doesn't write about places he hasn't visited himself, which has meant countless research trips to remote regions of the American Southwest and Mexico. It is this kind of empirical rigor and pursuit of certainty that he has often claimed to admire in scientists, particularly those he brushed shoulders with at his home away from home, the Santa Fe Institute in New Mexico.

Another example of McCarthy's almost maddening objectivity crops up in *All the Pretty Horses* (1992). Here McCarthy describes John Grady Cole and Lacey Rawlins breaking a wild horse at the lavish Mexican hacienda:

> Rawlins took one of the lengths of siderope from around his neck where he'd hung them and made a slipnoose and hitched it around the pastern of the hind leg and drew the leg up and halfhitched it to the horse's forelegs. He freed the catchrope and pitched it away and took the hackamore and they fitted it over the horse's muzzle and ears and John Grady ran his thumb in the animal's mouth and Rawlins fitted the mouthrope and then slipnoosed a second siderope to the other rear leg. Then he tied both sideropes to the hackamore [p. 104].

These absorptive and objective descriptions lend concreteness and credibility to the actions in the novel, as they are entirely attuned to accurate detail and utterly devoid of drama and emotional colors.

But they also, as Sara Mosle points out, create "suspense by placing us in the middle of the action, and then slowing it down. We experience, as if in real time, what his characters experience, without any hint of where the story is going." We see this as well in *The Road*, where the father's resourcefulness is constantly put to the test: "He pulled the bolt and bored out the collet with a hand drill and resleeved it with a section of pipe he'd cut to length with a hacksaw," writes McCarthy. "Then he bolted it all back together and stood the cart upright and wheeled it around the floor. It ran fairly true" (p. 16).

McCarthy reserves a more dramatic and ornate voice for his descriptions of landscapes, and has consistently displayed a deft sensitivity in his handling of the natural world. Vivid landscapes and natural visions rendered in striking detail saturate his work. In *All the Pretty Horses* Cole and Rawlins are caught in a rainstorm: "They watched a storm that had made up to the north. At sundown a troubled light. The dark jade shapes of the lagunillas below them lay in the floor of the desert savannah like piercings through to another sky," writes McCarthy. "The laminar bands of color to the west bleeding out under the hammered clouds. A sudden violetcolored hooding of the earth" (p. 137). During a nighttime hunting bivouac in *Cities of the Plain* (1998), the reader is struck with this desert vision:

> They sat against a rock bluff high in the Franklins with a fire before them that heeled in the wind and their figures cast up upon the rocks behind them enshadowed the petroglyphs carved there by other hunters a thousand years before.... To the south the distant lights of the city lay strewn across the desert floor like a tiara laid out upon a jeweler's blackcloth [p. 87].

This keen sensitivity for the natural world is something that has been intrinsic to McCarthy's muse from day one. Going back to over 30 years before *Cities of the Plain*, to McCarthy's first novel, *The Orchard Keeper* (1965), one finds that even a simple snowstorm has a touch of transcendence:

> Some time after midnight on the twenty-first of December it began to snow. By morning in the gray spectral light of a brief and obscure winter sun the fields lay dead-white and touched with a phosphorous glow as if producing illumination of themselves, and the snow was still wisping down thickly, veiling the trees beyond the creek and the mountain itself, falling softly, and softly, faintly sounding in the immense white silence [p. 131].

Even the devastated natural landscape of *The Road* is conveyed with compelling sensitivity and literary grace: "The soft black talc blew through the streets like squid ink uncoiling along a sea floor ... and the scavengers passing down the steep canyons with their torches trod silky holes in the drifted ash that closed behind them silently as eyes" (p. 181).

At other times, McCarthy's writing makes a great metaphysical leap, unfurling an omniscient narrative voice that suddenly intrudes upon the scene, bellowing from the cracked heavens. This is what fellow Pulitzer Prize–winning author William Kennedy has called the "exalted prose that is McCarthy's signature ... the linguistic excesses and the philosophizing for which he has been both venerated and mocked." It is an antiquarian voice akin to *Moby-Dick* or the Old Testament, yet still very much McCarthy's own, rushing out in an archaic tumble of words and bent to his distinct purposes.

In *Blood Meridian* (1985), the voice rings out in the pregnant moment before the murder of one Glanton Gang member by another: "Here beyond men's judgments all covenants were brittle," writes McCarthy. "About that fire were men whose eyes gave back the light like coals socketed hot in their skulls and men whose eyes did not, but the black man's eyes stood as corridors for the ferrying through of naked and unrectified night from what of it lay behind to what was yet to come" (p. 106). In that same novel, mounted Apache warriors unleash "high wild cries carrying that flat and barren pan like the cries of souls broke through some misweave in the weft of things to the world below" (109).

Another instance of this high, archaic oratory comes almost a decade later, when Billy cradles the dead she-wolf at the end of book 1 of *The Crossing*: "He took up her stiff head out of the leaves and held it or he reached to hold what cannot be held, what already ran among the mountains at once terrible and of a great beauty," McCarthy writes. "What blood and bone are made of but can themselves not make on any altar nor by any wound of war. What we may well believe has power to cut and shape and hollow out the dark form of the world surely if wind can, if rain can" (p. 127).

At these moments, McCarthy's language seems to burst free from the narrative and enter a different realm. Or as Will Blythe, writing in the *New York Times*, put it, "There is a way in which his writing delaminates from what it represents, and begins to sing by itself. The real hero of a McCarthy novel is the rhetoric."

Of course there is also a dark side to McCarthy's art, one that provides a compelling undertow to his beautiful prosaic flights. The writer's one constant and consistent preoccupation has been death and violence, and his novels often conjure up visions that other writers would never dare broach. In *The Road*, the man and boy come upon an abandoned campfire, where the "headless and gutted" corpse of an infant is "blackening on the spit" (p. 198), while in *Blood Meridian*, the kid encounters a mesquite bush that is adorned with dead babies, like some grisly, unthinkable ornaments "hung so by their throats from the broken stobs ... to stare eyeless at the naked sky" and "bloated, larval to some unreckonable being" (p. 57).

There is, of course, also the infanticide in *Outer Dark* (1968), or the serial killer who engages in acts of necrophilia in *Child of God* (1973), or the veritable bloodbath that constitutes McCarthy's nineteenth-century West in *Blood Meridian*. For McCarthy, violence is a fact of human existence; it is not symbolic, and it is something that must be confronted head-on and dealt with in all its lineaments.

It is interesting, however, that a writer known for such excesses — in his language, in his plumbing philosophical explorations, in his violent descriptions — should also come to be defined by such grammatical sparseness. For one, McCarthy's dialogue avoids quotation-mark usage and often attribution as well. (Somehow, though, the reader remains oriented as to who is speaking.)

Another striking quality of his dialogue is the tendency to lapse into Spanish, without any translation. His characters often engage in long, complex exchanges in that tongue before the narrative reverts back to English. Another symptom of his grammatical parsimony lies in his usage of commas and apostrophes — which appear only sparingly — and in his utter avoidance of semicolons, which McCarthy considers anathema. "There's no reason to blot the page up with weird little marks," he told Oprah Winfrey in 2007. He also noted that James Joyce was a "good model for punctuation. He keeps it to an absolute minimum" (Winfrey).

Despite all of his distinct tendencies, however, one should be cautious about trying to encapsulate McCarthy's style, as his canon itself is stylistically diverse. There is the dark Appalachian soul of his early Southern Gothics and the vast metaphysical expanse of his Western novels. There is the bursting-at-the-seams, "sloppy, baggy, shaggy" *Suttree* (1979) and the taut, blistering crime thriller *No Country for Old Men* (2005) (Bell, "A Writer's View," p. 7). And, of course, there is the riveting, sometimes impressionistic starkness of the Pulitzer Prize–winning *The Road*. What we see in McCarthy's catalogue is a compelling array of approaches and thematic matter and a style that is, by any standard, unparalleled and very much his own.

The Sunset Limited: A Novel in Dramatic Form

Cormac McCarthy's play *The Sunset Limited: A Novel in Dramatic Form* has been alluded to as "essentially an intellectual slugfest centered around two diametrically opposed points of view.... The ultimate question raised by McCarthy isn't should we live or die, but rather what should we do while we're living" (Siegel). The play premiered in May 2006 at the Steppenwolf Theater in Chicago, and then the same production moved to New York City for a short run in October of that same year. It featured actors Austin Pendleton (as "WHITE") and Freeman Coffey (as "BLACK") and was directed by Sheldon Patinkin.

The *New York Times* performance review was quite favorable, describing the play as "a poem in celebration of death" and comparing it to the work of Samuel Beckett (Zinoman). *Variety* magazine was less charmed by McCarthy's theater foray, however, claiming that the "inert" play "remains glued to the printed page" and "[neglects] drama for literary eloquence." The same review sized it up as "a talky play that goes nowhere and signifies far less than it thinks it does" (Stasio).

The play consists of two characters, named "BLACK" and "WHITE," monikers that represent both the characters' race and their opposing outlook on existence. (Here, as he so often does, McCarthy works with contradiction: BLACK possesses the more positive outlook of the two.) At the outset, we learn that BLACK, an ex-convict, has recently saved WHITE, a professor, from throwing himself in front of a subway train. Black is a man of faith, who espouses the teachings of the Bible, while White is an atheist and nihilist. The two sit in BLACK's New York City tenement apartment and pit their worldviews against each other. "I yearn for the darkness. I pray for death," WHITE says. "Real Death. If I thought that in death I would meet the people I've known in life I don't know what I'd do. That would be the ultimate horror" (p. 57).

Theatergoers unfamiliar with McCarthy's oeuvre may have been shocked by the bleakness of vision expressed by WHITE, but the author has worked with these notions before; in fact, a line spoken by the mother in the Pulitzer Prize–winning *The Road* (2006) works strikingly similar terrain: "As for me my only hope is for eternal nothingness and I hope it with all my heart," she says (p. 57). But never has McCarthy had a character undertake such a sustained and eloquent argument for personal obliteration as WHITE does.

Nevertheless, the compelling difference between WHITE and BLACK is the source of their beliefs. WHITE, the professor, has lived an intellectual life of ideas, and his belief system stems from that type of existence, an existence centered on study and books, on empiricism and the humanities. BLACK, on the other hand, has experienced what it is like to kill a man, endure prison, and then nearly die in a knife fight before turning to the church with a zeal borne of firsthand suffering. BLACK has had intimate encounters with bloodshed and violence and has sublimated his experience into conviction—and with this conviction he attempts to save the soul of WHITE (after he has literally saved him from being hit by a speeding train).

But WHITE's dark logic and rationality are relentless and often impossible for BLACK to pierce—though both parties bring great urgency to the table, making for a formidable philosophical standoff. In fact, in the end, neither is swayed from his convictions—neither WHITE from his intent to end his own life nor BLACK from his unwavering faith in God and His word.

The *New York Times* suggests that "it's best to view the characters as something other than real people in a piece of naturalism" (Zinoman). And the précis of the play at the Cormac McCarthy Society website takes largely the same tack, claiming that the author "aims at capturing the internal debate of the thoughtful individual seeking to navigate ... earthly existence, who hears ... the competing voices of, on the one hand, empirical reasoning and world-wearying experience and, on the other, hope and the transcendent spirit" (Luce, *Sunset Limited* synopsis). And this seems the best manner in which to approach *The Sunset Limited*, especially as it complicates any attempts to attribute WHITE's purely nihilistic views to the author himself, as is so often done.

Suttree

While many of McCarthy's novels could certainly be classified as unique, *Suttree* (1979) particularly stands out as distinct within the writer's catalogue. For one, it has somewhat of an autobiographical basis, taking up a central figure in McCarthy's native Knoxville, Tennessee (during the early 1950s), who has cast aside his genteel upbringing and abandoned all forms of family for an indigent life on a rickety houseboat. (Exactly *how* autobiographical it is can only be guessed at by critics.)

Here he fishes, pulling up his catch from the malodorous river bilge and drifting through the violent, grotesque underbelly of the city streets and environs. His adopted family consists of criminals, drunks, and the simply down-and-out. Taking a cue from James Joyce's *Ulysses*—and its central character, Leopold Bloom—Cornelius Suttree's "epic" journey is a grotesque and elliptical voyage through the seamiest parts of the city.

The dense novel is virtually bursting at the seams with characters, sub-plots, pungent descriptions, and esoteric sermonizing (from that omniscient narrative voice that occasionally bursts forth in McCarthy's novels). Writer Madison Smartt Bell considered it "unlike the other books, being sloppy, baggy, shaggy, and fundamentally unfinished, and yet ... ambitious" ("A Writer's View," p. 7). Indeed, *Suttree* is ambitious; it is also an extreme reading experience, an effusion of language riveted by gross humor, scatology, and random violence. The prose is as verdant, steamy, and overgrown as the very kudzu-choked forests of Tennessee.

There is also a sublime aimlessness to the plot, with no clear line of action driving it. Suttree simply drifts through Knoxville, fishing, drinking, checking in on pals, and occasionally running up against dumb, blind bad luck: An anonymous rock fastballed with remarkable accuracy off his head, a heavy floor buffer hoisted and smashed down upon his yielding skull, a deadly case of typhoid fever.

Nevertheless, as Vince Brewton points out, even the violent events in the novel "have neither a cumulative effect nor contribute to a narrative movement toward one central or conclusive moment" but are "inherently provisional" (p. 127). The same could be said of the whole yoked-together string of encounters that constitutes *Suttree*, which, despite its lack of narrative drive, remains a fascinating work on many levels.

In *Suttree*'s ambitious and gushing prose, we also see a different kind of writing than that in Cormac McCarthy's previous books, which had been tightly controlled, well-crafted visions — "perfect little books," as Madison Smartt Bell put it ("A Writer's View," p. 8). By contrast, *Suttree* is boundless, ungainly, vividly imagined, and clearly an indicator of things to come, for such later, weighty tomes as *Blood Meridian* (1985) and *The Crossing* (1994) share *Suttree*'s lush, darkly meditative style. And while James Joyce is the writer who is constantly evoked when discussing *Suttree*, surely we also see McCarthy stretching the limits of his prose toward his hero Herman Melville. (Some of the novel's scope and ambition may also derive from the fact that McCarthy plugged away at the book over two decades.) If you are looking for the root of *Blood Meridian*'s Melvillian oratory and bloody and brutal vision — it is here, in nascent form, on a smaller canvas (Knoxville instead of the historical West or the boundless oceans).

However, *Suttree*, while possessing very Southern Gothic moments, is less of that ilk than the previous three novels. At times the book reads more like the brutal realism of the economically and racially marginalized — and the characters' "marginalization makes them especially vulnerable to the violence that permeates all levels of the wasteland" (Giles, p. 84). This is a selective realism, through the lens of a certain strata of citizen — for many readers, it may come off as grotesque; for McCarthy, it is presented as a fact of life.

A man who lives in a makeshift hovel beneath a bridge has a different relationship to human waste. A man who must steal animals in order to feed himself has a different experience than those who shop in the grocery store. Thus, we encounter Harrogate in the early preparation stages of dinner: "the pig's fearcrazed eye looked up at him. A whitish matter was seeping from its head ... he brought the pipe down again over its skull, starting the eye from its socket" (p. 140).

Furthermore, a black man such as Ab who stays on the wrong side of the law and openly wages a pitched battle against the police in 1950s Tennessee must always live a hair's breadth from police-inflicted violence. "If you grow up in the South, you're going to see violence," McCarthy has stated. "And violence is pretty ugly" (Kushner). Perhaps the last word on McCarthy's alleged "grotesqueness" should be left to Flannery O'Connor, who once chafed at the Southern Gothic tag by bitingly remarking, "I have found that anything that comes out of the South is going to be called grotesque by the northern reader, unless it is grotesque, in which case it is going to be called realistic" (O'Connor, p. 40).

Another way in which *Suttree* diverges from most of McCarthy's canon is in the representation of "an intellectual focal character," though latter-day McCarthy characters such as the father in *The Road* (2006) and Sheriff Bell in *No Country for Old Men* (to a certain extent) could be described as such (Giles, p. 86). There is something thoughtful and noble about Suttree, despite his dissolute ways, and the book hints at but never fully addresses the deep psychological waters in him. We sense that he is intelligent; indeed, a sheriff who is acquainted with his past says, "I hear tell you're supposed to be real smart" (p. 157).

Also, the death of Suttree's young, estranged son and his break with his patrician roots add to his complexity. This complex portrait is furthered even more by the way in which he mentors Harrogate (one of McCarthy's most truly hilarious characters) and the way he looks after people such as Ab Jones, Daddy, and the ragman. In this way, Suttree seems influenced by the types of likeable anti-heroes that cropped up in the cinema of the 1960s and 1970s. There are certainly elements of Paul Newman's Luke in *Cool Hand Luke* (1967) or Jack Nicholson's portrayals of Randle Patrick McMurphy in *One Flew Over the Cuckoo's Nest* (1975) and Bobby Dupea in *Five Easy Pieces* (1970). (Suttree could be seen as a combination of all three.) Those who would balk at McCarthy drawing on such pop-culture fare should consider the author's own comments in *Time* magazine in 2007: "There are a lot of good American movies, you know," he said. "I'm not that big a fan of exotic foreign films. I think *Five Easy Pieces* is just a really good movie" (Ogden). No common reprobate, Suttree has the undeniable appeal of these cinematic anti-heroes.

There is also something much deeper and more figurative at work in *Suttree*, which springs from the central symbol of the Tennessee River and courses straight through Suttree himself. Traditionally, rivers represent a nourishing source of life, and fittingly Suttree makes his livelihood from the river. But in this novel the Tennessee River is also blighted, corrupted, and unhealthy; more importantly, it contains the dead. The novel opens with the corpse from a suicide being fished from its waters, and there are more corpses as well: the body of Leonard's father, which — having been wrapped in chains and dumped in the river — resolutely rises to the surface, as well as a dead baby that drifts by Suttree's boat.

The river represents an intermingling of life and death that also resonates elsewhere in the novel: "How surely are the dead beyond death. Death is what the living carry with them" (p. 153). This "death in life" motif is borne out in Suttree as well, who seems like the living dead at times. In fact, McCarthy terms Suttree and his cronies "the fellowship of the doomed" (p. 23). Suttree even has a dead doppelganger, a twin brother that "was born dead," a paradoxical phrase that has larger implications in the text (p. 17).

He encounters another death double when he returns to his houseboat to find a deceased man in his own bed, and it is interesting that the text never identifies who the man is or gives us enough information to differentiate it from Suttree (p. 465). In addition, while wandering the mountain glades, in the moments when starvation and exposure bring him to a point very near death, he senses a being that is moving just before him, "[s]ome doublegoer, some othersuttree" (p. 287). Not coincidentally, Suttree's stillborn twin had similarly led while Suttree followed: "we were like to the last hair.

I followed him into the world, me" (p. 14). This "death-double" imagery is consistent throughout the novel, first cropping up in the early pages: "He marches darkly toward his darkly marching shape in the glass of the depot door. His fetch come up from life's other side like an autoscopic hallucination, Suttree and Antisuttree, hand reaching to the hand" (p. 28).

We also see this co-mingling of life and death bear itself out in a photograph that the old witch Miss Mother shows Suttree. The image is of her grandmother, who is actually dead and lying in state in the photograph. A first, Suttree assumes he is looking at a photograph of a living person, as the corpse appears clear and vivid in the image. By contrast and paradox the very much alive (and at the time young) Miss Mother, who is also in the photograph, appears as a "grayed out patch, a ghost" that can be seen "yonder in that dead place" in a marginal area of the photograph (p. 279).

There are other descriptive passages that similarly blur the boundary between the dead and the living: For example, in Ab Jones' recently widowed wife Suttree witnesses "an eye for another kind of seeing ... to that still center where the living and dead are one" (p. 447). Additionally, in the book's final passage, a strangely ceremonial scene, a waterbearing boy offers Suttree up a dipper of water and he sees himself "twinned and dark and deep" in the child's eyes, yet again calling to mind Suttree's dead twin (p. 471). The book concludes with the image of a large hound, which is correlated in the final lines to a death hound from the underworld: "I have seen them in a dream, slaverous and wild and their eyes crazed with ravening for souls in this world. Fly them" (*ibid.*).

McCarthy's Knoxville comes off like a way station on the road to death, what Suttree terms a "terrestrial hell" (p. 14). In fact, most of his companions — those "thieves, derelicts, miscreants, pariahs ... murderers, gamblers, bawds, whores" with whom he spends his days — meet some kind of terrible end, leaving Suttree a rare survivor (p. 457). Critic Edwin T. Arnold considers Suttree's existence as "[f]or all practical purposes ... a state of purgatory" ("'Go to Sleep,'" p. 43), while the evocative opening incantation of the novel refers to Suttree's native environs as "*interstitial*," that is, a state "in between."

Death, as readers of Cormac McCarthy well know, is the author's very idiom. *Suttree* dwells constantly on its cusp, and no one describes the moment of death like McCarthy, his prose taking on a deeply pensive and deliberative cast, as if the death moment has opened up a secondary window through which to contemplate mysteries beyond human understanding. For example, in the shooting of Billy Ray Callahan, the infinitesimal moment between life and death is meditated upon:

> Billy Ray was standing there with a small discolored hole alongside his ruined nose. A trickle of thin blood started down his face.... For him perhaps it all was done in silence, or how would it sound, the shot that fired the bullet that lay already in his brain? These small enigmas of time and space and death [p. 376].

However, there are no morals to be drawn from *Suttree's* ruminations on death. As one assessment puts it, "There are no lessons to learn from *Suttree*, other than some vague acknowledgement of perseverance" (Forbes and Mahan, p. 66). There doesn't even seem to be much redemption in Suttree's leaving Knoxville and heading west at the end (for all we know, he could be en route to yet more mishaps), and the question of his relationship with his family remains unresolved.

Seeking resolution in *Suttree* is to miss the entire point of the reading experience; for, as previously mentioned, the book is an *extreme* reading experience, meant to take readers out beyond the margins of the familiar and into a realm that is flush up against death. We don't fully understand how Suttree came to break from his genteel roots and dwell here or what motivates him; McCarthy as usual steers wide of psychological implications.

For this and other reasons some critics, such as Vereen M. Bell (in the book *The Achievement of Cormac McCarthy*), have come to regard the novel as nihilistic. The very purposelessness of Cornelius Suttree's existence would seem to support such a view, but his heroic actions toward Harrogate and Ab (a truncated "Ahab" embarked on an all-consuming quest to destroy his own literally white whale, the police chief Tarzan Quinn) complicate this interpretation, as does Suttree's looking after the ragman.

Suttree could perhaps be termed a moral nihilist in his outright and aggressive rejection of organized religion, but again Suttree does have an ethical code that consistently comes to the fore: his refusal to take his share of mussels money from Reese, his selfless management of Joyce's prostitution earnings, his recovery of the Indian's boat. There is no mistaking the fact that Suttree is fundamentally "good" if often debauched; however in McCarthy's next book, *Blood Meridian*, the central character, the kid, is — at absolute best — ambivalent.

Upon the book's release in 1979, the *New York Times* review saw the character of Suttree as "a lost creature who can find no real hook into this world." The review also praised the novel's "rude, startling power" and viewed it as "personal and tough, without that boring neatness and desire for resolution that you can get in any well-made novel" (Charyn). In addition, the critic lauded the stylistic force of McCarthy's prose, which "creates images and feelings with the force of a knuckle on the head" (*ibid.*). Despite the power of its language, however, the book did not bring McCarthy to wider notice, and it remained relatively obscure until McCarthy's commercial success in the 1990s. In Knoxville, however, it has become a celebrated and hallmark book, much like James Agee's Pulitzer Prize–winning Knoxville-based novel, *A Death in the Family*.

See also Jones, Ab; Harrogate, Gene; Suttree, Cornelius

- *Further reading*

Charyn, Jerome. "Suttree." *New York Times Book Review*, February 18, 1979.
Giles, James Richard. "Violence and the Immanence of the 'Thing Unknown': Cormac McCarthy's *Suttree*." *Violence in the Contemporary American Novel: An End to Innocence*. Columbia: University of South Carolina Press, 2000, pp. 84–99.

Suttree, Cornelius

Cornelius Suttree, the titular character of Cormac McCarthy's fourth novel, *Suttree* (1979), is one of the author's most compelling early protagonists. There is even something heroic about the character, despite his abandonment of family and his commitment to a dissolute existence in the underbelly of Knoxville, Tennessee. And the book suggests but never fully explores the deep psychological waters in him.

The reader knows that he is relatively intelligent — perhaps too intelligent to be immersed in this kind of existence. In fact, a threatening sheriff says, "I hear tell you're supposed to be real smart" (p. 157). But Suttree's estrangement from his patrician roots and abandonment of wife and son only serve to make him more of a curiosity and fascination. Moreover, we witness firsthand his more noble qualities as he mentors Gene Harrogate and looks after people such as Ab Jones, Daddy, and the ragman.

Nevertheless, there is also something much deeper at work in the character of Suttree, something that resounds in the lines "How surely are the dead beyond death. Death is what the living carry with them" (p. 153). This "death in life" is central to understanding Suttree's Knoxville existence. McCarthy refers to Suttree and his cronies as "the fellowship of the doomed" (p. 23) and Suttree has a doppelganger, a twin brother that "was born dead" (p. 17).

He encounters another death twin when he returns to his houseboat to find a deceased man in his own bed — a man that is never satisfactorily differentiated from Suttree himself (p. 465). Additionally, in a mountain glade, suffering from starvation and exposure and lingering on the death precipice, he senses a death double yet again, "[s]ome doublegoer, some othersuttree" (p. 287). Suttree's Knoxville comes off like "a state of purgatory" (Arnold, "'Go to Sleep,'" p. 43), while the novel's mysterious opening incantation refers to Suttree's environs as "*interstitial*"—in-between.

In the book's final passage Suttree leaves Knoxville behind, and in a redolent and strangely ceremonial scene, a waterbearing boy offers Suttree a dipper of water and he sees himself "twinned and dark and deep" in the child's eyes — evoking, for the final time, Suttree's dead twin and the existence on the cusp of death that he is leaving behind (p. 471). The book concludes with a death hound, seemingly from the underworld: "I have seen them in a dream, slaverous and wild and their eyes crazed with ravening for souls in this world. Fly them" (*ibid.*). Suttree, though, is finally headed away from these death-life borderlands, perhaps toward a more purely "living" existence.

See also Jones, Ab; Harrogate, Gene; *Suttree*

Sylder, Marion

Marion Sylder is one of three protagonists in *The Orchard Keeper* (1965) connected to the book's grisly center: the old spray pit containing the decomposing body of Kenneth Rattner. Sylder is linked through his murder (in self-defense) of Rattner; John Wesley Rattner, Kenneth's son, is linked by heritage; and Arthur Ownby is linked by stewardship, keeping a "deadwatch" over the corpse and ritualistically laying cedar boughs over it for a period of seven years.

All three are additionally caught up in conflict with changing times: Ownby by virtue of his dogged adherence to ancient pastoral ways; while, for his part, young John Wesley simply can't seem to find a foothold between the ways of the old and the new as he comes of age in the community — a situation that will culminate in his abandonment of the community altogether.

But while Ownby remains a Southern Gothic stock type and John Wesley a relative *tabula rasa*, Sylder has contradictory impulses and light and dark aspects of his personality, emerging as McCarthy's most complete character in *The Orchard Keeper*. This is evidenced by Sylder's strivings for legitimacy on the one hand (factory work, fine clothes, impressive car) and his ultimately outlaw existence as a bootlegger on the other.

He at once seems to embrace the strictures of the community that he can't escape and reject the order they impose upon him. We also see the contradictory manifestations of the light and dark sides of his personality in his mentorship of John Wesley versus his predatory sexual trysts with young black women and his illicit disposal of Rattner's corpse. In the community, Sylder cuts an engagingly liminal figure, one foot deeply set in pastoral tradition (hunting, trapping) and another in modern urbanization (his glistening automobile, pressed gabardine, and ambition). Sylder's personal fastidiousness is one of his more compelling qualities. He calls to mind the accountant in Joseph Conrad's *Heart of Darkness* (1902) — the impeccably groomed man in his "starched collar" and "snowy trousers" who appears to Marlow like a vision, a person who, "in the great demoralization of the land ... kept up his appearance" (pp. 25–26).

And Sylder seems all too aware of some sanitary line between his native soil and himself, as if his accoutrements buffer him from the primordial dust that is his birthright. Tellingly, while engaged in a sordid tryst with one of the "country slatterns that hung on the city's perimeter like lost waifs," he "[e]xperimentally" wets a finger and draws "a white streak on the grime of her neck," as if gauging some sanitary boundary (p. 29).

Sylder also has the peculiar habit of ceremonially purchasing a pair of socks each Saturday, arriving at the shop "fresh-looking in starched khakis" and deliberating over his choice in a glass display case. Purchase made, he deliberately peels off his old socks, tosses them in the store stove and applies the fresh ones. Here, again, the under-things are a sanitary buffer between him and his native earth. But the clean socks both protect him and hide his mutation, the deformed foot that embodies the aberrations in his existence, much as his impeccable clothes and grooming can't conceal the "scar" of his connection to the tainted community — or perhaps who he really is: "On the back of his neck a scarlike gap between sunburn and hairline showed as he crossed the bar" (p. 14).

The white line mirrors the pale streak in the grime of the girl's neck, while the sunburn evokes the "redneck" epithet (p. 14). Moreover, as a prodigal son who returned to the community (with ultimately disastrous results), he serves as a prototype for John Wesley Rattner — yet another prodigal son who knows, through Sylder's example, that it's best to remain prodigal.

See also The Orchard Keeper; Ownby, Arthur; Rattner, John Wesley

Violence

The best initial guideline for a reader entering the violent narratives of Cormac McCarthy comes from Dana A. Phillips, who offered these cautionary words: "In

McCarthy's work," she wrote, "violence tends to be just that; it is not a sign or symbol of something else" (p. 435). In fact, violence is arguably the author's very idiom, and he has said that the only writers he takes seriously are those that directly confront issues of life and death. Throughout his career McCarthy has continually stared into the abyss of human violence, often without redemption or moralizing.

Nevertheless, when he turned his attention to the U.S.-Mexico borderlands, his unflinching and captivatingly vivid portrayals of bloodshed did seem to right a historical imbalance. Western historian Patricia Nelson Limerick has noted the American tendency to not face up "to the bitter reality of violence embedded in landscapes that Americans would later come to see as places of natural innocence, separated from the tragedy of history" (Foreword, p. xix). Karl Jacoby has also indicated how the "seeming inevitability of the western story" rooted in myths of the American frontier "has long desensitized us to both the region's violence and its other ways of being" (p. 6).

McCarthy's work moves strikingly against this grain, representing — particularly in *Blood Meridian* (1985) — what Vince Brewton has termed "informal violence ... violence that is fragmentary, unconsidered, 'random,' or 'senseless'" and not violence formalized by history, justice, or any moral codes (p. 122). Harold Bloom has described the novel as an "American ... tragedy of blood" that unflinchingly describes the "overwhelming carnage" that was very much the domain of the mid–1800s borderlands (p. 255).

Traditional historical narratives, by contrast, have the potential to "legitimize" or render rational mindless violence by giving it neatness and order and fitting it into a cause-and-effect or chronological sequence of events. But as Timothy Parrish and Elizabeth Spiller point out, the violence in McCarthy's border books is not aimed at the "compensatory pleasures of self-accusation." His renderings do, however, "remind us of how particularizing versions of history ... deny how we have become to be who we are" (p. 461).

We see another sort of "anti-history" in the detailing of events of the Mexican Revolution in the Border Trilogy, where that bloody epoch remains only in memory (though its inheritance and resonance is everywhere). And here is another case where the violence becomes the thing in the foreground, rendering all other details and facts subordinate. In *All the Pretty Horses* (1992), Dueña Alfonsa's narration of the events at the crucible of the revolution, the overthrow and execution of president Francisco I. Madera, highlights the specific and grisly details, particularly those of the torture and killing of the deposed president's brother, Gustavo.

She describes how "one of them came forward with a pick and pried out his good eye and he staggered away moaning in his darkness and spoke no more," and how a misshot revolver "tore away his jaw." Gustavo then "collapsed at the feet of the statue of Morelos. Finally a volley of rifle shots was fired into him." Even after his death, "[t]hey kicked his dead body and spat upon it. One of them pried out his artificial eye and it was passed among the crowd as a curiosity" (p. 237). In Alfonsa's rendering, all the ideals and politics that underpin the revolution dissipate into thin air and we are left with nothing but these acts, which she narrates in a stirringly cold and empirical manner.

And one can't help but think she shares the author's worldview when she proclaims, "What is constant in history is greed and foolishness and a love of blood and this is a thing that even God—who knows all that can be known—seems powerless to change" (p. 239). This is a worldview that finds its apotheosis in McCarthy's *The Road* (2006), in which the very world is blotted out, satisfying what the author himself has prophesied in an interview. In dismissing the idea that climate change would end civilization he proclaimed, "We're going to do ourselves in first" (Kushner).

See also History

- *Further reading*

Brewton, Vince. "The Changing Landscape of Violence in Cormac McCarthy's Early Novels and the Border Trilogy." *Southern Literary Journal* 37, no. 1 (Fall 2004), pp. 121–143.

Giles, James Richard. "Violence and the Immanence of the 'Thing Unknown': Cormac McCarthy's *Suttree*." *Violence in the Contemporary American Novel: An End to Innocence*. Columbia: University of South Carolina Press, 2000, pp. 84–99.

Jacoby, Karl. *Shadows at Dawn: A Borderlands Massacre and the Violence of History*. New York: Penguin Press, 2008.

"Wake for Susan"

This is a short story written by Cormac McCarthy while he was still a student at the University of Tennessee. This earliest known work by the author appeared in the university's student literary supplement, *The Phoenix*, in October 1959 and is attributed to "C.J. McCarthy, Jr." Of the work, McCarthy scholar Rick Wallach has written, "[P]redications of McCarthy's mature style are few and, except for a scattering of characteristic tags, this story could have been written by just about any nearly competent young author with an eye for naturalistic detail" ("Prefiguring Cormac," p. 15).

Nevertheless, Wallach does note of this immature early effort (which McCarthy has resisted having republished), "The narrative, even at this early stage of McCarthy's craft, is layered with ironies both subtle and biting" (*ibid.*, p. 16). Dianne C. Luce adds, "Though it carries few hints of the master of style and tone that McCarthy was to become, 'Wake for Susan' is a rather intricate experiment in narrative strategy" ("They Aint the Thing," p. 25).

The story describes a teenage boy, Wes, who is out exploring in the woods on a fall day. As often would become the case in Cormac McCarthy's later works, during the romp, Wes encounters remnants of the past, causing him to plunge backward into history (a largely imagined one). This evokes John Grady Cole's ride along an old Comanche trail in *All the Pretty Horses* (1992), Judge Holden's lectures among the Anasazi ruins, or even Llewelyn Moss' skirting among the rock pictographs in *No Country for Old Men* (2005).

Luce describes the tale as Wes' "coming to terms with human mortality and natural transitoriness through his act of creative imagination, an act triggered by his contact with the autumn woods and certain found or sought-after historical objects" (*ibid.*, p. 21). In the case of "Wake for Susan," it is first an expired rifle ball that stimulates Wes' historical imagination; the artifact causes him to summon the "ghosts of lean, rangy frontiersmen with powder horns and bullet pouches slung from their shoulders and carrying long-barreled, brass-trimmed rifles with brown and gold maple stocks" ("Wake for Susan," p. 3).

But it is his next encounter, with the gravestone of a 17-year-old girl that dates back to 1834, that becomes the centerpiece of the story and a historical whirlpool for his imagination: "From a simple carved stone, the marble turned to a monument; from a gravestone, to the surviving integral tie to a once warm-blooded, live person" (p. 4).

In reverie, Wes builds a whole life for the deceased Susan Ledbetter, one in which he becomes emotionally implicated. Emerging from the imagined history, he "wept for lost Susan, for all the lost Susans, for all the people; so beautiful, so pathetic, so lost and wasted and ungrieved" (p. 6). And if the youthful McCarthy shows a tendency toward a more "purple" brand of prose than his more calibrated later achievements, he also displays excess in his relatively liberal use of punctuation, the sort of marking up of the page (even with the taboo comma) that his later Spartan ethos toward grammar would never allow.

Nevertheless, "Wake for Susan" does indicate that certain thematic concerns were already rattling around in McCarthy's imagination as a neophyte writer, preoccupations that stay with him and come to drive some of his most lauded novels, most prominently what Luce describes as "the interaction of memory, imagination, and artifact" ("The Road and the Matrix," p. 204).

• *Further reading*

Luce, Dianne. "The Road and the Matrix: The World as Tale in *The Crossing*." *Perspectives on Cormac McCarthy*, eds. Edwin T. Arnold and Dianne C. Luce. Jackson: University Press of Mississippi, 1999, pp. 195–220.

_____. "'They Aint the Thing': Artifact and Hallucinated Recollection in Cormac McCarthy's Early Frame-Works." *Myth, Legend, Dust: Critical Responses to Cormac McCarthy*, ed. Rick Wallach. Manchester, UK: Manchester University Press, 2000.

The Western

"The image of the West for writers ... underwent some major revision in the later part of the twentieth century," writes critic David H. Evans. "[T]he Western novel, long the unchallenged territory of the pulp specialist, was increasingly staked out by literary sodbusters with more serious ambitions — such as Larry McMurtry, Thomas Berger, and above all Cormac McCarthy" (pp. 862–863). McCarthy was already an established and critically acclaimed writer — if not a widely read one — when he took up the trope of the U.S.-Mexico borderland with 1985's *Blood Meridian*, a novel that replaced so many myths and images of the American Western with a mindless (and captivatingly rendered) savagery and philosophical discoursing on history and the bloody core of civilizations.

Blood Meridian reveled in what Vince Brewton has termed "informal violence ... violence that is fragmentary, unconsidered, 'random,' or 'senseless'" (p. 122). This was not violence attached to justice, codes, or honor — it was not the arranged showdown of *High Noon*. Rather, McCarthy's books "tend to dispense with the heavy moralism that accompanies most representations of violence in the traditional Western," writes Mark A. Eaton. "[T]he violence in *Blood Meridian* and to a lesser extent in the border trilogy is presented simply as one of the hard facts of frontier life" (p. 157). And while *Blood Meridian*, like so much of McCarthy's work (and like many Westerns), is bound up with the idea of the quest or journey—covering great swaths of land and including numerous geographical locations in the U.S. and Mexico—ultimately "the reader experiences a collapse of time and space so that only the ceaseless repetition of violence remains foregrounded, enacted in a kind of no-place of desolation" (Brewton, p. 131).

John Grady Cole, of *All the Pretty Horses* (1992), also undertakes a journey typical of the Western, galloping across the plains, deserts, and mountains. But he embarks on his quest self-consciously, aware that he is attempting to return to some kind of historical and mythic cowboy existence, "only to discover that no such return is possible" (Spurgeon, p. 42). Nevertheless, there is something "heroic"—in the old mode of the Western—about John Grady Cole and Billy Parham, the Border Trilogy protagonists, even though the books they inhabit call the myths and histories of the American West into question. (The kid, of *Blood Meridian*, despite his evolution in the novel, remains a largely ambivalent character that never quite approaches heroism.) But all of that collapses at the end of *Cities of the Plain* (1998), when McCarthy slams shut the frontier on Billy Parham and the cowboy becomes an old man who has seen all of the lineaments of his existence swallowed into an existential void. (Billy wonders aloud to the stranger toward the end of *Cities of the Plain*, "Where do we go when we die?" The man replies, "I don't know ... where are we now?" [p. 268].)

McCarthy's next Western, *No Country for Old Men* (2005), is arguably not a Western at all, but a potboiler thriller set in the 1980 U.S.-Mexico borderlands. But Sheriff Bell does come from a ranching and cowboy tradition familiar to those who have read the Border Trilogy—and the novel does seem to answer the question of what replaced the Western. But the answer McCarthy chooses for us is drug trafficking, which the author sees as an evil of the region that perhaps even Judge Holden, from *Blood Meridian*, could not have anticipated. Sheriff Bell mediates, "I think if you were Satan and you were settin around tryin to think up something that would just bring the human race to its knees what you would probably come up with was narcotics. Maybe he did" (p. 218).

And if we can trace an arc of commentary through McCarthy's Western novels and beyond them, perhaps *The Road* (2006)—though not set in the borderlands at all—is the culmination; for it is what the apocalyptic imagery in his borderlands works have hinted at all along: the end of the world as we know it.

See also All the Pretty Horses; The American Southwest; *Blood Meridian*; Borderlands; *Cities of the Plain*; *The Crossing*; History; *No Country for Old Men*

Whales and Men

Whales and Men (undated) is a screenplay written by Cormac McCarthy that, as of this writing, remains unpublished and unproduced. While the exact era of its composition is uncertain, Edwin T. Arnold indicates that it was likely written "based on internal evidence, in the mid-to-late 1980s, a decade during which McCarthy wrote a number of screenplays for film, none of which has yet been produced" (*Whales and Men* synopsis). During that same decade, the novels *Cities of the Plain* (1998) and *No Country for Old Men* (2005) saw first light as potential screenplays.

Whales and Men, which as of this writing is only available in the Cormac McCarthy Papers in the Southwestern Writers Collection at Texas State University–San Marcos library, is a primarily dialogue-driven work about the nature of whales, particularly their communication ability. The characters include a marine biologist (Guy Schuler) likely "based in part on McCarthy's friend and noted [marine animal expert] Roger Payne" (*ibid.*). Payne actually inscribed his 1995 book-length study *Among Whales* "to Cormac McCarthy" and furthermore noted that "Cormac McCarthy read nearly the entire text and made innumerable improvements to it" (p. 8). The 1992 *New York Times* interview with McCarthy noted, "At the MacArthur reunions he spends his time with scientists, like the physicist Murray Gell-Mann and the whale biologist Roger Payne, rather than other writers" (Woodward, "Venomous Fiction").

Other characters in the screenplay include a wealthy explorer (John Western), his girlfriend (Kelly McAmon), and a freewheeling Irish aristocrat (Peter Gregory). The screenplay is set in Florida, Ireland, and Sri Lanka. And as is typical for McCarthy, he uses the nature of whales as a wedge into probing philosophical questions.

In fact, some of the insights that fall from the characters' mouths are ideas that McCarthy will later wrestle with in the Border Trilogy. "What had begun as a system for identifying and ordering the phenomena of the world had become a system for replacing those phenomena," claims Peter Gregory in *Whales and Men*. "Language is a way of containing the world. A thing named becomes that named thing" (pp. 57–58; quoted in Lilly, pp. 149–150). This calls to mind the semiotic deliberations that will crop up in the Border Trilogy — for example, when Quijada tells Billy, "The world has no name. The names of the cerros and the sierras and the deserts exist only on maps. We name them [so] that we do not lose our way" (*The Crossing*, p. 387).

Women

One of the prime criticisms leveled at McCarthy's work is his portrayal of women. Women are rarely the focus of his novels, and when they do appear, they are not as fleshed-out and complex as the male characters. In 2005, the *New Yorker* noted this "claustrophobically male-locked" quality of McCarthy's fiction, and claimed the writer "has a tendency to omit half the human race from serious scrutiny" (Wood). In her TV interview with Cormac McCarthy, Oprah Winfrey pointed out, "There's not a lot of engagement with women in your books," to which McCarthy conceded, "Women are tough. I don't pretend to understand women."

Writing in London's *Guardian* in 1994, after the great success of *All the Pretty Horses* (1992), one journalist declared of McCarthy's male characters, her pen dripping with sarcasm, "Their lives are free, literally, of everything pedestrian: free of routine, of money, even of women, who intrude only rarely, as women should, offering platefuls of food, freshly laundered shirts, and occasionally, their bodies" (Bennett). A *Washington Post* critic opined that "women found *[All the] Pretty Horses* boringly macho" (Dirda, "End of His Tether"), while London's *Independent* proffered, "McCarthy's world is an existential one in which men face two choices — either to battle or to die; the female characters, meanwhile, cook and sew or sell themselves on the street" (Bradfield, "Mystery").

Indeed, in the wake of *All the Pretty Horses*, McCarthy has come to embody a distinct brand of literary masculinity, and a survey of his female characters pulls up few compelling renderings. The mother in *The Road* (2006) only exists as a memory, as she chose to take her own life rather than face the brutal post-apocalyptic world of the novel. In *No Country for Old Men* (2005), Carla Jean, Llewelyn Moss' wife, is a fretting, adoring character who takes direction from her husband. The central female character in *Cities of the Plain* (1998) is a young epileptic prostitute who spends the novel waiting for John Grady Cole to marry her and free her from her grim existence. In *The Crossing* (1994), a young Mexican girl that Billy Parham and his brother Boyd save actually becomes the brothers' undoing, as Boyd takes off with her, abandoning Billy, and then turns up dead.

In *All the Pretty Horses* (1992), John Grady Cole's mother, with whom he has only a tangential relationship, actually represents a threat to the very way of life celebrated in the novel, that of the cowboy rancher, when (after the death of John Grady's grandfather) she chooses to sell off the ranch that has been in the family for generations. Dueña Alfonsa, in the same novel, may be the one exception to the criticism leveled at McCarthy in that she is a powerful presence with a penetrating intellect and a feminist slant. "I am not a society person," she tells Cole. "The societies to which I have been exposed seemed to me largely machines for the suppression of women. Society is very important in Mexico. Where women do not even have the vote" (p. 230). But even she is shrewish and ultimately responsible for causing John Grady much hardship and suffering.

One academic critic even went so far as to suggest that in the Border Trilogy, each of McCarthy's books actually "excludes the potentially significant female characters as part of a process of the obviation of women" (Sullivan, "Boys Will Be Boys," p. 229). The same academic took an even more ominous stance on the female portrayals in McCarthy's fiction in another essay, claiming that, throughout the writer's canon, "female sexuality [was] inextricably bound up with death and, therefore, posed as a source of masculine dread" (Sullivan, "Evolution," p. 68). Nevertheless, McCarthy, like Ernest Hemingway before him, does seem to be an easy target for such criticism, as he unapologetically takes up masculinity as part of his very idiom. For, as novelist Jennifer Egan asserted, Hemingway and McCarthy represent the "apotheosis of a form of literary masculinity that features men in contention with the natural world, testing their expertise against it and finding, in their mastery of it, meaning — even grace."

Appendix A: Chronology of the Borderlands Works

1833: "The kid" is born. (*Blood Meridian*)

1846–1848: The Mexican War

1847: The kid, 14, runs away from home. (*BM*)

1848: The kid is shot in St. Louis. (*BM*)

Spring 1849: The kid first encounters Judge Holden, in the town of Nacogdoches, Texas. (*BM*)

July 1849: The members of the Glanton Gang, bearing the impaled heads of Apache on poles, are welcomed as heroes in the city of Chihuahua. (*BM*)

December 1849: The governor of the Mexican state of Sonora contracts the Glanton Gang to provide Apache scalps. (*BM*)

1854: The Gadsden Purchase is finalized. The United States paid Mexico ten million dollars for a 30,000-square-mile portion of Mexico that would become part of Arizona and New Mexico. Despite lingering disputes, it established the Southwestern border of the United States.

1866: John Grady Cole's maternal ancestors settle in a one-room house on 2,300 acres of land in West-Central Texas. The land was once part of the Fisher-Miller Grant. (*All the Pretty Horses*)

1872: The house that John Grady Cole, his mother, and grandfather were raised in is built on the cattle ranch, which had grown to 18,000 acres. (*ATPH*)

1878: The kid, now 45 years old, shoots a boy in self-defense on the plains of North Texas. Judge Holden murders the kid in a town (possibly the site of the future Abilene) near the Clear Fork of the Brazos River in Texas. (*BM*)

1883: The first barbed wire is put up on the Grady family ranch. (*ATPH*)

1886: All of the buffalo have vanished from the lands containing the Grady family ranch. (*ATPH*)

April–August 1898: The Spanish-American War

1898: The last two of John Grady Cole's eight maternal great uncles are killed in Puerto Rico during the Spanish-American War. (*ATPH*)

1910–1920: The Mexican Revolution

February 1913: Mexican president Francisco I. Madero and his brother, Gustavo A. Madero, are executed during the period of the Mexican Revolution known as the "Ten Tragic Days" (*La decena trágica*).

June 1914: Alejandra Rocha's grandfather is killed in a plaza in Zacatecas, Mexico, during the revolution. (*ATPH*)

1939–1945: World War II

1941: At the opening of *The Crossing*, Billy Parham is 16 and his brother Boyd is 14. Billy's first two crossings into Mexico — with the wolf and with Boyd — transpire this year.

December 1941: The United States declares war on Japan on the 8th and on Germany on the 11th.

December 1941: After his second journey into Mexico (with Boyd), Billy crosses the border back into the United States at Columbus, New Mexico, and unsuccessfully tries to enlist in the military. (*The Crossing*)

1942–1943: Billy drifts, working at ranches in the North Texas panhandle and then heading south to work on numerous small ranches. (*C*)

March 1944: Billy, now 20 years old, visits his old neighbor Mr. Sanders at the SK Bar Ranch before crossing back into Mexico for the third time, this time to search for his brother Boyd. (*C*)

April 1944: While searching for Boyd, Billy re-encounters the traveling opera company, now masquerading as a *lotería* caravan, at a fair in Madera, Mexico. (*C*)

May 1944: Billy hears a woman singing the *corrido* about his brother Boyd in a hotel garden in Casas Grandes. (*C*)

July 1945: In the final passages of *The Crossing*, Billy is awakened by the detonation of an atomic bomb in the New Mexico desert (near San Lorenzo and the Black Range) — presumably the Trinity test explosion.

March 1949: John Grady Cole and his terminally ill father ride together for a last time, crossing through the low hills from Tom Green County into Coke County. John Grady Cole's grandfather, the last to bear the Grady name, dies. The Grady ranch (in the unincorporated community of Knickerbocker, Texas, just outside of San Angelo) is planned for sale, and John Grady and Lacey Rawlins set off on horseback for Mexico. (*ATPH*)

April–June 1949: John Grady Cole and Lacey Rawlins work breaking wild horses at the Hacienda de Nuestra Señora de la Purísima Concepción. (*ATPH*)

June 1949: The closing on the sale of the Grady Ranch. (*ATPH*)

Thanksgiving Day 1949: John Grady Cole crosses the border back into the United States near Langtry, Texas. (*ATPH*)

December 1949: John Grady Cole appears before a judge in Ozona, Texas, to offer testimony regarding Jimmy Blevins' horse and tells the judge the story of his time in Mexico. (*ATPH*)

February 1950: John Grady Cole heads northwest from the border country toward his onetime home region in Tom Green County. (*ATPH*)

March 1950: John Grady Cole reunites with Lacey Rawlins in Knickerbocker, Texas, and returns his horse to him. (*ATPH*)

Fall 1952: Billy Parham, now 28 years old, and John Grady Cole, now 19, are employed at Mac McGovern's Cross Fours Ranch in Alamogordo, New Mexico, not far from the titular cities of the plain, El Paso, Texas, and Juárez, Mexico. (*Cities of the Plain*)

August 1966–May 1968: Llewelyn Moss, a protagonist in *No Country for Old Men*, serves in the Vietnam War.

Winter 1980: The action of *No Country for Old Men* takes place.

Spring 2002: In the epilogue of *Cities of the Plain*, Billy is now 78 years old. He works as an extra in a movie and then becomes itinerant.

Fall 2002: Billy is taken in by a family near Portales, New Mexico, who provide him a shed room in which to sleep. (*CP*)

Appendix B: Topics for Discussion, Research, and Study

The Orchard Keeper

1. Explain the significance of the opening scene, wherein a wrought-iron gate is embedded in the trunk of an old elm tree.
2. Compare, contrast, and analyze the orientation of the three main characters — John Wesley Rattner, Arthur Ownby, and Marion Sylder — toward their community.
3. Describe how the conflict between the old ways and the new plays out in *The Orchard Keeper*.
4. What commentary is suggested by the repeated "cat" imagery?
5. Why is Arthur Ownby the title character of the novel when so much of the narrative focuses on the coming-of-age tale surrounding John Wesley Rattner?

Outer Dark

6. Propose how the three malevolent figures might not be literal figures at all, but aspects of Culla.
7. What do Culla's and Rinthy's respective (and very different) journeys in the novel say about them?
8. Does the vagueness regarding time period and setting enhance or take away from the story? Explain.
9. Indicate the elements in *Outer Dark* that are like a Brother's Grimm fairy tale (particularly the Grimm tale "Brother and Sister"). What can be deduced about *Outer Dark* through this comparison?

Child of God

10. Explain how this novel can be seen as more of a bildungsroman than a work of horror.
11. Explain and support the novel's insistence that Lester Ballard is a child of God, just like anyone else.

12. What effect does the plumbing of Ballard's unexpected emotional depths late in the novel have on the overall narrative?
13. What effect does the often grotesque and caricatured writing style have on the tale?
14. Support critic Edward J. Pacientino's assertion, "Without delving into sentimentality, McCarthy nonetheless demands our consideration for such an essentially unsympathetic character" (p. 199).
15. What is the significance of the description of the autopsy of Lester Ballard's body?

Suttree

16. Explain how the Knoxville underbelly described in the novel represents a sort of "death in life" co-mingling.
17. What is the significance — on a more emblematic level — of the dead man that Suttree finds in his bed? Relate it to the many other "doubles" in the novel, including Suttree's stillborn twin, the "doublegoer, some othersuttree" in the mountain glades (p. 287), and the image of "Suttree and Antisuttree, hand reaching to the hand" (p. 28).
18. What sort of racial commentary emerges from the portrait of Ab Jones and his pitched war of attrition with the local police?
19. Should one characterize the ending of *Suttree* as uplifting, ambivalent, or ultimately hollow? Explain.

Blood Meridian

20. Esteemed literary critic Harold Bloom has written, "I venture that no other living American novelist ... has given us a book as strong and memorable as *Blood Meridian*." He also claimed that the "fulfilled renown of *Moby-Dick* and of *As I Lay Dying* is augmented by *Blood Meridian*, since McCarthy is the worthy disciple of both [Herman] Melville and [William] Faulkner" (pp. 254–255). Assuming that Bloom's praise is warranted, what is it about this novel that deserves such accolades?
21. Is Judge Holden immortal, as he claims? Explain.
22. What post-colonial commentary emerges from the fact that Judge Holden is at once a paragon of "civilized" man and capable of terrible savagery?
23. Neil Campbell has described *Blood Meridian* as an "excessive, revisionist, and contradictory narrative" that "both rewrites the histories of the West ... and maintains and utilizes many of the Western archetypes familiar in this genre of writing" (p. 217). Support this reading of the novel.
24. Is there a moral and ethical evolution in the kid? Explain.
25. How can one justify the sheer bloodletting and brutality that is vividly rendered in the novel?
26. Judge Holden proclaims that man's "spirit is exhausted at the peak of its achieve-

ment. His meridian is at once his darkening and the evening of his day" (pp. 146–147). Explain how this is a key idea for reading the book.

27. How do the opening quotes from Paul Valéry and Jacob Boehme and the 1982 newspaper snippet — reporting that anthropologists have discovered "a 300,000-year-old fossil skull" that "shows evidence of having been scalped" (p. 1) — pertain to the novel that follows?

28. How does one explain the book's mysterious epilogue, in which a lone figure progresses across the plain "by means of holes which he is making in the ground. He uses an implement with two handles and he chucks it into the hole and he enkindles the stone in the hole with his steel hole by hole striking the fire out of the rock which God has put there" (p. 337)?

All the Pretty Horses

29. Explain how *All the Pretty Horses* both upholds and questions the myths and romance of the Western genre.

30. Despite taking place decades after the end of the Mexican Revolution, all of the Border Trilogy books resonate with memories of that bloody epoch. What is the function of the Mexican Revolution in the Border Trilogy?

31. What is Dueña Alfonsa's purpose for narrating to John Grady Cole the events surrounding the execution of Mexican president Francisco Madero and his brother, Gustavo?

32. What does Jimmy Blevins' death represent to John Grady Cole?

33. How does John Grady Cole's perspective on Mexico evolve throughout the novel?

34. Why does Alejandra show John Grady Cole the spot in the plaza in Zacatecas where her grandfather was killed during the revolution?

35. When asked by Rawlins where his country is, why does John Grady Cole respond, "I don't know where it is. I don't know what happens to country" (p. 299)?

The Crossing

36. Explain the difference between the three crossings in the novel and link them to the title. Why is the title singular ("crossing")? What figurative "crossings" are also explored in the book?

37. Why does Billy Parham abandon home to bring the pregnant she-wolf to Mexico?

38. How does the author use the idea of the *corrido* to explore larger issues in the novel?

39. What is the purpose of the lengthy tale of the heretic that the Mormon hermit relates to Billy?

40. What is the literary function of Billy's frequent and apocalyptic dreams?

41. What does Quijada mean when he says to Billy, "Your brother is in that place which the world has chosen for him.... And yet the place he has found is also of his own choosing. That is a piece of luck not to be despised" (pp. 387–388)?

42. What significance can be gleaned from the gypsy's tale of the two identical biplanes that crashed in the high desert mountains of Sonora during the Mexican Revolution?

43. The primadonna from the opera company says to Billy and Boyd, "You will see. It is difficult even for brothers to travel together on such a voyage. The road has its own reasons and no two travelers will have the same understanding of those reasons" (p. 230). Explain the meaning of her words as they apply to the two brothers.

44. Explain the significance of the final scene in *The Crossing*. If this is indeed the Trinity test explosion of the atom bomb, how does this event fit into a larger worldview established in the trilogy?

Cities of the Plain

45. How is this novel, which brings together the individual heroes of the previous two trilogy books, John Grady Cole (*All the Pretty Horses*) and Billy Parham (*The Crossing*), disorienting in its opening pages for those familiar with the characters?

46. How does the title's biblical allusion — "cities of the plain" (Sodom and Gomorrah) — play out in this work?

47. Reviewer Sara Mosle wrote that "McCarthy is concerned not just with the history of the American Southwest but with all the 'cities of the plain'" and the "brief moment between a culture's existence and extinction — this is the border that McCarthy's characters keep crossing and recrossing" (p. 16). Explain how this idea applies to the novel *Cities of the Plain*.

48. The stranger at the end of the novel tells Billy, who is now an old man, that one's life "vanishes at its own appearance. Moment by moment. Until it vanishes to appear no more ... is there a point in time when the seen becomes the remembered? How are they separate?" (p. 273). How is this statement significant to the tale of Billy, as witnessed in both this novel and in *The Crossing*?

49. What is the meaning behind the following exchange between Billy and the kind woman that has taken him in at the end of the novel? "I'm not what you think I am. I ain't nothing. I dont know why you put up with me," Billy says, to which she responds, "Well, Mr. Parham, I know who you are. And I do know why. You go to sleep now" (p. 291).

No Country for Old Men

50. Compare the character of Anton Chigurh to Judge Holden. How are they similar? What ultimately distinguishes one from the other?

51. Compare William Butler Yeats' "Sailing to Byzantium," from which the title of this novel is taken, to *No Country for Old Men*. How does McCarthy adapt and reconfigure the ideas from the Yeats poem?

52. How does *No Country for Old Men* display a thread of continuity with McCarthy's other border novels?
53. Some reviewers found Sheriff Bell's meditations highly evocative, while others thought they weighed down the main driving action of the novel. Show how the italicized Sheriff Bell chapters are crucial to *No Country for Old Men*.

The Road

54. Author William Kennedy, reviewing the book for the *New York Times*, termed the character of the boy as a "designated but unsubstantiated messiah." Is there enough in the novel to suggest that the boy is truly some sort of messianic figure?
55. Compare the character Ely to the biblical prophet Elijah and *Moby-Dick*'s Elijah (which is rooted in the biblical). What can one interpret from the ideas that the Ely of *The Road* espouses in his conversation with the boy's father?
56. What can be said of the father's relationship with God, to whom he occasionally speaks?
57. How does McCarthy offer a completely unprecedented and fresh take on the post-apocalyptic genre with *The Road*? Compare it to notable books of the genre such as Stephen King's *The Stand* (1978) or Richard Matheson's *I Am Legend* (1954).
58. How does one read the final passage of the novel, about the "brook trout in the streams in the mountains" so that it makes sense in the larger scheme of the narrative?

Bibliography

PRIMARY SOURCES

McCarthy, Cormac. *All the Pretty Horses*. New York: Knopf, 1992; first Vintage International edition, 1993.
_____. *Blood Meridian, or The Evening Redness in the West*. New York: Random House, 1985; first Vintage International edition, 1992.
_____. *Child of God*. New York: Random House, 1973; first Vintage International edition, 1993.
_____. *Cities of the Plain*. New York: Knopf, 1998; first Vintage International edition, 1993.
_____. *The Crossing*. New York: Knopf, 1994; first Vintage International edition, 1995.
_____. *The Gardener's Son* (television play), 1977; published as *The Gardener's Son: A Screenplay*, Hopewell, NJ: Ecco Press, 1996.
_____. *No Country for Old Men*. New York: Knopf, 2005; Vintage Movie Tie-In edition, 2007.
_____. *The Orchard Keeper*. New York: Random House, 1965; first Vintage International edition, 1993.
_____. *Outer Dark*. New York: Random House, 1968; first Vintage International edition, 1993.
_____. *The Road*. New York: Knopf, 2006; first Vintage International edition, 2006.
_____. *The Stonemason: A Play in Five Acts*. Hopewell, NJ: Ecco Press, 1994.
_____. *The Sunset Limited: A Novel in Dramatic Form*. New York: Dramatists Play Service, 2006.
_____. *Suttree*. New York: Random House, 1979; first Vintage International edition, 1992.
Credited to "C.J. McCarthy, Jr.": "Wake for Susan." *The Phoenix* (University of Tennessee), October 1959, pp. 3–6.
Credited to C.J. McCarthy: "A Drowning Incident." *The Phoenix* (University of Tennessee), March 1960, pp. 3–4.

SECONDARY SOURCES

Abbey, Edward. *Desert Solitaire: A Season in the Wilderness*. Tucson: University of Arizona Press, 1968.
_____. *One Life at a Time, Please*. New York: Macmillan, 1988.
Abbott, Jacob. "Memoirs of the Holy Land." *Harper's Magazine* 5, no. 24 (October 1852), p. 577 (University of Michigan collection, digitized by Google).
Anderson, Benedict. *Imagined Communities: Reflections on the Origin and Spread of Nationalism*. Revised ed. London and New York: Verso, 1991.
Arnold, Edwin T. "'Go to Sleep': Dreams and Visions in the Border Trilogy." *A Cormac McCarthy Companion: The Border Trilogy*, eds. Edwin T. Arnold and Dianne C. Luce. Jackson: University Press of Mississippi, 2001.
_____. "The Last of the Trilogy: First Thoughts on *Cities of the Plain*." *Perspectives on Cormac*

McCarthy, eds. Edwin T. Arnold and Dianne C. Luce. Jackson: University Press of Mississippi, 1999, pp. 221–248.

_____. *Outer Dark* synopsis from the Cormac McCarthy Society website. http://www.cormacmc carthy. com/works/outerdark.html/. Accessed May 2009.

_____. "A Stonemason Evening." *The Cormac McCarthy Journal Online*, 2002. http://www.cor macmccarthy.com/journal/Default.htm.

_____. *Whales and Men* synopsis from the Cormac McCarthy Society website. http://www.cor macmccarthy.com/works/ whalesandmen.html/. Accessed June 2009.

"Author Cormac McCarthy receives PEN award." *USA TODAY*, May 4, 2009. http://www.usato day.com/life/books/news/2009–05–04-mccarthy-pen_N.htm.

Authors: William Faulkner. Discovery Channel documentary. http://videos.howstuffworks.com/ hsw/20055-authors-william-faulkner-video.htm.

Bancroft, Collette. "A Detour at the End of 'The Road.'" *St. Petersburg Times*, April 23, 2007, "Floridian," 1E.

Barra, Allen. "Delving into Post-Apocalypse." *The Philadelphia Inquirer*, September 25, 2006. http://www.lexis-nexis.com/.

Battersby, Eileen. "A Hard Crossing into the Future." *The Irish Times*, June 27, 1998, p. 67.

Bell, Madison Smartt. "The Man Who Understood Horses." *The New York Times Book Review*, May 17, 1992, p. 9.

_____. "A Writer's View of Cormac McCarthy." *Myth, Legend, Dust: Critical Responses to Cormac McCarthy*, ed. Rick Wallach. Manchester, UK: Manchester University Press, 2000.

Bennett, Catherine. "Home Thoughts: Write 'Em Cowboy." *The Guardian* (London), December 15, 1994.

Berry, K. Wesley. "The Lay of the Land in Cormac McCarthy's *The Orchard Keeper* and *Child of God*." *The Southern Quarterly* 38, no. 4 (2000), pp. 61–77.

Bettelheim, Bruno. *The Uses of Enchantment*. New York: Alfred A. Knopf, 1976.

Bhabha, Homi K. *The Location of Culture*. New York: Routledge, 2004.

Bilton, Alan. *An Introduction to Contemporary American Fiction*. New York: New York University Press, 2003.

Birkerts, Sven. "The Lone Soul State." *The New Republic*, July 11, 1994, pp. 38–41.

Bloom, Harold. *How to Read and Why*. New York: Scribner, 2000.

Blythe, Will. "Existence Precedes Essence. Yup!" *The New York Times*, June 9, 2002. http://nytimes. com/2002/06/09/books/existence-precedes-essence-yup.html.

Bradfield, Scott. "The Twilight Cowboy." *The Independent*, June 13, 1998. http://www.indepen dent.co.uk/life-style/books-the-twilight-cowboy-1164609.html.

_____. "When the Mystery Is That There Is No Mystery." *The Independent* (London), April 17, 1993.

Brancano, Manuel. *En/Clave de Frontera*, ed. Urbano Viñuela Angulo. Oviedo (Spain): Universidad de Oviedo, 2007.

Brewton, Vince. "The Changing Landscape of Violence in Cormac McCarthy's Early Novels and the Border Trilogy." *Southern Literary Journal* 37, no. 1 (Fall 2004), pp. 121–143.

Brickman, Barbara Jane. "Imposition and Resistance in Cormac McCarthy's *The Orchard Keeper*." *The Southern Quarterly* 38, no. 2 (2000), pp. 123–134.

Brickner, Richard P. "Child of God" (book review). *The New York Times Book Review*, January 13, 1974. http://nytimes.com/1974/01/13/books/mccarthy-child.html.

Brown, Bill. "Reading the West: Cultural and Historical Background." *Reading the West: An Anthology of Dime Westerns*, ed. Bill Brown. Boston: Bedford, 1997, pp. 1–40.

Bryant, J.A., Jr. *Twentieth-Century Southern Literature*. Lexington: University Press of Kentucky, 1997.

Bulkeley, Kelly. *Dreaming in the World's Religions*. New York: NYU Press, 2008.

Burns, Richard. "Bloody Episodes in the Setting Sun." *The Independent*, March 11, 1989.

Busby, Mark. "Into the Darkening Land, the World to Come: Cormac McCarthy's Border Cross-ings." *Myth, Legend, Dust: Critical Responses to Cormac McCarthy*, ed. Rick Wallach. Manchester, UK: Manchester University Press, 2000.

Caldwell, Gail. "Lone Star Cauldron." *The Boston Globe*, July 24, 2005, p. D6.

_____. "The Unsheltering Sky: Cormac McCarthy Completes His Trilogy of Man's Fate in the Borderlands." *The Boston Globe*, May 10, 1998. http://www.boston.com/globe/search/stories/books/cormac_mccarthy.htm.

_____. "What Bond between Dog and Master — And Master and Mutt." *The Boston Globe*, September 10, 1995.

Campbell, Neil. "Liberty beyond Its Proper Bounds: Cormac McCarthy's History of the West in *Blood Meridian*." *Myth, Legend, Dust: Critical Responses to Cormac McCarthy*, ed. Rick Wallach. Manchester, UK: Manchester University Press, 2000, pp. 217–226.

Chamberlain, Samuel. *My Confession: Recollections of a Rogue*. Lincoln: University of Nebraska Press, 1987.

Charyn, Jerome. "Suttree." *New York Times Book Review*, February 18, 1979. http://nytimes.com/1979/02/18/books/mccarthy-suttree.html.

Chollier, Christine. "Autotextuality, or Dialogic Imagination in Cormac McCarthy's Border Trilogy." *A Cormac McCarthy Companion: The Border Trilogy*, eds. Edwin T. Arnold and Dianne C. Luce. Jackson: University Press of Mississippi, 2001, pp. 3–36.

Coles, Robert. Review of *Child of God. The New Yorker*, August 1974, pp. 87–90.

Conrad, Joseph. *Heart of Darkness and the Secret Sharer*. Ed. Franklin Walker. New York: Random House, 1981.

Cornwell, Rupert. "Saul Bellow, Nobel-Winning Master of Melancholy, Dies." *The Independent* (London), April 6, 2005.

Danzen, J. Daniel. "Oprah's Interview with Cormac McCarthy." *Flak Magazine*. http://www.flakmag.com/books/cormacoprah.html.

Daugherty, Leo. "Gravers False and True: *Blood Meridian* as Gnostic Tragedy." *Perspectives on Cormac McCarthy*, eds. Edwin T. Arnold and Dianne C. Luce. Jackson: University Press of Mississippi, 1993, pp. 157–172.

Delbanco, Andrew. *Melville: His World and Work*. New York: Alfred A. Knopf, 2005.

Diebel, Linda. "U.S. Accepts Blame in Narco-War." *Toronto Star*, June 3, 2009, p. A7.

Dirda, Michael. "At the End of His Tether." *The Washington Post Book World*, June 5, 1994.

_____. "The Last Roundup." *The Washington Post Book World*, May 24, 1998.

Donoghue, Denis. "Teaching Blood Meridian." *The Practice of Reading*. New Haven, CT: Yale University Press, 2000, pp. 258–278.

Draper, Robert. "The Invisible Man." *Texas Monthly*, July 1992.

Eaton, Mark A. "Dis(re)membered Bodies: Cormac McCarthy's Border Fiction." *Modern Fiction Studies* 49, no. 1 (Spring 2003), pp. 155–180.

Edberg, Mark Cameron. *El Narcotraficante: Narcocorridos and the Construction of a Cultural Persona on the U.S.-Mexico Border*. Austin: University of Texas Press, 2004.

Egan, Jennifer. "Men at Work: The Literary Masculinity of Cormac McCarthy." *Slate*, October 10, 2006. http://www.slate.com/id/2151300/.

Ellis, Jay. "McCarthy Music." *Myth, Legend, Dust: Critical Responses to Cormac McCarthy*, ed. Rick Wallach. Manchester, UK: Manchester University Press, 2000.

_____. *No Place for Home: Spatial Constraint and Character Flight in the Novels of Cormac McCarthy*. Boca Raton, FL: CRC Press, 1996.

Ellis, Markman. *The History of Gothic Fiction*. Edinburgh, Scotland: Edinburgh University Press, 2000.

Evans, David. "The West of the Story." *Modern Fiction Studies* 54, no. 4 (Winter 2008), pp. 862–869.

Faulkner, William. *The Unvanquished* (the corrected text). New York: Random House, 1991.

Fleming, Michael. "Field Takes Universal's 'Creed.'" *Variety.com*, June 1, 2009.

Flood, Alison. "Cormac McCarthy Archive Goes on Display in Texas." *The Guardian* (London), May 18, 2009. http://www.guardian.co.uk/books/2009/may/18/cormac-mccarthy-archive-texas.

Flora, Joseph M., Lucinda Hardwick MacKethan, and Todd W. Taylor, eds. *The Companion to Southern Literature*. Baton Rouge: Louisiana State University Press, 2002.

Folks, Jeffrey Jay, and James A. Perkins. *Southern Writers at Century's End*. Lexington: University Press of Kentucky, 1997.

Forbes, Bruce David, and Jeffrey H. Mahan. "From American Dream to American Horizon: The Religious Dimension in Louis L'Amour and Cormac McCarthy." *Religion and Popular Culture in America*. Berkeley: University of California Press, 2000, pp. 56–76.

Giles, James Richard. "Violence and the Immanence of the 'Thing Unknown': Cormac McCarthy's *Suttree*." *Violence in the Contemporary American Novel: An End to Innocence*. Columbia: University of South Carolina Press, 2000, pp. 84–99.

Gonzales, Michael J. *The Mexican Revolution: 1910–1940*. Albuquerque: University of New Mexico Press, 2002.

Guillemin, Georg. *The Pastoral Vision of Cormac McCarthy*. College Station: Texas A&M University Press, 2004.

Gussow, Mel, and Charles McGrath. "Saul Bellow, Who Breathed Life into American Novel, Dies at 89." *The New York Times*, April 6, 2005. http://nytimes.com/2005/04/05/books/0406wire-bellow.html.

Hamnett, Brian R. *A Concise History of Mexico*. Cambridge, UK: Cambridge University Press, 1999.

Hart, John Mason. *Revolutionary Mexico: The Coming and Process of the Mexican Revolution*. Berkeley: University of California Press, 1997.

Hass, Robert. Review of *The Crossing*. *New York Times Book Review*, June 12, 1994, p. 31.

Hill, Douglas. "PAPERBACKS: Novels to Rattle the Chains in the Southern Gothic Cellar." *The Globe and Mail* (Canada), October 20, 1984.

Hinton, Diana Davids, and Roger M. Olien. *Oil in Texas: The Gusher Age, 1895–1945*. Austin: University of Texas Press, 2002.

Hobbes, Thomas. *Leviathan; or The Matter, Forme & Power of a Commonwealth, Ecclesiasticall and Civill*. 1651. Cambridge, UK: Cambridge University Press, 1904.

Holloway, David. *The Late Modernism of Cormac McCarthy*. Westport, CT: Greenwood Press, 2002.

Horn, John. "An Apocalypse You Can Bear." *The Los Angeles Times*, August 17, 2008. http://articles.latimes.com/2008/aug/17/entertainment/ca-road17. Retrieved December 13, 2008.

Hughes-Hallett, Lucy. "Almost Divine." *The Sunday Times* (London), June 7, 1998.

Jacoby, Karl. *Shadows at Dawn: A Borderlands Massacre and the Violence of History*. New York: Penguin Press, 2008.

James, Caryn. "Is Everybody Dead Around Here?" *The New York Times Book Review*, April 28, 1985, p. 31.

Jarrett, Robert L. *Cormac McCarthy: Twayne's United States Author Series*. New York: Twayne Publishers, 1997.

Johansson, Frans. *The Medici Effect: Breakthrough Insights at the Intersection of Ideas, Concepts, and Cultures*. Boston, MA: Harvard Business Press, 2004.

Jones, Malcolm, Jr. "Literary Lion in the Desert." *Newsweek*, May 18, 1992.

Josyph, Peter. "Tragic Ecstasy: A Conversation with Harold Bloom about Cormac McCarthy's *Blood Meridian*." *Southwestern American Literature* 26, no. 1 (Fall 2000), pp. 7–20.

"The Judge from Blood Meridian, by Cormac McCarthy." *The Daily Telegraph* (London), September 20, 2008, ART, p. 2.

Jung, Carl Gustav. *Psychology and Religion*. New Haven, CT: Yale University Press, 1992.

Kakutani, Michiko. "On the Loose in Badlands: Killer with a Cattle Gun." *The New York Times Book Review*, July 18, 2005. http://nytimes.com/2005/07/18/books/18kaku.html?_r=1.

Kaplan, Amy. "Romancing the Empire: The Embodiment of American Masculinity in the Popular Historical Novel of the 1890s." *American Literary History* 2 (1990), pp. 659–90.

Kastenbaum, Robert. *On Our Way: The Final Passage through Life and Death*. Berkeley: University of California Press, 2004.

Kennedy, William. "Left Behind." *The New York Times Book Review*, October 8, 2006. http://nytimes.com/2006/10/08/books/review/Kennedy.t.html.

King, Martin Luther, Jr. "Letter from a Birmingham Jail," April 16, 1963. African Studies Center, University of Pennsylvania. http://www.africa.upenn.edu/Articles_Gen/Letter_Birmingham.html/. Accessed July 26, 2009.

Kirn, Walter. "Texas Noir." *The New York Times Book Review*, July 24, 2005. http://nytimes.com/2005/07/24/books/review/24KIRNL.html.

Kooser, Ted. "American Life in Poetry: Column 148." http://www.americanlifeinpoetry.org/columns/148.html/. Accessed June 3, 2009.

Krauze, Enrique. *Mexico: Biography of Power*. New York: HarperCollins, 1998.

Kushner, David. "Cormac McCarthy's Apocalypse." *Rolling Stone*, December 27, 2007.

La Botz, Dan. *Democracy in Mexico: Peasant Rebellion and Political Reform*. Cambridge, MA: South End Press, 1995.

Lee McCarthy Obituary. *The Bakersfield Californian*, March 29, 2009. http://www.legacy.com/obituaries/bakersfield/obituary.aspx?n=lee-mccarthy&pid=125527543.

Lent, Jeffrey. "Blood Money." *The Washington Post*. July 17, 2005. http://www.washingtonpost.com/wp-dyn/content/article/2005/07/15/AR2005071500732.html.

Lilly, James D. "Of Whales and Men: The Dynamics of Cormac McCarthy's Environmental Imagination." *The Greening of Literary Scholarship: Literature, Theory, and the Environment*, ed. Steven Rosendale. Iowa City: University of Iowa Press, pp. 149–164.

Limerick, Patricia Nelson. Foreword to *Shadows at Dawn: A Borderlands Massacre and the Violence of History*, by Karl Jacoby. New York: Penguin Press, 2008.

_____. *The Legacy of Conquest: The Unbroken Past of the American West*. New York: W.W. Norton, 1988.

Limón, José E. *Mexican Ballads, Chicano Poems: History and Influence in Mexican-American Social Poetry*. Berkeley: University of California Press, 1992.

Luce, Dianne. "Ambiguities, Dilemmas, and Double-Binds in Cormac McCarthy's *Blood Meridian*." *Southwestern American Literature* 26, no. 1 (Fall 2000), pp. 21–46.

_____. "The Road and the Matrix: The World as Tale in *The Crossing*." *Perspectives on Cormac McCarthy*, eds. Edwin T. Arnold and Dianne C. Luce. Jackson: University Press of Mississippi, 1999, pp. 195–220.

_____. *The Sunset Limited* synopsis from the Cormac McCarthy Society website. http://www.cormacmccarthy.com/works/sunsetlimited.htm.

_____. "'They Aint the Thing': Artifact and Hallucinated Recollection in Cormac McCarthy's Early Frame-Works." *Myth, Legend, Dust: Critical Responses to Cormac McCarthy*, ed. Rick Wallach. Manchester, UK: Manchester University Press, 2000.

Mars-Jones, Adam. "Psycho Dramas: A Compelling Killer Is Central to Cormac McCarthy's Typically Lean and Stylish Novel." *The Observer* (London), November 6, 2005, reviews section, p. 15.

Martin, Douglas. "Shelby Foote, Historian and Novelist, Dies at 88." *The New York Times*, June 29, 2005. http://www.nytimes.com/2005/06/29/books/29foote.html.

Martínez, Oscar Jáquez. *U.S.-Mexico Borderlands: Historical and Contemporary Perspectives*. Lanham, MD: Rowman & Littlefield, 2003.

Maslin, Janet. "The Road through Hell, Paved with Desperation." *The New York Times*, September 25, 2005, p. E1. http://www.nytimes.com/2006/09/25/books/25masl.html.

Bibliography

McCaffrey, James M. *Army of Manifest Destiny: The American Soldier in the Mexican War (1846–1848)*. New York: New York University Press, 1992.

McGrath, Charles. "At World's End, Honing a Father-Son Dynamic." *The New York Times*, May 27, 2008. http://www.nytimes.com/2008/05/27/movies/27road.html.

McMurtry, Larry. *Oh What a Slaughter: Massacres in the American West (1846–1890)*. New York: Simon & Schuster, 2005.

Mehta, Sonny. Speech at 1992 National Book Awards, accepting for Cormac McCarthy's *All the Pretty Horses*. http://www.nationalbook.org/nbaacceptspeech_cmccarthy.html. Accessed June 3, 2009.

Melville, Herman. HM to Sarah Morewood, September 1851, in *Correspondence*. Evanston: Northwestern University Press; Chicago: Newberry Library, 1993, p. 206.

_____. *Moby-Dick: or; the Whale*. Evanston, IL: Northwestern University Press, 1988.

Miano, Sara Emily. "Take the Money and Run." *The Times* (London), November 5, 2005.

Morrison, Gail Moore. "*All the Pretty Horses*: John Grady Cole's Expulsion from Paradise." *Perspectives on Cormac McCarthy*, eds. Edwin T. Arnold and Dianne C. Luce. Jackson: University Press of Mississippi, 1999, pp. 175–194.

Mosle, Sara. "Don't Let Your Babies Grow Up to Be Cowboys." *New York Times Book Review*, May 17, 1998, p. 16.

Murdoch, David Hamilton. *The American West: The Invention of a Myth*. Reno: University of Nevada Press, 2001.

National Book Foundation website. http://www.nationalbook.org/index.html/. Accessed June 3, 2009.

"National Briefing. Southwest, New Mexico: A Mass for Border Crossers." *The New York Times*, November 3, 2004.

New Perspectives on the West. "Frederick Jackson Turner." The West Film Project and WETA, 2001. http://www.pbs.org/weta/thewest/people/s_z/turner.htm. Accessed July 24, 2009.

"Not a Pretty Sight: New Fiction." *The Economist*, July 30, 2005.

"Obama Administration Announces National Strategy to Reduce Drug Trafficking and Flow of Bulk Cash and Weapons across Southwest Border." *Biotech Business Week*, June 22, 2009.

O'Connor, Flannery. *Mystery and Manners: Occasional Prose*. Eds. Robert Fitzgerald and Sally Fitzgerald. New York: Macmillan, 1969, p. 40.

Ogden, Eric. "A Conversation between Author Cormac McCarthy and the Coen Brothers about the New Movie *No Country for Old Men*." *Time*, October 18, 2007. http://www.time.com/time/magazine/article/0,9171,1673269,00.html.

O'Hara, Helen. "Exclusive: Scott Talks Blood Meridian." *Empire* (UK), November 19, 2008. http://www.empireonline.com/News/story.asp?NID=23714.

Pacientino, Edward J. *The Enduring Legacy of Old Southwest Humor*. Baton Rouge: Louisiana State University Press, 2006.

Palmer, Louis H., III. "Southern Gothic and Appalachian Gothic: A Comparative Look at Flannery O'Connor and Cormac McCarthy." *Journal of the Appalachian Studies Association* 3 (1991), pp. 166–76.

Papineau, David. "BOOK REVIEW/Quantum leap of model professor: The Quark and the Jaguar." *The Independent*, July 17, 1994. http://independent.co.uk/arts-entertainment/book-review — quantum-leap-of-model-professor-the-quark-and-the-jaguar — murray-gelman-little-brown-1899-pounds-1414474.html. Retrieved January 3, 2009.

Parrish, Timothy B., and Elizabeth Spiller. "A Flute Made of Human Bone: *Blood Meridian* and the Survivors of American History." *Prospects* 23 (1998), pp. 461–481.

Payne, Roger. *Among Whales*. New York: Scribner, 1995.

PEN American Center. http://www.pen.org/.

Phillips, Dana. "History and the Ugly Facts of McCarthy's *Blood Meridian*." *American Literature* 68, no. 2 (June 1996), pp. 433–460.

Pick, Daniel, and Lyndal Roper, eds. *Dreams and History*. London: Psychology Press (Taylor & Francis Group), 2004.

Pilkington, Tom. *State of Mind: Texas Literature and Culture*. College Station: Texas A&M University Press, 1998.

Praz, Mario. "Hemingway in Italy." *Hemingway and His Critics*, ed. Carlos Baker. New York: Hill & Wang, 1961, pp. 116–130.

Prescott, Orville. "Still Another Disciple of William Faulkner," *The New York Times*, May 12, 1965. http://www.times.com/books/98/05/17/specials/mccarthy-orchard.html.

Quinones, Sam. "Mexico under Siege: Senators Take Concerns to the Border." *The Los Angeles Times*, March 31, 2009, p. A11.

Ragan, David Paul. "Values and Structure in *The Orchard Keeper*." *Perspectives on Cormac McCarthy*, eds. Edwin T. Arnold and Dianne C. Luce. Jackson: University Press of Mississippi, 1999.

Ratcliffe, Sophie. "New Fiction." *The Daily Mail* (London), October 28, 2005.

Rea, Steven. "Cowboy Tale Lost on Dusty Trail." *The Philadelphia Inquirer*, December 24, 2000.

Rebein, Robert. *Hicks, Tribes, and Dirty Realists: American Fiction after Post-Modernism*. Lexington: University Press of Kentucky, 2001.

Romero, Rolando. "Border of Fear, Border of Desire." *Borderlines* 1, no. 1 (1993), pp. 35–70.

Ryan, Matthew. "The Dystopian Rendering of Ideology and Utopia in Cormac McCarthy's *The Road*." Centre for Comparative Literature and Cultural Studies, Monash University (Australia). http://arts.monash.edu.au/cclcs/research/papers/dystopian-rendering.pdf.

Saltzman, Arthur. Book review: *The Spaces of Violence* (by James R. Giles). *Modern Fiction Studies* 53, no 4 (Winter 2007), pp. 895–898.

Sanborn, Wallis R. *Animals in the Fiction of Cormac McCarthy*. Jefferson, NC: McFarland, 2006.

Sánchez, Martha I. Chew. *Corridos in Migrant Memory*. Albuquerque: University of New Mexico Press, 2006.

Savage, D.S. *The Withered Branch: Six Studies in the Modern Novel*. London: Eyre & Spottiswoode, 1950.

Scoones, Jacqueline. "The World on Fire: Ethics and Evolution in Cormac McCarthy's Border Trilogy." *A Cormac McCarthy Companion: The Border Trilogy*, eds. Edwin T. Arnold and Dianne C. Luce. Jackson: University Press of Mississippi, 2001, pp. 131–160.

Scott, A.O. "Lost Souls Adrift across a Barren Mesa." *The New York Times*, December 25, 2000. http://www.nytimes.com/2000/12/25/movies/film-review-lost-souls-adrift-across-a-barren-mesa.html.

———. "Touch of Evil in West Texas." *The New York Times*, May 21, 2007.

Siegel, Barbara, and Scott Siegel. Performance review of *The Sunset Limited: A Novel in Dramatic Form*. *TheaterMania*, October 30, 2006.

Singletary, Otis A. *The Mexican War*. Chicago: University of Chicago Press, 1962.

Sipchen, Bob. "Abbey: Rage on the Range." *The Washington Post*, January 5, 1988, p. B2.

Smith, Damon. "A Great Western Is Shot to Pieces." *Western Daily Press* (Bristol, UK), May 24, 2001, p. 37.

Stacy, Lee, ed. *Mexico and the United States*. Tarrytown, NY: Marshall Cavendish, 2003.

Stambaugh, J.J. "Cormac McCarthy House Burns." Knoxville.com, January 28, 2009. http://www.knoxville.com/news/2009/jan/28/mccarthy-house-burns/. Retrieved February 9, 2009.

Stasio, Marilyn. Performance review of *The Sunset Limited: A Novel in Dramatic Form*. *Daily Variety*, October 31, 2006.

Stevens, Anthony. *Jung: A Very Short Introduction*. New York: Oxford University Press, 1994.

Spurgeon, Sara L. *Exploding the Western: Myths of Empire on the Postmodern Frontier*. College Station: Texas A&M University Press, 2005.

Suchlicki, Jaime. *Mexico: From Montezuma to the Fall of the PRI*. Washington, D.C.: Brassey's, 2001.

Sugg, Katherine. "Multicultural Masculinities and the Border Romance in John Sayles's *Lone Star* and Cormac McCarthy's Border Trilogy." *The New Centennial Review* 1, no. 3 (Winter 2001), pp. 117–154.

Sullivan, Nell. "Boys Will Be Boys and Girls Will Be Gone: The Circuit of Male Desire in Cormac McCarthy's Border Trilogy." *A Cormac McCarthy Companion: The Border Trilogy*, eds. Edwin T. Arnold and Dianne C. Luce. Jackson: University Press of Mississippi, 2001, pp. 228–254.

_____. "The Evolution of the Dead Girlfriend Motif in *Child of God* and *Outer Dark*." *Myth, Legend, Dust: Critical Responses to Cormac McCarthy*, ed. Rick Wallach. Manchester, UK: Manchester University Press, 2000, pp. 68–77.

Tatum, Stephen. *Cormac McCarthy's* All the Pretty Horses: *A Reader's Guide*. New York: Continuum Books, 2002.

"Texas State Acquires Cormac McCarthy Archives." *The Associated Press*, January 14, 2008.

Tidmore, Kurt. "Lighting Out for the Territory." *Washington Post Book World*, May 3, 1992, p. X1.

Timberg, Scott. "Shameless Pleasures." *Los Angeles Times*, July 27, 2008, p. F9.

Trilling, Lionel. "Hemingway and His Critics." *Hemingway and His Critics*, ed. Carlos Baker. New York: Hill & Wang, 1961, pp. 61–70.

Turner, Frederick Jackson. *The Frontier in American History*. New York: Henry Holt, 1921.

Updike, John. "Both Rough and Tender." *Due Considerations: Essays and Criticism*. New York: Ballantine Books, 2007.

Wallach, Rick. "Prefiguring Cormac McCarthy: The Early Stories." *Myth, Legend, Dust: Critical Responses to Cormac McCarthy*, ed. Rick Wallach. Manchester, UK: Manchester University Press, 2000, pp. 15–20.

Ward, Geoffrey C. *The West: An Illustrated History*. New York: Little, Brown, 1996.

Warner, Alan. "The Road to Hell." *The Guardian* (London), November 4, 2006. http://www.guardian.co.uk/books/2006/nov/04/featuresreviews.guardianreview4.

Wegner, John. "'Mexico para los Mexicanos': Revolution, Mexico, and McCarthy's Border Trilogy." *Myth, Legend, Dust: Critical Responses to Cormac McCarthy*, ed. Rick Wallach. Manchester, UK: Manchester University Press, 2000.

_____. "Wars and Rumors of Wars in Cormac McCarthy's Border Trilogy." *A Cormac McCarthy Companion: The Border Trilogy*, eds. Edwin T. Arnold and Dianne C. Luce. Jackson: University Press of Mississippi, 2001.

Willey, Basil. *The Seventeenth-Century Background: Studies in the Thought of the Age in Relation to Poetry and Religion*. London: Routledge & Kegan Paul, 1934.

Williamson, Geordie. Review of *The Road*. *Weekend Australian*, September 30, 2006.

Winchell, Mark Royden. *Reinventing the South*. Columbia: University of Missouri Press, 2006.

_____. *Too Good to Be True: The Life and Work of Leslie Fiedler*. Columbia: University of Missouri Press, 2002.

Winfrey, Oprah. Television interview with Cormac McCarthy, *The Oprah Winfrey Show*, June 5, 2007.

Witliff Collections website for the Cormac McCarthy Papers in the Southwestern Writers Collection at the Texas State University–San Marcos library. http://alkek.library.txstate.edu/swwc/archives/writers/cormac.html.

Wong, Hertha Dawn. *Louise Erdrich's Love Medicine: A Casebook*. New York: Oxford University Press, 2000.

Wood, James. "Red Planet: The Sanguinary Sublime of Cormac McCarthy." *The New Yorker*, July 25, 2005. http://www.newyorker.com/archive/2005/07/25/050725crbo_books.

Woodward, Richard B. "Bernard Madoff and Anton Chigurh: The Con Man as Serial Killer." *The Huffington Post*, December 22, 2008. http://www.huffingtonpost.com/richard-b-woodward/bernard-madoff-and-anton_b_152860.html.

_____. "Cormac Country." *Vanity Fair*, August 2005.

_____. "Cormac McCarthy's Venomous Fiction." *The New York Times*, April 19, 1992. http://www. nytimes.com/books/98/05/17/specials/mccarthy-venom.html.

Worcester, Donald E. *The Apaches: Eagles of the Southwest*. Norman: University of Oklahoma Press, 1992.

Yardley, Jonathan. "In All Its Gory." *The Washington Post*, March 13, 1985, p. B2.

Zinoman, Jason. "A Debate of Souls, Torn between Faith and Unbelief." *The New York Times*, October 31, 2006. http://theater.nytimes.com/2006/10/31/theater/reviews/31suns.html.

Index

Index

Index